Ezra Pound and 20th-Century Theories of Language

Ezra Pound is one of the most significant poets of the twentieth century, a writer whose poetry is particularly notable for the intensity of its linguistic qualities. Indeed, from the principles of Imagism to the polyphony of his Cantos, Pound is central to our conception of modernism's relationship with language. This volume explores the development of Pound's understanding of language in the context of twentieth-century linguistics and the philosophy of language. It draws on largely unpublished archival material in order to provide a broadly chronological account of the development of Pound's views and their relation to both his own poetry and modernist writing as a whole. Beginning with Pound's contentious relationship with philology and his antagonism towards academia, the book traces continuities and shifts across Pound's career, culminating in a discussion of the centrality of language to the conception of his Cantos. While it contains discussions around significant figures in twentieth-century linguistic thought, such as Ferdinand de Saussure and Ludwig Wittgenstein, the book attempts to recover the work of theorists such as Leonard Bloomfield, Lucien Lévy-Bruhl, and C.K. Ogden, figures who were once central to modernism, but who have largely been pushed to the periphery of modernist studies. The picture of Pound that emerges is a figure whose understanding of language is not only bound up with modernist approaches to anthropology, politics, and philosophy, but which calls for a new understanding of modernism's relationship to each.

James Dowthwaite was born and raised in Winchester and studied, first, at Royal Holloway, University of London, before completing his doctorate at The Queen's College, University of Oxford in July 2016. He now teaches English and American literature at the University of Jena, having previously taught at the University of Göttingen. He lives in Heidelberg with his wife.

Routledge Studies in Twentieth-Century Literature

For more information about this series, please visit: https://www.routledge.com

Ezra Pound and 20th-Century Theories of Language

Faith with the Word

James Dowthwaite

Routledge
Taylor & Francis Group

NEW YORK AND LONDON

First published 2019
by Routledge
52 Vanderbilt Avenue, New York, NY 10017

and by Routledge
2 Park Square, Milton Park, Abingdon, Oxon, OX14 4RN

Routledge is an imprint of the Taylor & Francis Group, an informa business

First issued in paperback 2021

Library of Congress Cataloging-in-Publication Data
Names: Dowthwaite, James, 1989– author.
Title: Ezra Pound and 20th-century theories of language : faith with the word / James Dowthwaite.
Description: New York, NY : Routledge, 2019. |
Series: Routledge studies in twentieth-century literature ; 60 | Includes bibliographical references and index. |
Identifiers: LCCN 2019013721 (print) | LCCN 2019016351 (ebook) | ISBN 9780429292316 (Master) | ISBN 9781000005547 (Pdf) | ISBN 9781000012361 (epub) | ISBN 9781000018882 (Mobi) | ISBN 9780367262747 | ISBN 9780367262747(hardback :alk. paper) | ISBN 9780429292316(ebk)
Subjects: LCSH: Pound, Ezra, 1885–1972—
Knowledge—Language and languages. | Pound, Ezra, 1885–1972—Influence. | Language and languages—Philosophy—History—20th century. | Linguistics.
Classification: LCC PS3531.O82 (ebook) | LCC PS3531.O82 Z596 2019 (print) | DDC 811/.52—dc23
LC record available at https://lccn.loc.gov/2019013721

ISBN: 978-0-367-26274-7 (hbk)
ISBN: 978-1-03-209227-0 (pbk)
ISBN: 978-0-429-29231-6 (ebk)

Typeset in Sabon
by codeMantra

For my family, British and German,
with love and gratitude

Contents

Acknowledgements

Any academic work is, at root, a collaboration. Primarily, this work is product of my engagement with four academic institutions and the staff members there. First, Royal Holloway, where I was first introduced to the work of Ezra Pound by Will Montgomery. In terms of this project specifically, I would like to thank Tim Armstrong for his continued support over the years, and Finn Fordham for patiently listening to my ideas and assisting with the very earliest stages of this project.

Second, the Faculty of English Language and Literature at the University of Oxford, where I was able to pursue the question of Pound's theory of language as a doctoral project. There is no one to whom this project owes more than Rebecca Beasley, whose supervisions during my doctoral studies and whose continued support, help, and care towards this project and its author have been a source of both inspiration and strength. I could not have dreamed of a better supervisor. I would also like to thank Rhodri Lewis for his support for my work throughout my time at Oxford. The project also benefitted greatly from discussions with Ronald Bush, Laura Marcus, Hannah Sullivan, Helen Barr, and David Barnes at various stages, and I am grateful for their expert help along the way. I would also like to thank my doctoral examiners, Kate McCloughlin and Daniel Katz, for their crucial help and their insightful comments on how to take the project forward. Their comments have been with me throughout this process and I am deeply grateful for them.

Since my move to Germany I have been extremely lucky to have worked at two great institutions. First, the University of Göttingen, where I was able to present research relating to this topic at the research colloquium and where I was given the opportunity to teach Pound's work. As it stands now, this project emerged from lengthy discussions with Andrew Gross, whose help with the manuscript, extensive knowledge of modern poetry, and whose friendship have been a source of constant strength over the last few years, and he has my deepest gratitude. I would extend my warmest thanks to the staff and students of the American Studies department at Göttingen: they are a credit to their institution.

The final institution which must take some responsibility for this project is the University of Jena. I would like to thank Dirk Vanderbeke and his research colloquium for the time taken to discuss the project, and assistance with editing in the final stages, as well as their support. I would like to thank Jena for providing such a warm and hospitable environment in which I could finish this project, and my particular thanks go to the students who have had to suffer through my numerous references to my work. It was very much written with them in mind.

I would also like to thank the staff at the Beinecke Library at the University of Yale for their kind assistance and warm welcome during a five-week research stay in 2015. In addition, I would like to thank the staff at the William Ready Division of the Archives and Research Collections at McMaster University for their help with the C.K. Ogden fonds, the staff at the Department of Manuscripts and University Archives, Cambridge University Library, Cambridge University, and at the University College London Special Collections, at the National Archives in Kew. In terms of the writing of this project, special mention must go to the staff at the Anglistik library, University of Heidelberg, for their accommodation. The staff of all of these institutions perhaps do not realise how much they make possible. All academic work is built on their shoulders. I am deeply grateful.

In addition, there are a number of individuals whom I must thank. Helen Carr and Richard Parker for their kindness and support during my time attending and organising the London Cantos Reading Group: the discussions that took place there were essential for this project and they are always in my thoughts. I would also like to thank Massimo Bacigalupo for his long-term interest in and support for this project, and for his comments regarding certain aspects of the manuscript.

I would also like to thank Christopher Wait at New Directions for his kind help in answering all of my questions. I would like to thank them for permission to quote from the following works: Unpublished material by Ezra Pound, New Directions Pub. acting as agent, copyright ©2018 by Mary de Rachewiltz and the Estate of Omar S. Pound. Reprinted by permission of New Directions Publishing Corp; Excerpts from THE CANTOS OF EZRA POUND copyright ©1934 by Ezra Pound. Reprinted by permission of New Directions Publishing Corp; By Ezra Pound, from ABC OF READING, copyright ©1934 by Ezra Pound. Reprinted by permission of New Directions Publishing Corp; By Ezra Pound, from GUIDE TO KULCHUR, copyright ©1970 by Ezra Pound. Reprinted by permission of New Directions Publishing Corp; By Ezra Pound, from SELECTED LETTERS 1907–1941 OF EZRA POUND, copyright ©1950 by Ezra Pound. Reprinted by permission of New Directions Publishing Corp.

I would also like to thank Michelle Salyga and Bryony Reece at Routledge for their faith in this project and the fantastic support they have given me. I would also like to thank the reviewers of the manuscript for their immensely kind words and suggestions. I have tried to do them justice.

Last but not least, I would like to thank my family: my mother and father, for their constant love, support, and humour, all three of which are essential to anything I do. I would also like to thank my sister, Francesca, stepfather, David, and my stepmother, Mo, for the same. My grandmothers, Corinne and Olive, have given me the emotional framework to complete this project, and my grandfathers, Eric and Syd, are there in any successes it may have. Any failures, they are mine alone. Last of all, I must thank my wife, Mailin, for her patience, love, support, and brilliance. Not one word of this book would have been possible without her.

Abbreviations

Works by Ezra Pound

ABC/R	*ABC of Reading* (New York: New Directions, 1934)
GK	*Guide to Kulchur* (New York: New Directions, 1938)
LE	*Literary Essays* (New York: New Directions, 1968)
SL	*Selected Letters*, ed. D.D. Paige (New York: New Directions, 1950)
SR	*The Spirit of Romance* (London: Dent, 1910)

Citations of the *Cantos* (New York: New Directions, 1996) are inserted parenthetically after the quotation or reference in the form of 'Canto number. Page number(s)'.

Introduction
The Word beyond Formulated Language

Why does it matter what Ezra Pound thought about language? There are three reasons: first, because Pound has been paradigmatic to our understanding of modernism since he first published 'A Few Don'ts by an Imagiste' with its famous definition of the image as 'that which presents an intellectual and emotional complex in an instant of time', a definition which remains seminal to our understanding of what it is that the language of poetry does.[1] Second, because the broader paradigm of twentieth-century letters, whether literature or philosophy, is language, and Pound was not only contemporaneous with many of the great conceptual shifts in the understanding of language, but he was at the forefront of a literary culture which embraced and rejected them in equal measure. Third, because Pound's work offers an alternative to structuralist and post-structuralist accounts of literary language, with their focus on the nature and structure of the linguistic sign. The terminologies and frameworks of post-Saussurian accounts of language have brought numerous advances to our subject, but there is a sense in which they strain against the material when we use them to study modernism. By looking at Pound's life and work in relation to contemporaneous debates in language, we can lay a foundation for an understanding of modernist accounts of language which allows greater commerce between criticism and texts. With regard to poetic language, Pound writes in 'A Serious Artist' (1913): 'you can be wholly precise in representing a vagueness' (*LE*, 44). The purpose of this book is to outline why that might be the case, and to explore the problems it raises.

Pound's life (1885–1972) covered a period of literary and philosophical history in which faith in language, as opposed to the metaphysical ideas or the external reality it supposedly mediated, became a central aspect of philosophical enquiry. Pound's unique and significant voice provides crucial insight into the way in which we can understand the relationship between language and literature in the twentieth century; this by virtue of both his extensive and complex oeuvre and his historical vantage point. Pound was not only a significant poet in his own right, but was a central node in the modernist nexus. There are numerous problems in attempting to understand the trajectory of Pound's career in relation to the most famous writers on language in the twentieth century, chief among them that Pound was notoriously idiosyncratic in his choice of sources. Were scholars to put together a reading list of key texts of twentieth-century linguistic and philosophical thought, it would be unlikely that Pound would have read many of the works listed. The difficulty for Poundian scholarship has been finding a balance between doing justice to Pound's views on his own terms and relating this to wider modernist and historical debates. One of the major problems in historicising Pound is the diversity of his interests and his own view of history as an equilibrium. As he claims in *The Spirit of Romance* (1910), he wanted an approach which would 'weigh Theocritus and Mr Yeats with one balance' (*SR*, 8). Where he found no satisfactory answers in his own time, he would reach back into the past and consider the point as no less current. His use of Dante's *De Vulgari Eloquentio*, the Confucian odes, or his attempt to recover certain methodologies of scholasticism all demonstrate this approach to history. From the point of view of the historian of twentieth-century letters, Pound is a somewhat frustrating figure. His preference for obscure or underappreciated figures leads to us finding not Edmund Husserl, Friedrich Nietzsche, Ferdinand de Saussure, or Ludwig Wittgenstein, but instead Ernest Fenollosa, C.K. Ogden, Leo Frobenius, and George Santayana. However, it is essential that we understand his relation to the major figures of modernist thought. This leaves the historian with two options: first, to understand the ways in which Pound responds to the same concerns and debates as his contemporaries; second, to understand affinities between Pound and his contemporaries in terms of common roots and sources.

In order to understand Pound's role in twentieth-century debates around language, it is worth first sketching some of the key ideas in the period in which he lived. The late nineteenth century had seen the emergence of a series of challenges to the apparently long-held epistemological and cultural assumptions of Western philosophy, and language was no exception. From Friedrich Nietzsche's and Soren Kierkegaard's challenges to Western metaphysical traditions to scientific positivism in the late nineteenth century to Edmund Husserl's and Martin Heidegger's phenomenologies of the early twentieth, Pound conducted his work in a period of philosophical and literary upheaval. Faith in language as a stable medium of thought and communication was severely challenged. The great shift of philosophy from epistemology, from the study of how we know, to ontology, the question of being itself, had a great effect on the ways in which we can conceive objective reality, our relationship to it, and the way we represent it. The Western metaphysical tradition was challenged from a number of directions, and language became central to this concern: speech shifted from being understood as the main medium through which we encounter reality to being conceived as that which constitutes reality itself. There was a broad shift to the following position: as our experience of reality is always bound through language, it is only through an intense study of the interior logic of language that we can understand our relationship to the world, and the cultures, art forms, people, and ideas it contains. This is what Richard Rorty has termed the 'linguistic turn' in philosophy.[2]

Identifying the 'linguistic turn' is both a matter of conjecture and relativity. One place to begin is the work of Gottlob Frege and his theory of reference.[3] Frege conceived of language in mathematical terms, treating it as a series of logical propositions. In his *Grundlage* (1884), written one year before Pound's birth, Frege proposed that sentences have meaning by virtue of being true or false, and this truth or falsehood is determined by each of the components of a sentence having a meaning, a reference, or, in Frege's terms, *Bedeutung*.[4] In his *Sinn und Bedeutung* (1892), Frege further expands his view by demonstrating that *Bedeutung* cannot be all that determines our understanding of language. While 'Earth' clearly refers to the planet Earth, it is not clear what the reference for 'Odysseus' is, and yet we are still able to understand stories told about the mythical character. Frege refers to this as the *Sinn*, or the 'sense' of a proposition, sentence, or text. Thus, a name, such as Odysseus, can have sense even if it does not have a direct reference.[5] In 1905, Bertrand Russell challenged this view in his 'On Denoting', a seminal text in the so-called analytic tradition. Russell held that such as Odysseus are really shorthand descriptions. Thus 'Odysseus' does not necessarily refer to an individual object, but rather functions as a shorthand version of a description such as 'the main character of the *Odyssey*'.[6] Russell's student, Ludwig Wittgenstein, expanded such treatments of language and logic in his *Tractatus Logico-Philosophicus*, wherein he explored the ways in which '*the limits of my language* mean the limits of my world', a notion in which the boundaries of human perception and the capacity of human speech are seen as one and the same for the speaking subject.[7]

In some senses, however, what is often conceived of as a 'linguistic turn' was, in fact, a 'semiotic turn', in which the multifaceted issue of linguistic communication was brought to focus on the notion of the sign: that is, the unification of material and conceptual components of language, and the way they 'point' towards external objects in reality. From the perspective of intersections between literary and linguistic treatments of language, the most influential figure has been Ferdinand de Saussure, whose *Course in General Linguistics* (1916) was both a summation of the linguistic approach and the seminal text in the foundation of semiotics, or the study of signs. Saussure was a professor of Sanskrit philology and, after his death, his *Course* was assembled out of lecture notes taken down by his students. Although Saussure's text is a summary and survey of many aspects of linguistic study, it has become most famous for its formulation of the linguistic sign. Saussure distinguishes, first, between the various objects of linguistic study: *le langage* (language – as a general concept), *la langue* (an individual language, or tongue), and *la parole* (speech).[8] He also outlines the two approaches to linguistic study: a linguist can study language diachronically, that is, language change across time, or synchronically, which constitutes a study of language use at any single point in time.[9] The focus of structuralism is generally on the latter, the object of linguistics being language qua language. Saussure outlines an argument for the psychological construction of all human speech. Language, he argues, is composed of signs which refer to objects, or referents. The linguistic sign is itself made up of two parts: a sound image, or *signifier* (such as the word *tree*), and a mental concept, or *signifier* (such as an image of a tree in one's mind). As Saussure writes, 'the linguistic sign unites, not a thing and a name, but a concept and a sound-image'.[10] Following the work of the American philologist William Dwight Whitney, Saussure then asserts the fundamental arbitrariness of the linguistic sign: there is no fundamental link between the particular composition of the phonemes in the sound image, or *signifier*, and the particular image that comes to the speaker's or listener's mind. Rather, the connection between *signifiers* and *signifieds* is based on convention and communal use. That does not mean, however, that one can simply shift the meanings of words at will. Language, Saussure points out, is not so much communally determined or agreed upon, as it is culturally predetermined; all language users are born into a linguistic community both the language of which and the rules governing it have, by and large, long since been established. Saussure's formulation of the linguistic sign has provided one of the bases for structuralism and for the general science of semiotics – or the study of ways in which signs and sign-systems structure our lives – of which he hoped linguistics would form a subcategory.

The semiotic foci of structuralist linguists culminated in the emergence of post-structuralist theory in the 1960s, the point at which Pound stopped writing. It is here that the development of the linguistic-semiotic understanding of language had its most fruitful encounter with literature. In his famous essay 'The Death of the Author', Roland Barthes explores the implications of the focus on language in the twentieth century in terms of challenging the authority given to writers in determining the meaning of a given text:

> Linguistics has recently provided the destruction of the Author with a valuable analytic tool by showing that the whole of the enunciation is an empty process, functioning perfectly without there being any need for it to be filled with the person of the interlocuters. Linguistically, the author is never more than the instance writing, just as *I* is nothing other than the instance saying *I*: language knows a 'subject', not a 'person', and this subject, empty outside of the very enunciation which defines it, suffices to make language 'hold together', suffices, that is to say, to exhaust it.[11]

This is a radical inversion of our intuitive assumptions about language. Where one may believe that grammatical categories such as the pronoun *I* are constituted by the existence of individuals, Barthes argues that it is, in fact, the other way around, and we are led through our linguistic conventions towards an unstable understanding of reality. According to this theory, literature does not necessarily point towards an external reality, but rather self-referentially draws attention to language's fundamental and paradoxical status as the arbiter of reality. Should one use a methodology of this kind to read Pound, for example, it would run up against the current of his own faith in the relationship between literature and lived experience. As was the case with Pound, should one take a more holistic approach to language, relegating the notion of 'signs' to a less privileged place, Barthes's dismissal of speaking subjects (and the authority of the author), while immensely influential in and of itself, functions poorly as an explanation of the modernist understanding of language.

This brings us to the work of Martin Heidegger, whose career and notoriety, as Jean-Michel Rabaté points out, contains many parallels with Pound.[12] In his late essay 'Poetry', Heidegger appears to argue a similar thesis to Barthes, with his famous dictum that 'language speaks, not the man'.[13] Heidegger attempts to isolate the function of language as language, readily admitting that individuals use language, but that it is not clear what language is as such, as divorced from those who use it. Heidegger's more phenomenological approach and unique terminology allow him a way of thinking about language outside of previous traditions, and in thinking about poetry, he developed the following thesis: the naming of things which occurs in language, and especially in poetry, 'does not hand out titles, it does not apply terms, but it calls into the word'.[14] That is to say that rather than language being a system of signs which point outwards to an external world, it is a kind of summoning, a creative act which calls the world inwards towards the speaking subject, thereby becoming the medium by which we, as writers and readers, encounter the world.

Certain questions can be drawn out from this: to what extent did Pound's aesthetic innovations intersect with these philosophical and ideological revolutions? How far did Pound's ideas about language reflect, challenge, engage with or ignore those of his time? And, most significantly, what influence did his understanding of language have on his work? In this book, I trace the development of Pound's understanding of language, from his early years as a student studying modern languages at Hamilton College and the University of Pennsylvania to the lyrical reflections of his *Pisan Cantos*, conceived when he was held in an open-air cage, isolated from his library and companions, for his part in supporting Mussolini's Fascist government. It is worth remembering, however, that Pound's work was, above all, literary. Insofar as there is a literary approach to language, language as considered by the poet as opposed to the linguist or the philosopher, Pound sought at all points to hew close to it. As a way of introduction to this subject, it is perhaps best to begin by situating Pound in relation to what was primarily a literary discussion in order to determine the exact place of language (as a subject in and of itself) in Pound's early career.

Le Mot Juste

The first question that needs to be determined regarding the relationship between modernist poetry and writing is: what is *poetic* language? Perhaps the best introduction to the question of language in twentieth-century literature is Hugo von Hofmannsthal's 'Letter of Lord Chandos', published in 1902. Hofmannsthal imagines a letter, dated 22 August 1603, sent from the fictional writer Lord Chandos to the English philosopher Francis Bacon, a figure who would, incidentally, become important for Pound. In his letter, Chandos apologises for having cut off correspondence with Bacon over the previous two years and for failing to have produced any literary work in that time. His failure, he explains, resulted from an existential crisis in which his previous understanding of the unity of the world fell apart: 'everything disintegrated into parts, these parts again into parts'; a crisis which ruptures Chandos's perception of the connection between word and world, for 'single words floated around [him]' and he was 'led into the void'.[15] Chandos retreats into the stable world of classical culture, but fails to find solace, and finds himself unable to write. Accepting his situation, he concludes that he cannot write another book, explaining to Bacon:

> And this for an odd and embarrassing reason which I must leave to the boundless superiority of your mind to place in the realm of physical and spiritual values spread out harmoniously before your unprejudiced eye: to wit, because the language in which I might be able not only to write but to think is neither Latin nor English, neither Italian nor Spanish but a language none of whose words is known to me, a language in which inanimate things speak to me and wherein I may one day have to justify myself before an unknown judge.[16]

Hofmannsthal, in the guise of Chandos, raises a number of issues that would become central to twentieth-century linguistics, literature, and philosophy. The first is whether or not Chandos's crisis is one of thought or language, and whether there is a distinction between the two. Is Chandos able to comprehend his crisis even if he does not have the language to express it? Does the letter expose the general limits of language or the limits of Chandos's personal understanding of the world? Does the fact that Hofmannsthal is able to express Chandos's crisis in clear prose suggest that these crises can in fact be overcome in a refined use of language? Or, ultimately, does Hofmannsthal's text simply gesture towards the abyss between the world and the language we use to express it? Although Hofmansthal did not provide the answer to these questions himself, one way into this problem is a literary principle central to the development of the realist prose tradition and which Pound would later import into his poetics: *le mot juste.*

The concept *le mot juste*, or 'the exact word', is most often attributed to Gustave Flaubert, whose literary practice revolved around a language of precision, choosing the most appropriate word to characterise or describe the objects, scenes, or people that he wished to get across. For Flaubert, *le mot juste* was indicative of an aesthetic and philosophical temperament. Writing to the novelist George Sand in 1876, Flaubert explains his literary process:

> The anxiety for external beauty which you reproach me with is for me a METHOD. When I discover a bad assonance or a repetition in one of my phrases, I am sure that I am floundering in error; by dint of searching, I find the exact expression which was the only one and is, at the same time, the harmonious one. The word is never lacking when one possesses the idea.[17]

Flaubert notes the materiality of his artistic medium on stylistic grounds, disapproving of unwanted, merely literary flourishes. But these questions of style are then connected to a philosophical and psychological faith in harmony between word and concept. It can seem difficult to reconcile Flaubert's concept of an 'exact' phrase with an understanding of language as a system of arbitrary signs, but it is worth noting that Flaubert refers only to the relationship between words and ideas. He does not refer to what constitutes the harmoniousness of word and concept, be it determined by use, history, society, natural law, or God, but rather simply asserts that a differentiated concept demands a word which differentiates it. In general terms, then, we can say that the notion of *le mot juste* is the principle that differences in language should always stand for conceptual differences, and that, in using a different word or phrase, one differentiates one concept from another.

The importance of Flaubert for Pound is attested to in numerous places, but nowhere more striking than in *Hugh Selwyn Mauberley* (1920), Pound's satiric, semi-autobiographical verse assessment of life as a literary 'modern' before, during, and after the trauma of the First World War. In the opening poem of the *Mauberley* sequence, 'Ode pour l'Election de Son Sepulchre', Pound includes a critique of his own career up to that point, one in which he was 'bent resolutely on wringing lilies from the acorn':

> His true Penelope was Flaubert
> He fished by obstinate isles;
> Observed the elegance of Circe's hair
> Rather than the mottoes on sun dials.[18]

Comparing himself to Odysseus, Pound sees himself as having navigated the misdirection of Anglophone literary culture; where the cultural norm is the analysis of 'mottoes on sun dials', Pound's poetic thrust is towards the 'elegance' of divine beauty. This is not a mere celebration of aesthetic values over materialistic ones, but a unification of the aesthetic and the ethical in the figure of the *mot juste*. Throughout the various adventures of literary modernism, Flaubert weaves and unweaves the tapestry of language, a loyal, yet threatened, linguistic homestead.

Yet Pound was by no means the first to insist on the values of the *mot juste*. A generation earlier, Walter Pater, whom Pound would later deride for the 'softness' of his writings and convictions, had argued for the value of the *mot juste* as a principle.[19] Pater built upon Flaubert's ideas in his collection of essays, *Appreciations* (1889). See, for example, his opening statement in 'Style', which asserts that 'all progress of mind consists for the most part in differentiation'.[20] Pater's essay is an early attempt to outline the value of the Flaubertian *mot juste* in English, and in it we find the role of the artist defined as the discrimination of differences in images and the rendering of this in appropriate language. For Pater, this is at the centre of the literary craft:

> The one word for the one thing, the one thought, amid the multitude of words, terms, that might just do; the problem of style was there! – the unique word, phrase, sentence, paragraph, essay, or song, absolutely proper to the single mental presentation or vision within.[21]

The role of the writer, then, is the careful, exhaustive search for the word or phrase that corresponds to what the writer sees in a way no other would. This must then be transmitted to the reader, which Pater describes in terms of an artistic address to an audience: 'I want you to see precisely what I see'.[22] At this point, Pater seems to approach a radical individualism, with the question of what constitutes the 'proper' word being its relation to the personal vision of the writer, rather than to an external reality. However, again with the assistance of Flaubert, he claims that

> for every lineament of the vision within, the one word, the one acceptable word, recognisable by the sensitive, by others 'who have intelligence' in the matter, as absolutely as ever anything can be in the evanescent and delicate region of human language. The style, the manner, would be the man, not in his unreasoned and really uncharacteristic caprices, involuntary or affected, but in absolutely sincere apprehension of what is most real to him.[23]

The correctness of a word is determined, then, by the sincerity with which a writer describes the apprehended object. Such an understanding has a tendency to slip into essentialism, but Pater's meaning is some-what different. What is significant here is the phrase 'recognisable by the sensitive', that is, the correct word is not simply one which draws the attention of the writer onto the thing described, but one that would draw the attention of others as well. Pater is careful to draw his terms on a conceptual plane rather than a material one, and the assumption at the basis of his thought is that if we share a language, we share certain conceptual elements as well. The object of good writing, then, is to draw these conceptual and linguistic elements as closely together as possible.

The possibility of stylistic precision, as suggested by Flaubert and Pater, is one that is in equal parts clinical and mystical; while there is a clear attempt to represent subjectivity on an objective plane, this often has recourse to a series of essentialist metaphors. There is always a conceptual gap in such explanations, as can be seen in Pater's admission that language is an 'evanescent and delicate region'. Pound notes this conflict in his essay series 'I Gather the Limbs of Osiris' (1912), where he claims that poetry must retain its powers of 'vague suggestion' as 'our life is, in so far as it is worth living, made up in great part of things indefinite, impalpable'. Because the arts present these impalpable things to us, they matter so greatly to humanity. Poets thus aim to exploit the vagaries of human language in the elucidation of images, thoughts, and sensations, rather than the elucidation of language itself: it is on this point that poetry and linguistics divide. As Pound explains,

> The artist discriminates, that is, between one kind of indefinability and another, and poetry is a very complex art. Its media are on the one hand the simplest, the least interesting, and on the other the most arcane, more fascinating. It is an art of pure sound bound in through an art of arbitrary and conventional symbols. In so far as it is an art of pure sound, it is allied with music, painting, sculpture; in so far as it is an art of arbitrary symbols, it is allied to prose. A word exists when two or more people agree to mean the same thing by it.[24]

There is a temptation here, of course, to recast Pound's words in Saussurian terms, but by the time Pound was writing this statement, the arbitrariness of language was something of an intellectual truism for those who had studied language at university, as Pound had. Pound's terms capture not only the material basis of poetry: the cadences, rhythms, sounds and written marks, rhymes, and alliterations that we submit to analysis, but also the conceptual side, the process behind the poem's production, the linguistic laws and communities which serve to limit it, and the functions and effects that it has.

It is notable that Pound's material 'pure sound' does not include those 'arbitrary symbols'.[25] Contrary to the assumptions typical of the 'linguistic turn', Pound does not associate this arbitrariness with a systemic analysis of the linguistic matrix. 'Arbitrary' has become a kind of literary shorthand for 'unnatural', but Pound's lifelong dedication to technique, praxis, and later Aristotelian *techne* distance him from an analysis based on language as system. Where Roman Jakobson, for example, sees linguistics and poetics as sub-disciplines of an overarching semiotics, Pound begins not with the sign but with the image, the technique, or the creative impulse: the sign in use.[26] While it is of course naïve to separate language use from the linguistic matrixes in which a speech act occurs, and such a radical separation is not licensed anywhere by Pound, it is significant that his discussions of language are always focussed on the nature of signification or the thing signified, rather than a discussion of the structural relations of the signs themselves.

Pound's most famous innovation of the *mot juste* tradition is, of course, the image: an importation of Flaubert's prose principle into poetics. The impulse that encouraged Richard Aldington, H.D., and Pound to develop poetic Imagism can be traced to the ideas being discussed at The Poet's Club in London between 1908 and 1914. The secretary of the club was the poet and philosopher, T.E. Hulme, who was greatly influenced by the work of French philosopher Henri Bergson. Hulme formulated well the linguistic problems to which the 'image' and the *mot juste* respond. Unlike Pound, Hulme provides more overtly philosophical material for critics to work with. Although Pound was always at pains to play down the influence that Hulme's ideas had on his own, the latter's essays and talks revolve around the same questions that Pound sought to answer. In 'Romanticism and Classicism' (published posthumously in 1924), Hulme thinks through the problems facing poets at the turn of the century in terms that characterise modernist poetic practice:

> The great aim is accurate, precise and definite description. The first thing is to recognise how extraordinarily difficult this is. It is no mere matter of carefulness; you have to use language, and language is by its very nature a communal thing; that is, it expresses never the exact thing but a compromise – that which is common to you, me and everybody. But each man sees a little differently, and to get out clearly and exactly what he does see, he must have a terrific struggle with language; whether it be with words or the technique of other arts. Language has its own special nature, its own conventions and communal ideas. It is only by a concentrated effort of the mind that can hold it fixed to your own purpose.[27]

Hulme's recognition of language as a communal, conventional, and yet unstable system is a perfect synthesis of problems to which the philosophy of language attends. According to Hulme, language is an imperfect medium for the communication of individual thought (not to say objects and external reality), poets in fact seek to overcome and compensate innate linguistic problems. Hulme continues to define prose as like algebra, which he sees as 'concrete things embodied in signs or counters which are moved about according to rules'. He argues that in prose, one only returns those signs or counters to the things they represent at the end of the process, thus introducing inevitable delay and confusion. Poetry, he argues, is an attempt to avoid this process with a freshness and clarity of presentation:

> Poetry, in one aspect, at any rate, may be considered as an effort to avoid this characteristic of prose. It is not a counter language, but a visual concrete one. It is a compromise for a language of intuition which would hand over accusations bodily. It always endeavours to arrest you, and to make you continuously see a physical thing, to prevent you gliding through an abstract process. It chooses fresh epithets and fresh metaphors, not so much because they are new, and we are tired of the old, but because the old cease to convey a mind.[28]

The basic unit of poetry is not the same as ordinary language, in this sense: the basic meaningful unit of poetry is not necessarily the word, but the image. The image is, in the end, the result of a poetic struggle to overcome what Hulme sees as the deficiencies of common, conventional language; the problem for Hulme, as for the post-structuralists later, is that this escape from common language cannot truly escape. Poetry is thus conceived as a more definite and accurate form of compensation.

Although Pound shared much of Hulme's convictions, and clearly derived much of his framing of the image from him, there are a number of important differences in their thought. Where Hulme sees poetry as an attempt to overcome language's inherent failure to represent the mental apprehension of objects, Pound sees this as something of a fallacy. In 'I Gather the Limbs of Osiris', Pound describes the attempts to capture an event such as sunrise in language:

> It is bad poetry to talk much of the colours of the sunrise, though one may speak of our lady 'of rosy fingers' or 'in russet clad', invoking an image not present to the uninitiated; at this game the poet may surpass, but in the matter of the actual colour he is a bungler. The painter sees, or should see, half a hundred hues and varieties, where we see ten; or, granting we are ourselves skilled with the brush, how many hundred colours are there, where language has but a dozen crude names? Even if the poet understands the subtleties of gradation and juxtaposition, his medium refuses to convey them. He can say all his say while he is ignorant of the reality, and knowledge of the reality will not help him say it better.[29]

Pound's difference from Hulme here is subtle but significant. Where Hulme sees poets as inevitably trapped by their medium, Pound overcomes this apparent problem by suggesting an attempt such as the representation of colour in poetry is misdirected. Language is not, in this case, an inevitably imperfect medium for the representation of reality, but rather simply the wrong medium. We may think of Dante's description of the sunrise in *Purgatorio*: 'Dolce color d'oriental zaffiro/ che s'accoglieva nel sereno aspetto del mezzo' ['soft colours of oriental sapphire/ gather themselves about the serene aspect of the horizon'].[30] The reader's attention is directed towards the impression and articulation by means of a metaphor (the oriental sapphire), rather than by plain description. Contrary to Hulme, who argues that language is inherently flawed, Pound discerns that it is not language itself which is flawed, but the use to which it is put.

At the time in which Pound wrote 'I Gather the Limbs of Osiris', Pound shared with Hulme a distinction between the language of poetry and common speech. Pound dismisses as a fallacy the notion that poetry should mimic ordinary language, and, echoing Milton, he claims 'works of art attract by a resembling unlikeness'. That is, readers are attracted to poetry by coming into contact with the familiar 'arranged more finely': the distinction between poetic language and ordinary language is a question of form and use. Pound then advances to explain the importance of 'technique', which would remain a constant throughout his career, which he defines as 'the clinch of the expression on the thing intended to be expressed'.[31] Pound's formula includes the intentionality between the image perceived and the perceiver; poetic language is distinguished by the creative process, rather than by its passive inheritance of language's inherent structures. This intense connection between expression and thing expressed is a dynamic process dependent on the active participation of writer and reader.

The struggle to determine the experience beyond language, the effort to capture the richness of perceived phenomena that cannot be delimited in ordinary words, is at the centre of the creation of one of Pound's most famous poems, 'In a Station of the Metro'.

> The apparition of these faces in a crowd;
> Petals on a wet, black bough.[32]

Pound's two-line poem is prized for its fine, precise quality, its author making use of principles discerned from both Western and Eastern literary traditions. He overlays two images, the one of the ghostly quality of passing people in the city; the other of a natural world, the petals departed from their stems and caught on the trees in a storm. Pound's account of the impression that this poem captures, included in his memoir

of the life of the painter Henri Gaudier-Brzeska (published 1916), is
written in terms similar to those used by Hofmannsthal:

> Three years ago in Paris I got out of a 'Metro' train at La Concorde,
> and saw suddenly a beautiful face, and then another and another,
> and then a beautiful child's face, and then another beautiful
> woman, and I tried all that day to find words for what this had
> meant to me, and I could not find any words that seemed to me wor-
> thy, or as lovely as that sudden emotion. And that evening, as I went
> home along the Rue Raynouard, I was still trying and I found, sud-
> denly, the expression. I do not mean that I found words, but there
> came an equation...not in speech, but in little splotches of colour.
> It was just that – a 'pattern,' or hardly a pattern, if by 'pattern' you
> mean something with a 'repeat' in it. But it was a word, the begin-
> ning, for me, of a language in colour.[33]

The revelatory quality of Pound's impression was not reflected in the
composition of the poem, however. Initially, Pound struggled with his
'language in colour' and composed a thirty-line poem. Eventually, he
was able to reduce it to the two lines of the poem in its final form. In
Pound's rendering of his impression, his 'image', the conventional languages that he had inherited would not serve his purposes and could
not be used to capture the complexity of the instant, much like Lord
Chandos's 'language none of whose words is known'. As Pound writes,
'any mind that is worth calling a mind must have needs beyond the
existing categories of language'. In this sense, 'all poetic language
is the language of exploration', a notion that leads him to conclude that
'the image is itself the speech. The image is the word beyond formulated
language'.[34] When we read 'In a Station of the Metro', then, the two images form a kind of sentence in a language beyond the conventional signs
of ordinary speech or writing; Pound's imagistic poetry shifts meaning
from the interplay of the words onto the interplay of the images they
describe. The intention is that we see beyond the word to the vision, as if
we experience the vision ourselves. The purpose of the imagistic poem,
in this sense, is to bind through in language the uniqueness of an experienced image. To speak of the meaning of an imagist poem is to speak of
the 'meaning' of phenomena.

What does this say about language and the nature of reference? And
where does this map on the landscape of linguistic thought in the twentieth century? A simple theory of reference, such as Saussure's, is only
of partial assistance. Pound rejects association with French Symbolism,
claiming that the Symbolists 'degraded the image to the status of a
word', that is, one thing standing for another. Symbolism, for Pound,
is a proliferation of the semiotic, an extension of the already symbolic
into another symbolic realm, whereas he conceives of a poetics which

must come to rest on the concrete and the definite, on the real. Pound's 'image' is not a symbol of external reality, but is a measure of our experience of reality; it is on these grounds that Pound compares his work with the visual arts:

> The image is the poet's pigment. The painter should use his colour because he sees or feels it. I don't much care whether he is representative or non-representative. He should *depend*, of course, on the creative, not upon the mimetic or representational part in his work. It is the same in writing poems, the author must use his *image* because he sees it or feels it, *not* because he thinks he can use it to back up some creed or some system of ethics or economics.
>
> An *image*, in our sense, is real because we know it directly. If it have an age-old traditional meaning this may serve as proof to the professional student of symbology that we have stood in the deathless light, or that we have walked in some particular arbour of his traditional paradiso, but that is not our affair. It is our affair to render the *image* as we have perceived or conceived it.[35]

Pound does not claim that this language beyond words, nor the words that he uses to gesture towards it, reflects external reality as such, but rather that it is a mode of consciousness. His definition of 'the real' is one that negotiates between subjective experience and external reality, and his 'image' speech is the medium in which this is done. Poetry thus emerges as a meditation on states of consciousness and modes of being, all of which are 'beyond formulated language'. Pound's argument suggests that, although a poet's medium is words, the base material of poetry is the image. *Le mot juste* is thus that which best communicates the image 'beyond formulated language' and cannot simply be abstracted as a principle of language alone. Although the 'linguistic turn' encourages us to expect Pound to view language as both the material and subject of poetry, he saw it, first and foremost, as a tool put to use, directed towards subjects beyond linguistic matrices. The use of language is, for Pound, a multifaceted, creative process, always with the capacity to extend beyond itself. According to Pound, poetic language is, then, not an extension of ordinary speech, nor a privileged metalanguage intended to draw our attention to the function or disfunction of signs, but the ordering and patterning of images and melodies; its fundamental unit is not the word, but the image it calls.

Pound and Language in Literary Criticism

Although the genealogy of the *mot juste* and the image is reasonably well known, its linguistic implications for Pound have not been fully explored. From the stylistic treatments given by Donald Davie in *Ezra*

Pound: Poet as Sculptor (1964) and Hugh Kenner in *The Pound Era* (1971), Pound has been central to the way in which we conceive modernism. Although Pound's numerous statements have been crucial to our understanding of his poetic practice, treatments of Pound's work in relation to twentieth-century linguistic theories have been rare. The most sustained account of Pound's linguistic theory is Victor Li's essay 'Philology and Power: Ezra Pound and the Regulation of Language' (1987), a thorough treatment of both Pound's own statements and a number of his sources. Central to Li's contention is that Pound is a 'linguistic idealist'. The assumptions of linguistic idealism, Li explains, are manifest in three ways: '(1) language is secondary to some primary reality…(2) language's role is to represent or communicate aspects of that reality; and (3) language is most effective when it can communicate the real in the most unmediated and transparent way possible'.[36] Li's article, a substantial contribution to our knowledge of the ways in which Pound's understanding of language developed over the course of his career, explores his work in relation to these three points, all of which Li believes to have been based on a fallacious attempt to bring language closer to nature.

While there is a great deal to commend in Li's account, the notion of linguistic idealism, as well as its relation to Pound, requires some scrutiny. In the first instance, Li's definition of linguistic idealism is atypical, taking it to stand in this case for a belief that language is a direct representation of reality. Linguistic idealism, however, is most often associated with precisely the opposite view. Discussing the work of Ludwig Wittgenstein, G.E.M. Anscombe defines linguistic idealism as the belief that reality is the product of the languages we speak.[37] This is, contrary to Li's definition, an idealism which sees language as primary and reality as a reflection of its structures and practices. Continuing the debate, David Bloor offers a more moderate definition, defining linguistic idealism as 'the claim that some truths or realities are created by our linguistic practices'. As a result, Bloor argues, 'the contrast is with cases where language transmits or reflects an independent reality'.[38] Richard Rorty similarly defines linguistic idealism as a position in which 'what appears to us, or what we experience or what we are aware of, is a function of the language we use'.[39] It is clear, then, that what Li, in fact, outlines is a kind of linguistic realism, and this is to a great extent discernible in Pound's focus on the 'natural object' or his reliance on Fenollosa's theories.

Li's article raises a number of interesting questions about Pound's work, many of which are complicated by the charge of 'linguistic idealism'. The first problem is that Li suggests that the first point, language being secondary to an external reality, was one of Pound's major contentions; Pound's poetic practice leads us to a slightly modified view, which is that language is secondary to our conception of reality. The question of whether language is constitutive of reality or vice versa was of less a concern for Pound than for the way in which it mediates it. The second point, that it is the 'role' of language to represent or communicate real-ity, is again more a product of our critical heritage than a point raised by Pound's writing. The analysable relationship, in Li's understanding, is between language and external reality, and it fails to account for the experiential and intentional aspects at the root of poetic activity. Li be-lieves that Pound ascribes a particular role to language, but Pound rarely gives agency to abstract concepts or universals, and this does not reflect Pound's focus on particulars and specific usages. Li's third point, that Pound believes language to be most 'effective' when it communicates the 'real' requires the most investigation. While there is, indeed, a great deal of truth in Li's summary of Pound's belief, he focusses on the com-municative aspects of that formulation, when the focus is perhaps better directed at 'the real'. The terms under discussion here, idealism, realism, nominalism, conceptualism, and so on, are not theories of language, but theories of meaning and reality. The pertinent question Li deftly raises is, therefore: what does Pound's understanding of language tell us about his understanding of reality? In this case, it is inevitable that the debate shifts from language to questions of reality. A further question is, then: to what extent does Pound's understanding of language reflect a nomi-nalist approach to truth and reality? This question is the subject of the final chapter of this book.

Philip Kuberski's *A Calculus of Ezra Pound* (1992) takes a post-structuralist approach to Pound's corpus. Kuberski begins by consider-ing a curious remark of Jacques Derrida's in *Of Grammatology*. Derrida argues that Pound's and Fenollosa's writings represents a rejection of logocentrism. He contends that Pound and Fenollosa belong to a tra-dition of 'decentred' writing, which destabilises the supposedly fixed categories of being and language upon which the Western philosophical tradition has supposedly depended for centuries. As Derrida writes,

The necessary decentering cannot be a philosophical or scientific act as such, since it is a question of dislocating, through access to an-other system linking speech and writing, the founding categories of language and the grammar of the *episteme*. The natural tendency of *theory* – of what unites philosophy and science in the *episteme* – will push rather toward filling in the breach than toward forcing the clo-sure. It was normal that the breakthrough was more secure and pen-etrating on the side of literature and poetic writing: normal also that it, like Nietzsche, at first destroyed and caused to vacillate the tran-scendental authority and dominant category of the *episteme*: being. This is the meaning of Fenollosa whose influence upon Ezra Pound and his poetics is well-known: this irreducibly graphic poetics was, with that of Mallarmé, the first break in the most entrenched West-ern tradition. The fascination that the Chinese ideogram exercised on Pound's writing may thus be given all its historical significance.[40]

Derrida's notion of 'historical significance' is meant in the sense that we should be aware of the gravity of Fenollosa's and Pound's achievements and that their work should be considered as an embodiment of a Heideggerian reconsideration of the relationship between speech and being. By putting Pound in the same category of ontological thought as Nietzsche, Heidegger, and, in fact, himself, Derrida is reinterpreting the role of poetry. Although Pound's own philosophical outlook was far from this tradition, Derrida is, in fact, assigning poetry the same cultural and historical significance that Pound did, if in a radically different way. I will discuss this quotation and the problems it raises in more detail in Chapter 2, but one immediate problem is that Derrida misreads Pound's interest in the ideogram as a 'decentring', ontological endeavour. Not only does Pound rarely raise or question the notion of being in the context of Fenollosa, but Pound's work is far from 'decentred'. Rather, the *Cantos*, particularly in the late 1930s and afterwards record an attempt to return human culture, particularly European culture, to a lost centre. Pound's use of Fenollosa, were it to have a philosophical bent, would, in fact, be a radical re-centring of Western and oriental culture on to a shared basis in historical, natural, and (above all) poetic processes.

Derrida does not continue to explain how his terms relate to Pound's, nor how Pound fits into the tradition he assigns him, but Kuberski takes up this challenge. *A Calculus of Ezra Pound* is an engaging and deeply valuable assessment of the various ways in which Pound's work engages with language and semiotic ideas. While Pound's work has long interested post-structuralist critics, the *Cantos*, for all of their political gravity and controversy and all of their philosophical statements, tend to resist deconstructive analysis. One reason for this may be that Pound often names his sources and authorities in the text, giving the impression that binary oppositions that make up the poem are already laid bare. Another reason could be that Pound's sources are often outside of the dominant Western political and philosophical traditions upon which desconstructive analyses often focus as a point of opposition. Kuberski does not deconstruct the *Cantos* as such, but rather provides an exploration of the ways in which Pound's writing may or may not represent the 'break' that Derrida gestures towards in *Of Grammatology*. Kuberski argues that Pound's work can be characterised by tensions between a commitment to modernist poetics and a faith in anti-modern ideology and aesthetics (such as his belief in Mussolini, his treatment of Sigismundo Malatesta, or his use of Aristotelian notions of *techne*). Seen this way, Pound's is a project which works against the 'relativizing tendencies of Freud, Saussure, and Einstein' by attempting to 'put the word, self, and atom back together again'.[41] Kuberski concludes that with regard to language and writing, *The Cantos* are distinctly anti-modern, writing that 'Pound may, far from being an advocate of modernism, be seen as its first critic, and his poetry may be seen as an attempt to employ innovation to motivate the sign – not finally to sever it from ideological anchoring points'.[42] While Kuberski, like Li, provides an excellent account of the issues Pound raises for us today, the prism of semiotics distorts our ability to assess Pound's approach on its own terms. While literary studies begins its understanding of language with a theory of the sign, Pound's approach is far more holistic. As I have suggested, Pound rarely conceived of language as system. While Kuberski's interpretation of Pound in a semiotic context is an invaluable contribution, its focus on the semiotic aspects of language reduces what was for Pound a broad issue to a narrow focus on signs.

One way in which Pound's broad approach to language has been discussed is translation. In the last few decades, translation has become central to our understanding of literary language, and Pound has been at the centre of this discussion. Translation focusses our understanding of the relationship between words and phrases, thought, and the world, as well as the intense and intractable connection between language and culture. There has been a great deal of critical attention paid to Pound's work in relation to translation, from Ming Xie's 'Pound as Translator' to the broader studies of Laurence Venuti and Daniel Katz. These studies have served to build a clear picture of the ways in which translation infuses not simply Pound's understanding of the way languages and cultures interact, but also his entire poetic practice: as Daniel Katz has written, 'for Pound, poetry *is* translation'.[43] Understanding the importance translation held in Pound's conception of his work is essential for understanding the cultural negotiations of the *Cantos*. Echoing Pound's account quoted at the end of this introduction, Katz terms the language of the *Cantos* as 'post-English', as the text cannot be said to rely simply on the structures and vocabulary of any one linguistic code. As Katz explains, this is 'not only because [the *Cantos*] feature many foreign languages, but because no particular English remains against which the foreign tongues can be measured, it too having become an untethered "series of Englishes"'.[44] Translation is essential, therefore, in understanding three key aspects of Pound's poetics: the relationship between languages, language as cultural negotiation, and the language of the *Cantos*. As Katz's study reminds us, the *Cantos* do not simply take place in a 'series of Englishes', but also in Chinese, Egyptian hieroglyphs, French, German, Italian, and Spanish, among other national languages and diagrams. The poem fluctuates between translation and non-translation, blurring the distinction between the creative process behind the two. It is perhaps better, in light of the dynamism to which translation points, not to speak of Pound's theory of language, but rather his approach to languages. This subject is given more treatment in Chapters 2 and 3.

Another significant area of study is, of course, Pound's politics. In recent decades, from Robert Casillo's *A Genealogy of Demons* (1987) and

Tim Redman's *Ezra Pound and Italian Fascism* (1991) to current work by Matthew Feldman and David Barnes, critics have considered the role that Pound's fascism and anti-Semitism have played in his poetry.[45] Peter Nicholls frames Pound's politics in discussion of the relation between his economic theories and his language of 'rectification': that is, a desire for a clear and precise language conducive to good economics.[46] Nicholls draws on the essential unities between Pound's aesthetics and his politics, providing a clear model for Poundian scholarship wishing to work on either. In his *Language, Sexuality, and Ideology in Ezra Pound's Cantos*, Jean-Michel Rabaté deftly draws together the wide range of Pound's interests to focus on his critique of metaphysics through language and history, an approach that Rabaté links with Heidegger. The 1930s crystallise Rabaté's comparison, as both Heiddeger and Pound 'responded to the tide of history as it swept over Europe, while maintaining the claims of a foundational approach to language'.[47] Where Rabaté provides a Lacanian exposition of the way in which Pound posits the speaking subject as the 'Other' of language, my task in this book is always to maintain a closer relationship between the two. Nevertheless, as Rabaté demonstrates, one cannot speak of language alone. Culture, history, and psychology (and, as Rabaté suggests, sexuality, though this is beyond the scope of this book) all play a fundamental role in the determination of the linguistic structures that we inhabit and use; in Pound's case, there is the underlying question of the extent to which his own theories of culture, history, and psychology interact with language. Indeed, from the 1930s on, his understanding of all three became inflected with the racial and anti-Semitic theories he indulged. As Michael North has shown in his *The Dialect of Modernism* (1998), even Pound's technique of mimicking accents and dialects became a response to his interest in race.[48] Rabaté and North demonstrate that discussions of the relationship between language, language use, and literary style must take questions of culture or identity into account.

The Argument and Structure of the Book

One of the methodologies of this book has been to 'bracket off' both structuralist and post-structuralist treatments of language as far as possible in order to offer a recovery of Pound's work on the terms in which he himself would have understood it. This is not to challenge semiotic theories per se, but rather solely to allow a number of neglected voices to come through louder and more clearly. With the advent of semiotic models of language in the study of literature, Pound's work has often been appropriated into discourses and debates which, while eminently necessary, have blurred somewhat our notion of how he would have understood his work himself. The dominant approach to discussing the relationship between modernism and language has been to rely on structuralist or post-structuralist treatments of the linguistic sign. It is the role of linguistics, Saussure argues, to analyse the system of language as system, whether synchronically (that is, the system as it appears in an instant of time) or diachronically (changes in the system across time). Meaning is thus reduced to the interaction of signs and semiotic accounts of language are often further reduced to the analysis of the sign itself.[49] Applied to literary studies, it is the role of critics to formalise the structures of literary texts (whether intrinsic or intertextual) and to see the ways in which these arbitrary signs take effect in texts. With the advent of post-structuralism, the faith in the structure of these texts was challenged, most notably by Jacques Derrida, who critiqued Saussure's understanding of 'difference' as lacking a temporal quality. Derrida argues that Saussure relies on 'difference' as a kind of originary, 'transcendental signified', which, in fact, draws attention to the instability of the concept itself.[50] Saussure's understanding of all meanings as negatively constituted, Derrida argues, actually draws attention to the instability of language, seeing as signs by their nature stand for absences. Language, therefore, draws attention to our ontological instability. Literary texts, particularly literary modernism, according to such a view, draw attention to the ways in which language manifests this ontological instability. The problem with such a view is that, if literary analysis is too reductive to the status and structure of signs, and their interaction, the difference between texts is somewhat obscured. What unites both structuralism and post-structuralism is its focus on discussions of language through the lens of the sign; Pound's approach, by contrast, is, on the one hand, pragmatic and, on the other hand, holistic. While he grants the arbitrariness of linguistic signs, his work is far more concerned with the non-arbitrary aspects of language, its material conditions, physiology, its history, its cultural connections, and its psychological bases. This book is an attempt to understand Pound's theory of language in a way that does not reduce to the sign.

For all the manifold achievements of both structuralism and post-structuralism, there has recently been a movement towards revising the semiotic focus of the twentieth century. In her excellent recent study, *Saussure's Philosophy of Language as Phenomenology*, Beata Stawarska challenges the general conception that Saussure was the originator of structuralism and its focus on systemic analysis. Stawarska argues that Saussure really requires a phenomenological understanding of the relationship between signs, thought, and world in order to fully appreciate his ideas. Stawarska calls for a 'linguistic phenomenology' in which language is 'encountered subjectively, within the consciousness that a language user has of being involved in language-bound practices of speaking, listening, and writing'.[51] In many ways, I have attempted a similar revision of our understanding of Pound in particular, and modernism more generally. Rather than focus on the linguistic sign, I have tried to restore the debate around the literary understanding of language to the terms in which it was understood at the time, particularly with regard to thought. The nature of arbitrary signs was, of course, a part of this debate, but it had nothing like the centrality implied by scholarship in the structuralist and post-structuralist traditions.

In particular, I am interested in a recovery of the speaking subjects and creative acts. For all the merits of semiotic accounts of language, they have a tendency to subsume the notion of subjectivity within debates around language systems, culture, and ontology, and to reduce discussions around language to a focus on what Pound terms the most 'mundane' element of language, the sign. Where Pound writes of 'the clinch of the phrase onto the thing intended to be expressed', our critical inheritance encourages a reading which sees this in terms of a relationship between utterance and linguistic matrix, between sign and system. Seen thus, it is clear why Pound is often seen as a kind of linguistic reactionary with a faith in some natural connection between word and thing. A 'linguistic phenomenology' of the kind that Stawarska encourages, however, allows us to see this relationship in wider complexity by restoring the speaking subject and its activity, to expand beyond the sign into the totality of human experience. Pound's emphasis on poetry as craft, as an art of making, means we cannot reduce our understanding of language to a connection between signs and the systems governing them. It is the role of the poet to direct language towards intentional objects or ideas, and it is the extent of this directedness that constitutes poetic language.

Although I have spoken of the need to 'bracket off' structuralism, this is a solely theoretical exercise, and Saussure remains a prominent voice in this study. In another recent revision of Saussurian linguistics, Armin Burkhardt has argued that scholarship often ignores a significant distinction in Saussure's work between arbitrariness and 'motivation' (the assigning of meaning to a phrase on the basis of predetermined limits). In a close reading of the *Course in General Linguistics*, Burkhardt argues that the arbitrariness of linguistic signs is offset against and restricted by a process of 'motivating' signs towards objects or concepts: at the moment in which one selects a new work for a concept, one is limited by certain factors: be they historical meanings, social contexts, and aesthetic considerations. Forming a new word of compounds, for example, Burkhardt argues, cannot be arbitrary as 'compounds are always motivated (but not completely determined) by their components (at least not in a historical perspective)'.[52] In other words, the coining of phrases is always limited by certain conditions, including pre-existing linguistic forms. Saussure's most profound insight, according to Burkhardt, lies in demonstrating that over time even these 'motivated' signs lose their meaning and become arbitrary in conventional usage. The history of language is a process of fluctuation between motivation and arbitrariness: 'motivation stands at the beginning and arbitrariness at the end of a word's historical career'.[53] Pound's aesthetic and epistemological concerns lead him to stand resolutely at the outset of this linguistic arc.

The broadly chronological divisions that I have made in this book cannot be separated neatly. I have tried, however, to match them with important poetical and theoretic shifts in Pound's work. In this book, I have investigated five aspects of Pound's approach to language. In Chapter 1, I explore the ways in which Pound's background in philology, particularly Germanic philology, influenced his approach to poetry and translation. Pound's lifelong animosity towards the academic study of literature and language has obscured the numerous debts he owed it in his practice. In Chapter 2, I reassess Pound's understanding of Fenollosa's *The Chinese Written Character as a Medium for Poetry*, arguing that it is to be understood in terms of a modernist commitment to internal reality and consciousness, a discussion that requires disentangling from our current focus on semiotics. In Chapter 3, I explore Pound's linguistic relativism in relation to an anthropological shift in modernist culture. In particular, I look at the linguistic implications of Pound's reading of Lucien Levy-Bruhl and Leo Frobenius. Chapters 4 and 5 can be taken together as two related explorations of Pound's attempt to resolve the relationship between particulars and universals in language. In the former, I look at Pound's brief but enlightening engagement with international languages. Pound was interested in the work of C.K. Ogden and his Basic English project, exploring the ways in which Ogden's views of language correspond with Pound's. In the final chapter, I look at the final sections of Pound's *Cantos*, from the *Pisan Cantos* to 'Drafts and Fragments', reading them in relation to Pound's attempt to find an aesthetic and philosophical theory that will bind them together. In the 'Afterword', I attempt to pull out the implications that this has for Pound's understanding of language, and modernist debates around language's capabilities in general.

What I attempt in this book is a twofold recovery. On the one hand, I hope to lay the foundations for understanding Pound's career in light of his complex view of language, relating this not only to the traditions in which he saw himself working, but also to our broader understanding of modernism and linguistic theories. To modernist studies, I hope to contribute to the rediscovery of a number of strands of thought picked up not only by Pound, but by his contemporaries as well. On the other hand, and related to this first task, I hope to recover a literary understanding of language, distinct from the structuralist and post-structuralist ideas literary studies has inherited. By 'bracketing off', so to speak, the semiotic approach to language, I hope to restore to current debates a literary approach to language which draws on longstanding continuities and shifts in poetry and prose which consider the speaking subject, style, and notions of reality at their centre. In doing so, I suggest that the structuralist and post-structuralist focus on the linguistic sign is at once too reductive and too abstract to capture the various aesthetic, cultural, historical, psychological, political, and, above all, personal limitations which condition linguistic choices.

In 1934, Pound provided a retrospective account of the difficulties that he faced in establishing his poetic voice early in his career. As Pound makes clear, the problems he faced revolved around the history of language as well as the relationship between language and thought. They also, significantly, as I hope to show, indicate the importance of the individual mind in the use of language. Pound's retrospective account captures the problems he had in distinguishing himself from his forebears:

> What obfuscated me was...the crust of dead English, the sediment present in my own vocabulary – which I, let us hope, got rid of a few years later. You can't go round this sort of thing. It takes six or eight years to get educated in one's art, and another ten to get rid of that education.
>
> Neither can anyone learn English, one can only learn a series of Englishes. Rossetti made his own language. I hadn't in 1910 made a language, I don't mean a language to use, but even a language to think in.
>
> (*LE*, 193–194)

Language was, for Pound, the tool, the medium, and ultimately the form of thought. What this book is, then, is the story of a modernist poet's attempt to find a 'language to think in'. As with any language, there are contexts and histories and personal preferences that influence the phrases; there is an inherited grammar and syntax; there are rules to be obeyed for the sake of understanding. There is the ubiquitous problem of how to translate one language into another, and the difficulty of compensating for what is lost in the process: 'Shall two know the same in their knowing?' Pound asks in Canto XCIII, to which we may ask the respondent question: how would we know? (XCIII.651). There is, of course, language change across time and morphology; there is the difficulty in attending to the processes of meaning and the problem of how signs work. There is, as Pound was to discover towards the end of his career, the problem of silence in the face of the incommunicable: a problem raised by Hofmannsthal and Wittgenstein alike. Above all, however, there is the fact that human language binds us as a species (for all our division), and that poetry and literature generally, the art of language, depend upon its variety, its beauty and sublimity, and its uncanny success.

Notes

1 Ezra Pound, 'A Few Don'ts by an Imagiste', *Poetry: A Magazine of Verse*, 1:1 (1913), 200–206 (200).

2 See Richard Rorty, *The Linguistic Turn: Essays in Philosophical Method* (Chicago: University of Chicago Press, 1967).

3 See the discussion of number in §68 in Gottlob Frege, *The Foundations of Arithmetic: A Logico-mathematical Enquiry into the Concept of Number*, trans. J.L. Austin (New York: Harper, 1960), 79; and Michael Dummett, *Origins of Analytic Philosophy* (London: Bloomsbury, 2014), 6.

4 The German word *Bedeutung* is most commonly translated as 'meaning', but it, in fact, encapsulates a wider range of meanings than this: it lies somewhere between 'significance', 'intension', and 'use'.

5 Gottlob Frege, 'Sense and Reference', *The Philosophical Review*, 57:3 (1948), 209–230.

6 I have used this example for the sake of continuity, and Russell uses the examples of Walter Scott and the non-existent 'present King of France'. See Bertrand Russell, 'On Denoting', *Mind*, 14:56 (1905), 479–493.

7 Ludwig Wittgenstein, *Tractatus Logico-Philosophicus*, trans. D.F. Pears, and B.F. McGuinness (London: Routledge & Kegan Paul, 1961), 56.

8 Ferdinand de Saussure, *Course in General Linguistics*, ed. Charles Bally, Albert Sechehaye, and Albert Riedlinger, trans. Wade Baskin (New York: Philosophical Library, 1959), 9–10.

9 Saussure, *Course in General Linguistics*, 101–102.

10 Saussure, *Course in General Linguistics*, 66.

11 Roland Barthes, 'The Death of the Author' in *Music Image Text*, trans. Stephen Heath (London: Fontana, 1977), 142–148 (145).

12 Jean-Michel Rabaté, *Language, Sexuality and Ideology in Ezra Pound's Cantos* (Basingstoke: Macmillan, 1986), 2.

13 Martin Heidegger, 'Language' in *Poetry, Language, Thought*, trans. Albert Hofstadter (New York: HarperCollins, 1975), 185–208 (188). Heidegger's meaning here is somewhat lost in translation into English. Although it is quite clear that Heidegger argues that 'language speaks', the German word *Sprache* [language or speech] is linked to the verb *sprachen* [to speak], and so in Heideggerian terms the phrase 'die Sprache spricht' could very well be translated as 'language languages' or 'speech speaks', a notion which must be related to his argument that 'things thing' or 'humans human', that is, in arguing that *die Sprache spricht*, Heidegger is attempting to isolate the linguistic element without importing human values or agency in the way that later post-structuralists do. Heidegger resolutely does not personify speech.

14 Heidegger, 'Language', 196.

15 Hugo von Hofmannsthal, 'Letter to Lord Chandos' in *The Whole Difference: Selected Writings*, ed. J.D. McClatchy, trans. Tania Stern, and James Stern (Princeton: Princeton University Press, 2008), 69–79 (74).

16 Hugo von Hofmannsthal, 'Letter to Lord Chandos', 79.

17 Gustave Flaubert, *The George Sand-Gustave Flaubert Letters*, trans. Aimee L. McKenzie (London: Duckworth, 1922), 359–360.

18 Ezra Pound, *Hugh Selwyn Mauberley (Life and Contacts)* (London: Ovid Press, 1920), 9.

19 Ezra Pound, *Selected Letters, 1907–1941*, ed. D.D. Paige (New York: New Directions, 1951), 137.

20 Walter Pater, 'Style' in *Appreciations: with an Essay on Style* (London: Macmillan, 1889), 1–36 (1).

21 Pater, 'Style' 27.
22 Pater, 'Style', 28.
23 Pater, 'Style', 34.
24 Ezra Pound, 'I Gather the Limbs of Osiris: IX. On Technique', *The New Age*, 10:13 (1912), 297–299 (298).
25 There is, of course, a problem of terminology in the fact that the word 'semiotic' was not popularised at Pound's time, and so the word 'Symbolism' had a double meaning: In order to avoid this confusion, in the following, I will be explicit when referring to Symbolism in the semiotic sense, and Symbolism as a literary movement.
26 See Roman Jakobson, 'Closing Statement: Linguistics and Poetics' in *Style in Language*, ed. Thomas Sebeok (Cambridge, MA: MIT Press, 1960), 350–377.
27 T.E. Hulme, 'Romanticism and Classicism' in *Speculations: Essays on Humanism and the Philosophy of Art*, ed. Herbert Read (London: Kegan Paul, Trench & Trubner, 1924), 111–140 (132).
28 Hulme, 'Romanticism and Classicism', 134.
29 Ezra Pound, 'I Gather the Limbs of Osiris: X. On Music', *The New Age*, 10:15 (1912), 343–344 (343).
30 Dante Alighieri, *Purgatorio*, I.13–15. Translation my own.
31 Ezra Pound, 'I Gather the Limbs of Osiris: XI. En Breu Brisiral Temps Braus', *The New Age*, 10:16 (1912), 369–370 (370).
32 Ezra Pound, 'In A Station of the Metro' in *Lustra* (London: Elkin Matthews, 1916), 45.
33 Ezra Pound, *Gaudier-Brzeska: A Memoir* (New York: New Directions, 1960), 89.
34 Pound, *Gaudier-Brzeska*, 88.
35 Pound, *Gaudier-Brzeska*, 86–87.
36 Victor P.H. Li, 'Philology and Power: Ezra Pound and the Regulation of Language', *boundary 2*, 15:1 (1986–1987), 187–210 (189).
37 See G.E.M. Anscombe, 'The Question of Linguistic Idealism' in *From Parmenides to Wittgenstein* (London: Blackwell, 1981), 112–133.
38 David Bloor, 'The Question of Linguistic Idealism Revisited', in *The Cambridge Companion to Wittgenstein*, ed. David Stern, and Hans Sluga (Cambridge: Cambridge University Press, 1996) 354–382 (356).
39 Richard Rorty, "In Defense of Eliminative Materialism" in *Mind, Language and Metaphilosophy: Early Philosophical Papers*, ed. Stephen Leach, and James Tartaglia (Cambridge: Cambridge University Press, 2014), 199–207 (203).
40 Jacques Derrida, *Of Grammatology*, trans. Gayatri Chakravorty Spivak (Baltimore: Johns Hopkins University Press, 1976), 92.
41 Philip Kuberski, *A Calculus of Ezra Pound: Vocations of the American Sign* (Gainesville: University of Florida Press, 1992), 4.
42 Kuberski, *A Calculus of Ezra Pound*, 60.
43 Daniel Katz, *American Modernism's Expatriate Scene: The Labour of Translation* (Edinburgh: Edinburgh University Press, 2007), 75.
44 Katz, *American Modernism's Expatriate Scene*, 87.
45 See Matthew Feldman, *Ezra Pound's Fascist Propaganda, 1935–45* (Basingstoke: Macmillan, 2013); David Barnes, 'Fascist Aesthetics: Ezra Pound's Cultural Negotiations in 1930s Italy', *Journal of Modern Literature*, 34:1 (2010), 19–35.
46 See in particular Nicholls's chapters 'Pound and Fascism' (79–103) and 'A Metaphysics of the State' (104–124) in *Politics, Economics and Writing*.
47 Jean-Michel Rabaté, *Language, Sexuality and Ideology in Ezra Pound's Cantos* (Albany: State University of New York Press, 1986), 4.

48 See Michael North, *The Dialect of Modernism: Race, Language, and Twentieth-century Literature* (Oxford: Oxford University Press, 1998), 94–99.
49 Ferdinand de Saussure, *Course in General Linguistics*, 65–68.
50 Jacques Derrida, *Writing and Difference*, trans. Alan Bass (Chicago: University of Chicago Press, 1978), 280.
51 Beata Stawarska, *Saussure's Philosophy of Language as Phenomenology: Undoing the Doctrine of the Course in General Linguistics* (Oxford: Oxford University Press, 2015), 109.
52 Armin Burkhardt, 'The So-called Arbitrariness of Linguistic Signs and Saussure's "Realism"', in *Essays on Linguistic Realism*, ed. Christina Behme, and Martin Neef (Amsterdam: John Benjamins, 2018), 271–296 (286).
53 Armin Burkhardt, 'The So-Called Arbitrariness of Linguistic Signs and Saussure's "Realism"', 288–289.

1 'End Fact. Try Fiction'

Post-Philology in Pound's Early Writing

Pound's first critical publication was an article entitled 'Raphaelite Latin' defending aspects of Renaissance Latin poetry against what he felt was an undeserved reputation for 'literary barrenness'. This article was published in *Book News Monthly* in September 1906, when he had recently taken up doctoral study in Romance languages at the University of Pennsylvania, having previously completed an MA there, and a BPhil at Hamilton College. Pound's choice of subject matter, late Latin poetry, should be seen as medium rather than message. Pound used the occasion of his article to launch an attack on the academic methodologies of philology, the mother discipline of his own studies. Ostensibly his attack centres on the 'neglect' of the qualities of late Latin poetry:

> There are causes for this neglect. The scholars of classic Latin, bound to the Germanic ideal of scholarship, are no longer able to as of old fill themselves with the beauty of the classics, and by the very force of that beauty inspire their students to read Latin widely and for pleasure; nor are they able to make students see clearly whereof classic beauty consists. The scholar is compelled to spend most of his time learning what his author wore and ate, and in endless pondering over some utterly unanswerable question of textual criticism, such as: 'In a certain epigram,' not worth reading, and which could not get into print to-day, 'is a certain word *seca* or *secat?* The meaning will be the same, but the syntax is different'.[1]

Pound's characterisation of philological scholarship implies a dedicated yet limited focus on particulars and curiosities, without full attention to literature as a whole. During his time at the University of Pennsylvania (1901–1902, 1905–1907) and Hamilton College (1903–1905), Pound had become intimately acquainted with philology as both a discipline and a practice of reading texts. As David Moody has written, 'philology' would 'become the catchword for all that Pound thought wrong with the university teaching of literature as he experienced it', even if the antagonistic stances he took obscure a deeper, more complex relationship with the discipline.[2] Philology is an approach, Pound argues in 'Raphaelite

Latin', that takes too narrow a focus as the basis of study, basing its
methodology on the 'scientific' approach developed in Germany in the
early nineteenth century. He continues by describing the effect of the
perceived narrowness of philological study on the scholar:

> The scholar is bowed down to this Germanic ideal of scholarship,
> the life work of whose servants consists in gathering blocks to build
> a pyramid that will be of no especial use except as a monument, and
> whose greatest reward is the possibility that the servant may have
> his name on the under side of some half-prominent stone, where by
> chance – a slender one – some future stone-gatherer will find it. This
> system has three results; it makes the servant piously thank his gods
> that his period ends in A.D. 400, and that there are some stones he
> need not carry, some things written thereafter that he need not read.
> It also prevents his building a comfortable house for his brain to live
> in, and makes him revile anyone who tries to do so with the abject
> and utterly scornful 'dilettante'. No one knows the contempt and
> hatred that can be gathered into these few syllables until they have
> been hissed at him by one fully Germanized.[3]

Pound's vitriol and hyperbole is symptomatic of much of his criticism
and is particularly indicative of the attitude towards philology as a critical practice that he would come to adopt throughout his career. Nevertheless, what Pound's first article establishes is a dichotomy between
a 'Germanic' model of linguistic scholarship and a Romance literary
aesthetic (here Latin but later primarily Provençal) which, he believed,
the former tried to contain.

Philology provided Pound with the material for the early part of his
career and, inevitably, provided the framework for his earliest thought
on language, and yet the term appears almost entirely in the context of
Pound's attempt to define his project against it. The central contention
of this chapter is that Pound's use of the term 'philology' obscures the
immense debt that he owed to the discipline in providing him with a
solid foundation in the form of an historical understanding of language.
It was upon this foundation that Pound built his early career. That language is always historically determined, always textually mediated, and
always in a state of dynamic change are lessons we can draw from both
philology and Pound's oeuvre. Pound's criticism of philology thus speaks
to its role in literary analysis, rather than its linguistic dimensions. Although we find numerous instances of Pound's resentment towards philology as a literary study, we nowhere find instances of criticism of its
linguistic assumptions. Indeed, we find the precise opposite. By tracing
Pound's use of the word 'philology', and measuring it against his critical
and poetic practice, we can see that his attitude towards his former subject was far more complicated than his claims lead us to believe.

It is important, therefore, to draw a distinction between philology as a discipline and philology as a practice. While Pound attacks both at various points, it is far easier to see his continued affinity with the latter. As discipline, philology embodies what Pound calls the 'Germanized' model, a kind of sociocultural milieu in and of itself, a professorial approach to literature, and the restrictive atmosphere of university learning (as Pound conceived it). Philology as a practice encompasses an approach to the study of literature which, though Pound was dismissive of its subjugating literature to linguistic analysis, provided him with a set of critical tools which would serve him for the rest of his life. The tools included: an intense focus on the language of texts in relation to linguistic history, the use of etymology as the basis of arguments, an interest in morphology, a manuscript-led approach to literary scholarship (that is to say, a grounding of criticism in textual genesis), an understanding of history as textually mediated, a comparative approach to language and literature, and, above all, an intention to situate languages and texts within broader networks. There are numerous examples of the above in Pound's oeuvre: think of Pound's use of bibliographical notes in his *Personae*, his imitation of the logic of the Anglo-Saxon in the *Seafarer*, his poetic meditation on the cultural history of Homer's *Odyssey* as it passes from Greek to Latin to Pound's multifaceted English in Canto I (originally Canto III), the visibility and prominence of his research in the *Cantos*, the way citation is built into his poetics, and his interest in the relationship between prosody and the logic of language. In all of these cases, while there is a rejection of the disciplinary culture of philology, there is a reliance on his background in the practice.

Defining Philology

But what is philology? The best way to think about it is as a method of studying the linguistic dimensions of texts, bridging our modern division of literature and linguistics by bringing both within one historical discipline. In his authoritative recent study of the discipline and its history, James Turner loosely defines it as 'the multifaceted study of texts, languages, and the phenomenon of language itself'.[4] Turner's central argument is that philology is the common origin of all 'humanities' subjects in the contemporary university and, therefore, the spectre of philology haunts the academy even today. In particular, the modernist period emerges from Turner's study as a time in which philology dissipated, and yet this dissipation was one in which the discipline became part of the very fabric of modern thought. In many ways, this dissipation began in the mid- to late nineteenth century with the development of the Neogrammarian group at the University of Leipzig. The Neogrammarian hypothesis was one of the crowning achievements of nineteenth-century philology: drawing on the previous work of Jacob Grimm, philologists

such as Karl Brugmann, Berthold Delbrück, and Hermann Osthoff proposed the following principle: all sound change is regular and excep-
tionless, affecting all words in a language's environment. This change
is identical for all members of a speech community. The hypothesis
grounded philological study in the observation of diachronic and comparative change in languages. In their 'Neogrammarian hypothesis'
(1878), Brugmann and Osthoff argued for a focus on the idiolect, the
language as located in the individual speaker, moving towards modern
linguistics and away from a purely textual focus.[5]

Pound thus entered the modern language department at a crucial
juncture of philological history. In the early twentieth century, philology's twin aims, the study of language and the study of literature, separated (albeit uncleanly) into linguistics and literary studies, respectively.
Within literary studies, there was a further debate between those who
held fast to philological methodology and those who professed a more
aesthetically driven, critical approach. In his seminal study of the debates surrounding the development of modern language and literature
departments, Gerald Graff outlines two rival tendencies: philologists,
who were dedicated to the 'scientific' study of language, textual history,
and comparative grammar, and 'generalists', who saw literature as an
embodiment of a wider humanist spirit, and whose criticism focussed on
questions of literary value. Graff characterises the polarised extremity
of the 'generalist' and philological positions, respectively, as 'dilettantes
versus investigators: the one all interesting but untrue generalizations,
the other all true but sterile particularities, and evidently nothing in
between'.[6] In 'Raphelite Latin', Pound clearly nails his colours to the
'generalist' (or 'dilettante') mast, but this action should be seen in the
context of a rebellion against philology, more than an endorsement of
pure generalism.

By virtue of philology's dominance in the university and its centrality
to academic life by the time of the late nineteenth century, it may be that
it was simply too 'multifaceted' to yield a single definition. Indeed, there
seems to be little agreement on what philology's true object of study was:
literature or language. Although most accounts tend to emphasise that
it was a unification of the two, Pound, on the one hand, seems to have
felt the linguistic aspect of the discipline too dominant; Saussure, on
the other hand, complained of the predominance of the literary, writing
that '[philological criticism] follows the written language too slavishly
and neglects the living language'.[7] It is in this contrast that we can see
two things: first, that the multifaceted nature of philology had become
so strained by the early twentieth century that it could be interpreted in
completely opposed ways; second, we see a disciplinary chasm between
the modernist Pound and the structuralist Saussure.

As Pound suggests, philology was bound to its country of origin.
The American history of philology is one of constant exchanges with

Germany. American universities looked to their German counterparts. Germany was central, from the first American scholars who travelled to Göttingen to receive instruction in new university methodologies unavailable at home in the early nineteenth century (these included Edward Everett, George Bancroft, and, later, Henry Wadsworth Longfellow) to Daniel Coit Gilman and Andrew Dickson White, who were instrumental in the importation of the 'German model' during their premierships of Johns Hopkins and Cornell, respectively.[8] Both Gilman and White had studied at the University of Berlin, one of the world's leading centres for philological and linguistic research, from 1855 to 1856. As Pound writes in *Guide to Kulchur*, in a much more conciliatory mood than in 1906, 'the general belief during my youth in American beaneries was that one shd. go to Germany for systematized information' (*GK*, 219). An insight into the 'Germanic method' is provided by James Morgen Hart, who in 1874 recounted in somewhat romanticised terms his experience of studying philology in German universities:

> To make the method of instruction more evident, we have only to picture ourselves a man like George Curtius, of Leipsic, 'reading' on the Odyssey. He begins probably with a general introduction to the Homeric question, spending perhaps a fortnight setting forth his views and refuting the views of others. He then gives a detailed description of all the manuscripts of the poem, their comparative merits and deficiencies, and also the best modern critical editions. Then, following some generally received text, he translates, either carefully, line by line, or else rapidly, according as the passage may be difficult or easy. As he goes he makes historical, aesthetical, linguistic excursions. By the end of the semester he has probably finished only a few books. But his hearers, who have listened attentively and with minds prepared by their gymnasial training, have caught the essence of the poem and its relations, can henceforth study it for themselves.[9]

Hart's account largely consists as much of generalised summaries as it does of detailed experiences, aimed more at presenting something of the spirit of *Philologie* than in outlining university policy. In the case above, while Hart refers to the renowned philologist George Curtius (1820–1885) by name, the outline is largely speculative and based on a composite of lectures that he attended, as well as idealised depictions of a philological scholar. Pound, whose career is marked by those very 'historical, aesthetical, linguistic' excursions, presumably would have argued that they should have been the centre of pedagogic practice, rather than a grammar-translation method of teaching.

In the year before Pound's birth, 1884, H.C.G. Brandt, professor of German at Hamilton College, published his address to the Modern Language Association. In his address, he defended the 'scientific basis' of the

modern language department against what he believed to be three oppos-
·ing trends damaging the discipline: a 'utilitarian' (or 'dilettante') criticism
of literature, classical philologists being suspicious of new methods, and
complacency within modern language teachers themselves. He argued
passionately for the continuation of a scientific, rather than humanistic,
model, writing that 'a scientific basis dignifies our profession' by demanding professionalism, precision, and proof. But more than this, Brandt's argument is a passionate defence of the value of studying modern languages.
In his account, he cites the example of the Neogrammarians in particular,
suggesting that their achievements are an indication of the exciting possibilities that Germanic philology offered the scientists of language:

> We recognise these men as the foremost among those who have de-
> veloped within the last fifteen years the old humdrum, the empirical
> treatment of living languages into the scientific study of them today.
> They have done even more than that. Investigating the phenomena
> of *living* languages they have reached results which are a valuable
> contribution to the science of language and comparative philology.
> They have started a new branch of philology, viz. Phonetics, in-
> vented new methods of investigation, and gained deep insight into
> the nature of language.[10]

According to Brandt, philology as a practice and as an ideology of study
provided the student not only with a sound scientific basis, with the
nobility of proof and clear methodology, but also with access to current
and lively scholarship. Brandt was a moderniser, a practitioner of modern philology, as opposed to ancient or classical philology, and his emphasis on the value of studying living languages can be seen as a step in
the movement from philology to modern linguistics. There is, of course,
an implication in Brandt's address that to base the study of language
(and literature) on a non-scientific foundation would be undignified, and
in that sense the prejudices on either side of the debate are manifested in
this defence, but by and large it is a strong defence of philology's scientific bases. Brandt was still Professor of German when Pound attended
Hamilton College between 1903 and 1905, and Pound remembered his
former professor very fondly in a letter to John Quinn on 16 August
1915 as part of a list of admirable figures in the United States. Pound
also included his former professors Felix Schelling, Clarence Child,
Hugo Rennert (all of the University of Pennsylvania), as well as William
Pierce Shepard of Hamilton College.[11]

In fact, the period in which Pound entered university is often seen as
the moment at which philology entered into its phases of decline and
fall. In 2002, during his presidential address to the Modern Language
Association of America, Michael Holquist called for a return to philology in a paper entitled 'Why We Should Remember Philology'. This

echoed an earlier paper of Holquist's, 'Forgetting our Name, Remembering our Mother' (2000), in which he articulated the narrative of philology's decline and eventual disappearance by the time of the twentieth century. According to Holquist, philology is defined broadly as the study of language and literature for their own sakes.[12] He then argues that in the development of the nineteenth-century German university, philology became a specialised, narrower form of study, which comprised the dedicated linguistic and textual scholarship with which the term is most often associated today. At the heart of the word 'philology', then, is a separation between an original term encompassing the whole of the study of language and literature, and a narrower definition that developed out of the academy referring to practicalities of scholarship: a focus on details and variations, and a situating of study in relation to wider linguistic histories and developments. It was also focussed on textual scholarship, as opposed to critical or aesthetic evaluations.

Holquist proposes a narrative of decline and fall. Against this, one can posit one of assimilation and change, whereby the advent of linguistics and literary studies did not usurp philology as a discipline, but were natural outgrowths from it. This argument has been most fully articulated by Turner in his *Philology* (2014), which traces a longer narrative arch, rooting the origins of philology in ancient Greece, and explaining which traces of the discipline remain in the histories of the modern humanities. For Turner, the development of linguistics at the turn of the twentieth century was indeed a radical change in philology, but was not necessarily a radical departure from its humanistic roots.

> Perhaps the most accurate assessment is that, when the discipline of linguistics took its modern form around 1900, it stood betwixt and between. Part of it identifiably linked to the humanistic philological tradition. Other parts left that tradition far behind.[13]

Linguistics, then, developed from philology by adopting and adapting aspects of the latter discipline; the same can be said of literature departments, combining philological professionalism and scholarly ethos with wider critical concerns. Indeed, Turner's assessment is apt for a discussion of philology's place in the development of Pound's linguistic theories. Pound himself stood 'betwixt and between' philology's outgrowths in the early years of the twentieth century, negotiating between a sense of critical frustration and an inevitable scholarly learning. When he came to distance himself from philology, he still adopted and adapted much of what he had learned and put it to use in a linguistically charged poetic career that ran parallel to many of the developments of twentieth-century linguistics. As Turner concludes on the latter history of philology, in a phrase that applies equally well to the discipline's place in Pound's career, 'philology did not vanish. It went underground'.[14]

Pound's Encounter with Philology

For all his protestations, Pound's experience in philology was the foundation for his career. In 'A Visiting Card' (written 1942), Pound writes of how he considered the 'hours spent with Layamon's *Brut*, or copying a prose translation of Catallus by W. McDaniel; Ibbotson's instruction in Anglo-Saxon or W.P. Shepard's on Dante and the troubadours of Provence – more important than any contemporary influences'.[15] The narrative of Pound's university career is reasonably complex. First, owing to an exceptional score in Latin, he entered the University of Pennsylvania in 1901.[16] It was here that he met Hilda Doolittle and William Carlos Williams, whose lives and works became intimately intertwined with his own. His time at the university was unsuccessful, however, and he moved to Hamilton College, a liberal arts college in New York State, where his academic record improved markedly. In terms of philology and linguistics, Pound would have received an outstanding education in the latest research and methodologies. In particular, Pound seems to have come under the wing of William P. Shepard, who was one of the country's leading authorities on Provençal. Alongside Italian, French, and (later) Chinese, the Langue d'Oc provided Pound with a strong grounding for his interest in history (both political and literary), linguistic nuance, aesthetics, and poetic practice, a combination particularly apparent in the figures of the troubadours. Stuart McDougal alludes to the fact that Shepard, a well-travelled and renowned scholar of Provençal, would have exposed Pound to a number of philological trends.[17] Shepard had graduated from Hamilton College in 1891, before pursuing his studies in Provençal first at the University of Grenoble, then at the Sorbonne, and finally at the University of Heidelberg, where he studied for his PhD. In Europe, he was exposed to both the rapid development of Provençal as a subject and the German model of philological study.

At Hamilton, Pound had access to an extensive Romance collection at the library. In 1971, Rouben C. Cholakian, a later inheritor of Shepard's professorial chair at Hamilton, published a critical bibliography outlining the contents of his predecessor's personal library, providing commentaries on the most notable items. Cholakian explains Shepard's importance:

> It is due almost entirely to the efforts of William P. Shepard, Professor of Romance Languages at Hamilton College from 1896–1940, that this small school can boast today of its unusually extensive collection of Provençalia. During his long association with Hamilton, Professor Shepard guided the library in its purchase of works in Romance Philology and upon his death in 1948 bequeathed to it the major part of his own private collection.[18]

In searching through the items, we can establish a probable view of what would have been available to him as he began his studies in Romance languages. As would be expected, we find the spiritual father of the study of Provençal, Francois Raynouard, alongside the disciplinary founder, Friedrich Christian Diez, as well as a number of leading Provençal and Romance scholars. Assuming that Shepard (or Hamilton itself) owned them at the time of Pound's studies, the following books would all have been available either in the library or in Shepard's private collection: G.J. Adler's translation of Claude Charles Fauriel's *History of Provençal Poetry* (1860); Harriet Preston's *Troubadours and trouveres: New and Old* (1876); Antonio Restori's *Letteratura Provenzale* (1891); and Albert Stimming's *Provenzalische Literatur* (1893), which was also available as part of Gustav Gröber's *Grundriss der romanischen philologie* (1888), a seminal philological text, and one to which Pound would later refer favourably in *The Spirit of Romance* (1910). These texts would have provided Pound with enough evidence of the critical modes employed by 'Germanized' philology.

While little is known about the curricula of Pound's Bachelor's degree at Hamilton, rather more material is available relating to his return to the University of Pennsylvania for his Master's degree. Pound's notes taken from lecture courses on 'Philology' and 'Phonetics', for example, offer a great deal of insight into the kind of linguistic instruction that he gained at the university. Pound's notes on individual instances of sound change or explanations of etymological processes are far more detailed than his notes on individual philologists, suggesting that, as with the study of literature, there was more focus on practice than scholarly traditions. His notes from his 'Philology' course from 21 February 1906, for example, detail the particulars of sound change between Latin and late Vulgar Latin. The notes consist by and large of extensive details and examples of sound changes and linguistic laws. Phrases such as 'closed vowels all stay' and 'open vowels diphthongize and change', while seemingly innocuous, in fact, demonstrate Pound's acquaintance with one of the crowning achievements of German philology: the Neogrammarian hypothesis.[19] This shows that Pound's lifelong interest in language was founded upon sound linguistic practice and his linguistic knowledge on solid philological ground.

The notes are interspersed with references to various associations (such as the Modern Language Association), texts, and authors. One of the most often cited is Gaston Paris, a philologist and scholar who would retain Pound's respect even when he was disparaging of the discipline later in his career (Pound dedicated *ABC of Reading* to Paris and the French philologist-archaeologist, Salomon Reinach, 1858–1932). Paris balanced his dense philological scholarship – as seen in his *Les Plus anciens monuments de la langue française* (1875), his translation of *Grammaire des langues romanes* (1874–1878) by Friedrich Diez, or his

Manuel d'ancien français (1888) – with a dispensation towards expanding his research into more general aesthetic and biographical commentary, such as his *Penseurs et poetes* (1897) and *Légendes du Moyen Age* (1903). In 1872, Paris and fellow Romance scholar Paul Meyer founded the journal *Romania*. This was dedicated to the dissemination of contemporaneous research and thought relating to Romance languages. Pound cites the journal a number of times in his lecture notes.

Although Paris is by far the best represented, the majority of references are to dense bibliographical resources, such as Eduard von Wolfflin's *Archiv für lateinische Lexikographie und Grammatik* (1872), and large grammatical texts such as Gröber's *Grundriss der romanischen Philologie* (1888).[20] Literature was used as illustrative of linguistic research, and was not treated in aesthetic terms, an ethos against which Pound did protest, writing that the 'character of work must be looked to' in the middle of his notes during a lecture in philology on 24 January 1906.[21] This note may be the first recorded instance of his anti-philological stance. Pound was also aware of Walter Skeat's *An Etymological Dictionary of the English Language* (1888) and James Murray's *The Evolution of English Lexicography* (1900), both of which would have given Pound an indication of contemporary developments in the study of language. 'I endeavour, in every case', Skeat writes in the preface to the first edition, 'to exhibit [English's] relation to cognate tongues; and as, by this process, considerable light is thrown upon English by Latin and Greek, so also, at the same time, considerable light is thrown upon Latin and Greek by Anglo-Saxon and Icelandic'.[22] The comparative method which Pound employs in his criticism and in his poetic practice, his insistence on comparing and drawing out the relations between literary traditions in various different languages, mediated by time and place, corresponds to the instruction he received, as revealed in his notes.

By looking at the Catalogue of Courses offered by the University of Pennsylvania for the academic year 1905/1906, we can see that the department was unsurprisingly under the influence of the work of William Dwight Whitney, the leading American philologist of the late nineteenth century, and the 'starting point of American linguistics'.[23] Whitney's *Language and the Study of Language* was the primary text book in Morton Easton's 'Linguistics' course.[24] Having established himself as a leading figure in Indology at Yale, Whitney gave a series of public lectures on language in general in 1867, demonstrating that philological scholarship was capable of being expanded beyond linguistic particulars. Whitney argued that language was a purely conventionalised system of arbitrary signs, a notion which prompted Ferdinand de Saussure's semiotic programme at the University of Geneva, and which remains central to accounts of language today. As James Turner suggests, this was not an original point, and Whitney merely expanded upon an approach to language developed by the Scottish Common Sense philosophers a century earlier.[25] Indeed, one can trace the debate about the 'arbitrariness' of language back to the presocratics.[26] Whitney goes further, however, in the way in which convention creates relatively stabilised meanings out of an arbitrary system. He argues that the meaning of words is historically determined, and that diachronic philological study is required in order to explore the way in which meaning develops. It is easy to see the origins of modern linguistics' breadth of study (from psychological processes to sociolinguistics) in Whitney's broad approach.

However, it would be something of an error to see Whitney solely as the architect of modern scientific approaches to language. Whitney's work, rather than initiating a 'science' of language modelled on the natural sciences, in fact, comes closer to the German translation of the word: *Wissenschaft*, a kind of rigorous scholarship across the sciences and humanities. In his *Language and the Study of Language* (1867), he insists that linguists should not forget the humanistic element of language as an 'institution', that for all its materiality, it is still subject to human will, thought, and passion. Perhaps surprisingly, Whitney sets his stall against naturalism and materialism, often assumed to be correspondents of philology's intentions for language study:

> There is a school of modern philosophers who are trying to materialize all science, to eliminate the distinction between the physical and the intellectual and moral, to declare for naught the free action of the human will, and to resolve the whole story of the fates of mankind into a series of purely material effects, produced by assignable physical causes, and explainable in the past, or determinable for the future, by an intimate knowledge of those causes, by a recognition of the action of compulsory motives upon the passively obedient nature of man. With such, language will naturally pass, along with the rest, for a physical product, and its study for a physical science; and, however we may dissent from their general classification, we cannot quarrel with its application in this particular instance. But by those who still hold to the grand distinction of moral and physical sciences, who think the action of intelligent beings, weighing motives and selecting courses of conduct, seeing ends and seeking means to their attainment, to be fundamentally and essentially different from that of atoms moved by gravity, chemical affinity, and the other immutable forces of nature, as we call them – by such, the study of language, whose dependence upon voluntary action is so absolute that not one word ever was or ever will be uttered without the distinct exertion of the human will, cannot but be regarded as a moral science; its real relationship is with those branches of human knowledge among which common opinion is accustomed to rank it – with mental philosophy, with philology, with history.[27]

Whitney's warning comes as a contrast to the Sausurrian tradition of which he is often seen as a precursor: where Saussure's legacy lay in a distinct science of semiotics, a study of linguistic signs as operational in and of themselves, taking arbitrariness as the starting point of the sign and difference as the starting point of language, Whitney's argument is that such a science misses the point. Language should be located not only in a naturalistic social and evolutionary context, but also in psychological, textual, and historical contexts. Where Saussure takes the arbitrariness of language as the point of departure from Whitney's work, Whitney sees this arbitrariness in the context of something far more central: human nature and human will.

While Pound does not seem to have read Whitney in detail, his influence on the department in which Pound studied was vast, and it is for this reason that Pound's later statement in his essay series 'I Gather the Limbs of Osiris' (1911) that poetry is allied to prose 'as an art of arbitrary symbols' at the very least correlated with the Whitneyian ethos of his Alma Mater. If Pound's understanding of language was not drawn from Whitney directly, it was very much suffused with the same base set of assumptions about the twin symbolic (later, semiotic) and historical natures of language that Whitney's work had inculcated in his lecturers, as well as in many of his linguistic contemporaries. Pound's roots, though he often worked to deny them, lay very much intertwined with those of twentieth-century linguistics.

Rebellion against Philology

Pound's notes demonstrate that his antagonistic stance towards philology developed within the discipline. Returning to 'Raphelite Latin', we can see that Pound's vitriolic criticism of 'Germanised' philology expresses a grievance from a position of acquaintance. Although his writing uses the structure of the shorthand, Pound wrote from experience, and his relationship with the discipline cannot be seen solely in the terms he outlines. Anne Birien summarises Pound's position: 'philology had become corrupt enough to be reformed, but its teachings remained too essential to be dismissed or destroyed altogether'. Birien suggests that Pound's place in the American university system in the early part of the twentieth century provided a fruitful ground for his reformative zeal, in that 'individuals in and outside the academe vindicated both the need for and feasibility of the reform Pound envisioned'.[28] In essence, Pound's writing often asserts a total break from philology, even if his own literary project suggests a reconciliatory, reformist approach.

Pound's drafts of his college essays demonstrate that he was practising more 'generalist' critical techniques and standpoints while receiving, at least reluctantly, detailed instruction in philological history and practice. In response to this situation, Pound argues in an essay entitled

'Black Mirror' that criticism should have a creative vision, for the purpose of improving technique: an insight that is best represented by artists themselves. 'It is our aim to make our future criticism more constructive than destructive', he writes in a line that chimes with Graff's characterisation of philological dismissals of critics. He continues, writing that 'we are in perfect sympathy with those who want to see more criticism from the standpoint of the artist and less from that of the uncultivated public'.[29] Critical writing, Pound argues, is a matter that should be driven by those who practise art. It is not immediately clear who 'we' might represent, but as Pound was already writing poetry at this time, it may mean artists generally, positioning himself within a more aestheticist collective.

Pound's scholarship is one that calls for 'generalities', although we must be careful not to draw too fixed a binary opposition between philology and 'generalism'. Pound's arguments revolve around a failure to relate the particular to the general, and do not necessarily fall in favour of one, nor the other. Rather, he argues that scholarship should focus on significant works, and take care to relate the part to the whole, whether that particular generality be a text, a literary movement, or a style. What is clear from Pound's early writing is that his criticism of philology as a discipline revolves around its scholarly methodologies and its application to literature. Indeed, an early draft of a poem entitled 'Goal' (a mistyping of 'Gaol') demonstrates the complexity of Pound's relationship with his studies:

> Yea I will enter your prison
> Cramped mid the bands of your philology
> Ye that hold (holding) flowers naught but names and
> chemicals
> Yea will I stay behind the bars
> that hold poesy and ald men's loved writings
> To be science and no art.[30]

On the surface, Pound's characterisation of philology strikes one as simple enough: it is a discipline which constrains art, which sees the aesthetic qualities of a work as irrelevant to study, focussing instead on language alone (names) on the material composition of nature only (chemicals). As a metaphor, it seems to display little other than his boredom and contempt. Considering the choice of the image of a jail, however, the true complexity of Pound's relationship with his studies emerges. The speaker begins with an affirmation, reluctant though it may be; an acceptance of his place in this prison cell. The poem reads as a lamentation, but this only heightens the sense of inevitability: this is not a steadfast refusal and rejection of a discipline, but rather acquiescence into an unwanted fate. The 'bands of philology' are not ones Pound envisages escaping, and this provides a neat metaphor for Pound's poetic career. On the abandonment of his academic career, Pound sought at all points to distance himself from philology, to set his literary project up in opposition to it, and yet at all points he returned to the discipline, its practices, its basic assumptions, and his inescapable relationship with it.

Where one would expect something of a radical break from philology on Pound's part (particularly in the context of his later writing), what we see instead is a gradual disengagement. On the completion of his MA in 1906, Pound continued his postgraduate study for a further eighteen months in pursuit of a PhD on the plays of Lope de Vega. According to Pound, this was an error, though not quite for the reasons one would expect such a pronounced anti-philologist to give. Pound had wanted to write a thesis on a text 'OUTSIDE the list of classic authors included in the curriculum' (*GK*, 215–216) and was apparently discouraged by 'Prof MacD' (presumably Pound's Latin tutor, Walton Brooks McDaniel).[31] Recounting this over thirty years later, Pound clearly felt slighted on the grounds of wanting to do original research. Although he eventually abandoned academia in 1907 and embarked finally on his poetic career, that Pound was able to dedicate six years to the study of language and literature within a philological framework suggests that his relationship with the discipline was one of far deeper complexity than the outright hostility of his published work makes clear. Pound's abandonment of his PhD marks neither an abandonment of his interest in literary history nor, more significantly, his interest in theories of language nor scholarship. In the immediate aftermath of his leaving the University of Pennsylvania, Pound took a position teaching Romance languages at Crawfordsville, Indiana. Upon leaving his teaching post, Pound went to Europe in 1908 to begin his poetic career, eventually settling in London.

Pound spent six years of his life studying literature through the prism of linguistic scholarship, and the centrality of the analysis of language to understanding culture and civilisation remained throughout his career. Although the discipline, and academic life, may not have suited him, the theoretical and practical aspects of philology as an approach to language left an indelible mark. Whether they were conscious or unconscious, whether he accepted or rejected them, the early part of Pound's career marks a sustained engagement with dominant philological approaches to language and literature in the late nineteenth and early twentieth centuries.

Rescuing Literature from the 'Slough of Philology'

Pound's relationship with philology in the early part of his career should be understood in the context of a series of attempts to defend and define his own literary aesthetics: as Pound saw it, his theories of language, such as they may be isolated, emerge within the context of his artistic development, and not the other way around. In many ways, Pound's earliest prose writing should be seen as a loosely connected *apologia* for poetry, a series of defences in the mould of Phillip Sidney or Percy Bysshe Shelley. In *The Spirit of Romance* (1910), 'I Gather the Limbs of Osiris' (1912), and 'The Serious Artist' (1913), he outlines various aspects of a project dedicated to a comparative study of the 'best' in literature, a category which must be understood in line with his aesthetic principles. His prose writing at this time may bear the intentions of writing a *De Vulgari Eloquentia* (c.1302–1305) but, at all points, they are rooted in a background of philological scholarship.

Pound's aesthetic and literary break with philology was short lived, then. Between 1908 and 1909, Pound gave a series of lectures at London's Regent Street Polytechnic (now University of Westminster) on pre-Renaissance European Romance literature, which were published in 1910 under the title *The Spirit of Romance*. Pound's subtitle for the book, 'an attempt to define somewhat the charm of the pre-Renaissance literature of Latin Europe', implies a modesty of ambition overthrown by the book itself. The roots of Pound's most famous linguistic stances and much of his aesthetics can be found in *The Spirit of Romance*. The work of a young man, still under the influence of Swinburne and Dante Gabriel Rossetti, there is a subtlety to much (though not all) of Pound's writing and judgement that would, with time, be replaced by a more aggressive prose style. There is much within the pages of *The Spirit of Romance* that is recognisably Poundian as we know it, however, such as his definition of poetry as 'a sort of inspired mathematics, which gives us equations, not for abstract figures, triangles, spheres, and the like, but equations for the human emotions' (*SR*, 5).

Equally recognisably Poundian is the recalcitrant opening to the book. In the opening lines of the preface, Pound declares that 'this is not a philological work', an opening salvo drawn from his six years of apparent frustration at university. He continues to take aim at his former discipline (and, by extension, professors) in the rest of the preface:

> I have floundered somewhat ineffectually through the slough of philology, but I look forward to the time when it will be possible for the lover of poetry to study poetry – even the poetry of recondite times and places – without burdening himself with the rags of morphology, epigraphy, *privatleben* and the kindred delights of the archaeological or 'scholarly' mind. I make no plea for superficiality. But I consider it quite as justifiable that a man should wish to study the poetry and nothing but the poetry of a certain period, as that he should study its antiquities, phonetics or palaeography and be, at the end of his labours, incapable of discerning a refinement of style or a banality of diction.
>
> (*SR*, v)

What Pound offers instead is an approach to literature which outlines literary history, the development of certain literary aesthetics, and explicit value judgements on both: a literary scholarship 'which will weigh Theocritus and Mr Yeats with one balance' (*SR*, vi). Pound's language is interesting here, however. The main thrust of Pound's critical methodology is comparative, and the facets compared tend to fall into one or two categories: either there is a weighing of comparative literary merit, some advancement or discovery 'in the field' of literature as whole, or there is weighing of relative linguistic features. *The Spirit of Romance* is structured by the morphological development of the Romance languages, and although Pound seeks to divide his discussions up into subject matter and literary form, the structure of the book is historical.

The anti-philological stance Pound outlines in his introduction to *The Spirit of Romance* is not borne out in the text itself. He refers to Gustav Gröber's *Grundriss der romanischen philology*, a major philological collection which he had encountered during his time at Hamilton and the University of Pennsylvania:

> This is no attempt to at historical completeness. The 'Grundriss von Grüber' [*sic*] covers somewhat the same period and falls short of completeness in divers ways...to this admirable work I cheerfully commend anyone who has a passion for completeness. For, omitting though it does many of the facts concerning mediaeval literature, it yet contains references to some hundreds of other works wherein the curiosity of the earnest may in some measure be slaked.
>
> (*SR*, vii)

While this is true, *The Spirit of Romance* hinges upon Pound's extensive treatment of Arnaut Daniel, whom Gröber largely neglects. Pound's interest in Daniel can be compared to Dante Gabriel Rossetti's translations of Dante and Guido Cavalcanti, or with Robert Browning's use of Sordello in his eponymous long poem.[32] There is a subtle difference, however. Unlike Rossetti and Browning before him, Pound's reading of Daniel's language was informed by six years of university study in the field. Even if he was not an expert philologist himself, Pound had been exposed over a considerable period of time to the subject by expert philologists. Hence, we find reference in the text to Gröber, Gaston Paris (72–73, for example, where Pound engages with his interpretation of the Chancon de Roland), and W.P. Ker, a scholar and essayist who was at the time Quain Professor for English Literature at University College London. Pound's protestation that *The Spirit of Romance* is not a philological work, that he is resistant to the 'rags of morphology' and the intricacies of *Privatleben*, may well be a case of protesting too much.

The Spirit of Romance is an interesting text, full of astute observations about half-forgotten literary figures, and should be read as the first full treatment of Pound's literary aesthetics. Though Pound is generous in treating a wide variety of subjects in the book, the main focus of the text is on two poets who would become central to Pound's aesthetic: Dante Alighieri and Arnaut Daniel. The former's influence can be divided into two parts: first, *De Vulgari Eloquentia*, Dante's unfinished treatise on poetic language, part literary criticism, part linguistic theory. Lucia Boldrini has shown in her studies of Dante and Joyce the profound impact that this treatise had on literary modernism.[33] Dante's 'philology' as Carlos Riobó refers to it, had a profound influence on Pound, with its insistence of viewing linguistic material from an aesthetic perspective.[34] Dante selects words from various Romance languages (from Latin to his native Italian to Occitan) according to their material, sonic qualities, whether they are masculine, feminine, childlike, 'rustic', 'urbane', 'smooth', or 'hairy'. Dante encourages value judgements based on the sonic qualities of words, urging readers to consider 'how much you will need to sift out in order to keep only the best words'.[35] The application of aesthetic principles to the materiality of language is a project that Pound follows in his critical writing and in his poetry, submitting the contents of volumes of Romance philology to similar tests. Dante's second influence on Pound comes from his poetry and it lies in providing Pound with a paradigm of the kind of 'precise' language which he would assert throughout his career. See Pound's comment on the poetic quality of Dante's *Vita Nuova* and his *Commedia*: 'Dante's precision both in the "Vita Nuova" and in the "Commedia" comes from the attempt to reproduce exactly the thing which has been clearly seen. The "Lord of terrible aspect" is no abstraction, no figure of speech' (*SR*, 144). The seeds of Imagism lie in the language of visualisation which Pound reads into Dante's work.

Also central to the development of Pound's imagist aesthetic is Daniel. Dante had praised Daniel as 'il miglior fabbro' in his *Purgatorio* and included him among a list of revered poets in *De Vulgari Eloquentia*, but by Pound's time his voice was lost into relative obscurity. Pound claims that the reason for Daniel's neglect is twofold: first, he argues, 'poets have been unable to read his language' and, second, those scholars who have been able to read it 'have not known anything about poetry' (*SR*, 14). Pound had a foot in both camps. Interestingly, in a footnote, Pound makes an exception for W.P. Ker. We may add Ker's name to the list including Gaston Paris, Solomon Reinach, Emil Lévy, William Shepard, and Gustav Gröber: philologists whom Pound praises. Pound does qualify his exception by noting his disagreement with Ker's article 'Dante, Guido Guinicelli and Arnaut Daniel' which appeared in the January 1909 edition of the *Modern Language Review*, itself revealing in that it shows Pound was keeping abreast of the latest scholarship. In the article, Ker claims that Dante's praise for Arnaut Daniel in *Purgatorio* is hard to reconcile with his theory of language expressed in *De*

Vulgari Eloquentia. 'There is ingenuity, no doubt, in the way Arnaut drills his syllables and manages his difficult pattern of verse', Ker admits, 'but the ingenuity is very like that of the trivial early poets whom Dante depreciates'. He even goes further to argue that there is nothing of the 'noble harmony...the right proportion between the heptasyllable and the heroic line' that Ker claims is the great innovation of the *dolce stil nuovo*.[36] Pound's reading of Daniel is the precise opposite of Ker's.

Pound's treatment of Daniel in *The Spirit of Romance*, then, is both a defence of Provençal poetry (much like 'Raphelite Latin') and a recovery of Daniel's art from judgements of the kind given by Ker. Seen this way *The Spirit of Romance* is the first instance of Pound's post-philological project. In contrast to Ker's assessment of Daniel's harshness, we may set Pound's reading of his precision. According to Pound, '[Daniel] is never content with a conventional phrase, or with a word which does not convey his exact meaning; for which reason his words are often hard to translate'. Against this, he sets the second stanza of Daniel's *Si'm fos Amors de joi donar tant larga*, the original of which (taken from a 1902 British edition of the text) is given below alongside Pound's prose translation:

Pero s'ieu fatz lonc esper no m'embargaqu'en tant ric luoc me sui mes e m'estancc'ab sos bels digz mi tengra de joi larc;e segrai tant qu'om mi port a la tomba,qu'ieu no sui ges cel que lais aur per plom;e pois en lieis no's taing c'om ren esmertant li serai fis et obedienstro de s'amor, si'l platz, baisan m'envesta.[37]

Pound's rendering is thus:

Therefore a long delay will not put me off, for I have set myself toward so rich a place and 'pooled' myself about it; that with her sweet words along she would hold me bountied with joy, and I would follow her until they carry me to the tomb, for I am never one that leaves gold for lead; and since in her there is nothing that one could refine, so will I be true and obedient to her until out of her love, if it pleases her, she 'invest' me with a kiss.

(*SR*, 25)

Pound follows what was a convention of philological writing at the time in providing prose rather than verse translations. When he produced a verse translation a decade later, he sacrificed critical clarity for musical quality:

I am, spite long delay, pooled and contorted
And whirled with all my streams 'neath such a bank
Of promise, that her fair words hold me fast

In joy, and will, until in tomb I am halted.
As I'm not one to change hard gold for spalt,
And no alloy's in her, that debonaire
Shall hold my faith and mine obedience
Till, by her accolade, I am invested.[38]

What is interesting in Pound's treatment of this verse is that his reading of it forms an essential facet of his theory of poetic language, using Daniel much in the same way that Dante does in *De Vulgari Eloquentia*. He identifies Daniel as a key innovator in a tradition of the *mot juste*, the literary-linguistic principle at the heart of Pound's linguistic thought:

> Three times in this stanza the Provençal makes his picture, neither by simile nor by metaphor, but in the language beyond metaphor; by the use of the picturesque verb with an exact meaning. Firstly, 'pools himself' – the natural picture. Secondly, after the comparison of gold and lead, the metal worker's shop gives tribute, and is present to the vision in the technical word 'refine'. Thirdly, the feudal ceremony and the suggestion of its pageantry are in the verb 'invest'.
>
> (*SR*, 26)

Later on in the text, Pound defines this 'language beyond metaphor' as 'the more compressed or elliptical expression of metaphorical perception' (*SR*, 167). In his verse translation, interestingly, each of the verbs loses its force in an adjectival phrase: the reflective nature of 'pools himself' is not represented by 'I am...pooled', and while 'I am invested' has a beautiful cadence, it does not retain the force of 'she "invest" me with a kiss'. This is explained by the different aspects of Daniel's craft which Pound wishes to emphasise. While the verse translation captures the sonic qualities of Daniel's poetry – the material aspects of the language- the prose translation seeks to understand the 'verbal precision'. Pound only gestures towards the meaning of the 'language beyond metaphor', but in it we can identify the principles of Imagism as he would conceive them two years later. The natural object, in this case the image of a pool gathering, is used to bring about a supposed 'precision' (though Pound does not quite explain how), but is left to stand alone: it is not mixed with an abstraction, but the natural image appears as if summoned to clarify an abstract emotion or thought. What is also noticeable here is the way Pound argues that the 'feudal ceremony', that is the cultural-historical background of the poem's composition, is manifest in the image employed in the poem. This act of close reading in which the aesthetic elements of the poem are seen as symptomatic of a cultural period is a historical situating of poetic craft. In his interpretation of Arnaut Daniel, Pound's fundamental literary-linguistic principle, 'the picturesque verb with an exact meaning', is conceived within identifiably historical limits. It is here that we can see Pound's linguistic principles develop out of material introduced to him by philology.

In contrast to *The Spirit of Romance*, Pound's essay series 'I Gather the Limbs of Osiris' is far bolder and more assertive in detaching its author from his university training by emphasising the importance of studying poetic technique, of making value judgements, and of considering poetry as poetry, not as an example of linguistic history. In 'I Gather the Limbs of Osiris', Pound's plea for value judgements revolves largely around the categorising of significant authors as 'symptomatic' and 'donative', a value judgement applied to literary history.[39] But once one grants Pound this gesture, philology finds its way back in: his attempt to categorise, to use a 'scientific' method to analyse the aesthetic, and to relate literary works always to a language of particularity, of time and place, as well as to the history of the development of language, summons up its principles from the depths of philology. Pound's task is to outline a 'new method of scholarship', one which sets itself up in opposition to philology. This Pound calls 'the method of Luminous Detail', a method which he describes as 'most vigorously hostile to the prevailing mode of today – that is, the method of multitudinous detail, and to the method of yesterday, the method of sentiment and generalisation'.[40] The phrase 'detail' is usefully vague and flexible. At any one moment, it can mean a phrase, a poem, a writer, a rhythm, a meter, a musical intonation, an architectural form, an aesthetic principle, or a metaphysical idea. Pound's sole criteria is that it be 'luminous', by which he means that it contributes something of significance to the history of art. In many ways, Pound's idea comes to resemble that of canon formation, with its implicit value judgements and its aesthetic justifications. While he grants that philology has its place, he argues that the 'drudgery and minutiae of method concern only the scholar', drawing on a distinction between artists and scholars, between creativity and philology which fits well into Gerald Graff's characterisation of interdisciplinary conflicts in the early twentieth century. Pound extends his argument further, however, in seeing this philological impulse in the artistic production of the period, presenting the modern artist as a decisive break:

> The artist seeks out the luminous detail and presents it. He does not comment. His work remains the permanent basis of psychology and metaphysics. Each historian will `have ideas' – presumably different from other historians – imperfect inductions, varying as the fashions, but the luminous details remain unaltered. As scholarship has erred in presenting all detail as if of equal import, so also in literature, in a present school of writing we see a similar tendency.[41]

What Pound does not reveal, of course, is that the 'luminous detail' is often selected out of the mass of multitudinous details: he can make his argument with relative ease partly because he was exposed to this mass of details at university. Although he claims that the method of 'luminous detail' is 'vigorously hostile' to philology in terms of its selection of materials, and the reasons behind the selection, there are reasons to be sceptical towards the actual practice of Pound's new method. What emerges instead is a unification of philology with artistic creativity, a unification which stems, at least at root, from his immersion in both. Pound's argument rarely alights on the nature of the 'detail' itself, on how we should approach it, define it, and study it: he does not explain what the terms of the 'new method of scholarship' are, nor what, in fact, this 'new method' actually is in practice. His definition of the error of the old method of scholarship criticises it for a lack of discernment, rather than any specific practice. What Pound's 'new method', in fact, does, perhaps in a way that its advocate did not realise, is to redirect the methodologies of philological scholarship towards a critical standpoint: in this sense, Pound integrates his philological training into the new method, even if he defines it in contradistinction.

Another way in which Pound integrates philology is the insistence that there be a science of literature, a project about which he expressed doubt on many occasions, but nevertheless a programme to which he remained aligned his entire career. Where philological rigour was applied to the analysis of language in the form of historical linguistics, the method of 'luminous detail' calls for the principles of classification, etymological research, and close reading to be applied to the formal aspects of poetry. One sees this in Pound's discussion of Arnaut Daniel in fourth part of 'I Gather the Limbs of Osiris':

> He perceived, that is, that the beauty to be gotten from a similarity of line-terminations depends not upon their multiplicity, but upon their action the one upon the other; not upon frequency, but upon the manner of sequence and combination. The effect of `lais' in monorhyme, or of a canzon in which a few rhymes appear too often, is monotonous, is monotonous beyond the point where monotony is charming or interesting. Arnaut uses what for want of a better term I call polyphonic rhyme.[42]

Pound performs a masterful theorisation here, one based on years of acquaintance not only with Daniel's work itself but with commentaries on Daniel. His subject matter differs from philology in that his focus is on Daniel's genius – or at least the genius imbedded in the formal features of his poetry – but it retains a philological focus on close reading, an emphasis on the language itself, and an attempt to eliminate the vague, Romantic notion of literary prowess. Daniel's poetry is here presented as indicative of a theoretical discovery, one which Pound abstracts out of the verse. Pound's terms, though they are drawn from popular discourses on science rather than from centuries of linguistic research, demonstrate a tendency to present the artist as a theorist of the discipline; his forensic approach to language betrays a recourse to the very academic impulses which his vitriolic attacks on philology sought to discard.

Though it is bound through in a loose, non-academic style, and certainly does not contain the rigorous, critical orthodoxies of philological scholarship, Pound's work at the very least enters into dialogue with the discipline. Indeed, in the context of his work on Daniel, he reveals an anxiety about his task: 'I have spent six months of my life translating fifteen experiments of a man living in what one of my more genial critics calls a "very dead past". Is this justifiable in anyone who is not purely a philologist?'.[43] This, of course, begs a further question: to what extent does Pound's work on Daniel differ from philology? His distinction from either generalist or more Romantic accounts of artistic genius lies in his intention to tie literary innovation to an historical and cultural milieu, and his distinction from philology lies in his licence to speculate, as on the nature of Daniel's innovations:

> At a time when both prose and poetry were loose-jointed, prolix, barbaric, he, to all intents and virtually, rediscovered 'style'. He conceived, that is, a manner of writing in which each word should bear some burden, should make some special contribution to the effect of the whole. The poem is an organism in which each part functions, gives to sound or to sense something – preferably to sound *and* sense gives something.[44]

It is here that Pound's method of luminous detail connects with the Flaubertian *mot juste*, with the Hulmean 'image', and with Paterian 'style'. In each of these cases, a philosophy of language underpins a series of stylistic principles, with the emphasis on the latter, rather than the former – as opposed to his caricature of philology.

In 'I Gather the Limbs of Osiris', Pound moves between two imagined audiences, populated by figures of his past and present: an artistic one, in which he engages in speculations as to the nature of art; and a philological one in which he challenges a perceived sterility, a kind of dead historicism which diminishes the aesthetic legacy of the artist in favour of an emphasis of background. Pound explains philology to art, and art to philology. The commonality between these two audiences is language and the nature of symbolic (or, in modern terms, semiotic) communication. The link between the method of 'luminous detail' and 'multitudinous detail' is more a matter of which details one emphasises, rather than how they are treated specifically. What Pound does not reveal is that the 'luminosity' of his method is dependent on the 'multitudinous details' fading into the background. Pound's critical and poetical interests alight on the same details that are of interest to the philologist:

matters of etymology, the relationship between literary and linguistic history, and disciplinary categorisations. Where Pound differs from philology is more a question of the overarching subject which his writing serves: for Pound, this is the literary in and of itself, rather than the history of the English language. The method of luminous detail is, in many ways, a subversion of the hierarchy of philology: the aesthetic and the literary subjugating the linguistic. This is linguistics in the service of literature: a subversion of what Pound conceived as the philological order. Were Pound to have developed a programme for the method of 'luminous detail', it would have nevertheless been interrupted by the geopolitical upheavals merely two years later.

Propaganda, State *Kultur*, and Philology

In terms of poetry, Pound's notable contribution to our image of the First World War undoubtedly remains this haunting passage from *Hugh Selwyn Mauberley*, speaking to and for the generation of people who, though they saw no combat, saw society and culture disintegrate, receiving letters from abroad announcing the death of loved ones and friends.

> There died a myriad
> And of the best, among them,
> For an old bitch gone in the teeth
> For a botched civilization.[45]

Pound's stance towards that 'botched civilization' was rather less forthright in the war years, however. The reformative programme outlined in *The Spirit of Romance* and 'I Gather the Limbs of Osiris' became central to Pound's defence of 'civilisation' during the war. Pound's challenge to the predominance of philology, in particular, is of central importance in his war time writing. Pound came to argue that philology was an outgrowth of the alleged oppressive and suppressive nature of German state culture, or *Kultur*.[46] As a result, Pound's early career opposition to the privileged position of philology in academia intensified as part of his support of the allied war effort. As Vincent Sherry explains, anti-German war propaganda supplemented Pound's pre-existing prejudices against German philology:

> While Pound may well find philology to be the signature idiocy of German academic comprehensiveness (the opinion goes back to his experience of the system in his study, to the master's level, in romance language), this point of personal rebuke grows more virulent as a nationalist animus appropriates, animates, and expands it. The degree to which this propagandistic language takes over the passage may measure at once the dominant power of that political ideolect and the requisite strength of literary invention.[47]

Pound's antipathy towards German philology was supplemented by the war rather than initiated by it, but Pound's rhetoric gains a propagandist dimension during the war years. Between 1914 and 1918, Pound would continually challenge the place of philology in both academia and culture, arguing that it is representative of what he saw as a Germanic attitude in which the critical faculty of the individual is reduced to merely contributing minutiae to the detail of scholarship.

The war itself was to emphasise the role that nationality, race, and culture played in philological study. In particular, the heightened sense of the link between nationality and culture in years in and around the Great War served to highlight to Pound the ways in which language can manifest these issues. In his review of Joyce's *Portrait of the Artist as a Young Man*, Pound emphasises the difference in civilisation between the prose of Joyce and Flaubert and the situation of Europe in the early twentieth century:

> It is very important that there should be clear, unexaggerated, realistic literature. It is very important that there should be good prose. The hell of contemporary Europe is caused by the lack of representative government in Germany, *and* by the non-existence of decent prose in the German language. Clear thought and sanity depend on clear prose. They cannot live apart. The former produces the latter. The latter conserves and transmits the former.

While there may be reason to be somewhat sceptical of the sincerity of Pound's claim that the German language contributed to the war, this is a point of linguistic and moral unity that he would similarly find attractive in the writings of Confucius and in the ideology of fascist Italy. He goes on to give a concrete example of what he means:

> The mush of the German sentence, the straddling of the verb out to the end, are just as much a part of the befoozlement of Kultur and the consequent hell, as was the rhetoric of later Rome the seed and symptom of the Roman Empire's decadence and extinction. A nation that cannot write clearly cannot be trusted to govern, nor yet to think.[48]

There is reason to be sceptical here as Pound's acquaintance with the German language is somewhat ambivalent. In his *Cavalcanti*, Pound begs the following question: 'how can you have PROSE in a country where the chambermaid comes into your room and exclaims: "Schön ist das hemd!"' (literally, 'beautiful is that shirt!') (*LE*, 198). Pound's focus on the structure of the sentence, in English a poetic inversion, cannot simply be read as a dogmatic judgement of a foreign language; Pound was an admirer of Heinrich Heine and translated his poetry, as well as admitting in *Guide to Kulchur* to enjoying the humorous poems of *Das Stände-buch* (1568), and remembering fondly his studies in the *Minnesang* in 'A Visiting Card'.[49] German state *Kultur*, which Pound believed to have held philology and not literature as its bellwether of culture, is cast as a less 'advanced' and consequently more 'barbaric' state of civilisation. This, Pound argues, is the basis of the war between what he saw as a more 'civilised' allied force and a more 'barbaric' *Kultur* represented by Germany. This distinction would break down after the war, of course, as Pound similarly castigated the state of 'civilisation' in Britain and America, but in the midst of war, such judgements were not necessarily able to be openly expressed.

In a four-part essay series for *The New Age* in July 1917, entitled 'Provincialism the Enemy', Pound attached his resentment of the philological bias in the academy to the anti-Germanic sentiment bred by the First World War, arguing that *Kultur* and philology were outgrowths of an institutionalised provincialism. His argument begins by explaining his rationale for opposing the German model of academic research and instruction:

> It is evil because it holds up an ideal of 'scholarship' not an ideal of humanity. It says in effect: you are to acquire knowledge in order that knowledge may be acquired. Metaphorically, you are to build up a dam'd and useless pyramid which will be no use to you or to anyone else, but which will serve as a 'monument.' To this end you are to sacrifice your mind and vitality.[50]

Scholarship for the sake of scholarship is not justification enough for the philological method to be dominant. The notion of philology as 'evil', as if it corrupts the minds of its practitioners with an insidious intent, is a lot stronger than Pound's previous treatment of philology. The image of the pyramid recalls Pound's first published article, suggesting that the terminological and metaphoric framework with which he conceived philology remained unchanged for the best part of a decade.

Pound's position chimes with allied propaganda. Artistic, literary, philosophical, philological, and linguistic circles owed much to German scholars and thinkers, and as a result, professionals in these areas required a different rationalisation for anti-German sentiment. By the outbreak of the war, however, allied intellectual circles attempted to distance themselves from German heritage. Ford Madox Ford, for example, condemned philology as part of the general 'barbarism' of German *kultur*, as opposed to idealised leisureliness of English 'civilization'.[51] As Peter Buitenhuis has remarked, 'it is a curious spectacle to see this writer [Ford], who had spent much of his time before the war advocating professionalism in literature, demanding amateurism in the arts as well as everything else', but such ideological inconsistencies appear in war.[52]

Interestingly, Matthew Stibbe notes that the idea of a unified and strong *Kultur* as a bulwark against a liberal 'civilisation' was equally prevalent in German propaganda.[53]

In the first article in 'Provincialism the Enemy', Pound expands upon his anti-German and anti-philological positions and unifies the two more explicitly. 'Where the other phase of the idea, the slave of the state (i.e., of the emperor) idea has worked on the masses', Pound argues, 'the idea of the scholar as slave of learning has worked on the "intel-lectual"'.[54] His discussion is at its most advanced in the third essay in the series, which was published on 26 July 1917. What seems at the first glance an analogy, that German state oppression and control is like phil-ological scholarship, Pound develops into a direct assertion: namely, that philology is itself an extension of state oppression.

> The 'State' forgot the 'use' of 'man'; 'scholarship,' as a 'function of the state,' forgot the use of the individual, or, at least, mislaid it, secreted it for its own purpose. 'Philology' laid hold of the arts, and did its best to make them knuckle under. Kunstwissenschaft was exalted. The arts also were to become a function of the State, duly ordered and controlled. It is all exceedingly plausible. Germany was so provincial that she supposed the rest of the world would swal-low the bait and submit. America was so provincial that it took her several years to understand that militarism must be put down. Even now, she does not much understand; she is stampeded, thank God, in the right direction, toward the annihilation of Kaisers.[55]

Pound's argument is twofold: first, he argues that America should act politically to stop German militarism; second, the American university should reassess the place of philology in the outlook of the academy in order to better develop humanistic and artistic values. Pound portrays philology as a tool of suppression, acting to subject the arts to wider concerns around language and uniformity of culture. In this system, so Pound believes, individual expression is rejected in favour of uniform descriptions of isolated eras. Philology becomes for Pound the academic expression of the institution of provincialism.

In the final article, Pound's tone does become rather more conciliatory and less aggressive than in the preceding articles, and he expand upon his argument in favour of philology being subsumed into generalist criti-cal practice. Pound still contend that philology alone is a practice which stands against humanism, but conced that its uses are manifest in the study of literature.

> Such dehumanisation went on in the universities of Deutschland, subtly and with many exterior hues. There appeared to be no harm in it so long as it produced nothing more appalling than

'grundrissen' and 'Zeitschrifts fur blankische philologie': - parts
of which might conceivably be of some use and facilitate the reading of lost literatures. I know at least one German professor who
has produced a dictionary and remained delightfully human at the
age of about sixty-five. His abridgment would have helped me to
read troubadours if I had not learned to read them before I had
found it.[56]

The professor to whom Pound refers at the end is Emil Lévy, who ad-
vised Pound on the meaning of Arnaut Daniel's mistranscribed word
noigandres from a manuscript Pound had consulted in the Ambrosiana
library in Milan. Pound visited Lévy in Freiburg in 1912 to consult him
on the meaning of this word as he had put together a large dictionary
of Provençal. I will return to this discussion of Lévy below, as Pound
would remember this encounter a decade later in Canto XX. The gesture towards Lévy here does, however, slightly undermine Pound's opposition to philology. As Ann Birien argues, in terms that capture the
reformative nuances of Pound's arguments, he 'chose to eradicate the
evils of philology by sponsoring the kind of philology that legitimized
his own position, and thus kept at bay the kind that could easily harm
it'.[57] Philological details such as Lévy's intuition or Shepard's seminars
provided him with details, backed up by sources such as the *Grundrissen*, or works by Reinach and Paris, formed key parts of Pound's literary
and linguistic education, and served to colour his work with a reformed
philological practice.

In the immediate aftermath of the war, Pound turned his critical eye
away from Germany and Germanic philology and towards his native
and adopted homes: America and the United Kingdom. Pound's definition of the word 'philology' was extended from a critical approach
to literary and linguistic history into a catchword for the apparent
evils of print culture. In Canto XIV, written in the decade following
the war, we find the following description of the post-bellum Western
world:

> The slough of unamiable liars,
>   bog of stupidities,
> malevolent stupidities, and stupidities,
> the soil living pus, full of vermin,
> dead maggots begetting live maggots,
>   slum owners,
> usurers squeezing crab-lice, pandars to authority,
> pets-de-loup, sitting on piles of stone books,
> obscuring the texts with philology,
>   hiding them under their persons,

(XIV.63)

Pound's targets here are legion: from journalists, to publishers, to academics, he castigates a literary establishment in terms more direct, though far less affecting, than in *Hugh Selwyn Mauberley*. The notion of 'obscuring the texts with philology' captures the dual criticism that Pound maintains for the philological treatment of literature: first, the notion of 'hidden' texts implies that philological scholarship erects a monolith which prevents significant works of art from reaching the public; second, philology as a practice is an obfuscation of the 'luminous detail' that artists such as Pound wish to bring to the fore, a dulling of the message. The message which Pound clearly wishes to portray is that the discipline in which he was trained for half a decade at Hamilton College and the University of Pennsylvania could not be further from the poetic aesthetic he developed after it. This narrative is not, however, borne out in his work.

Post-Philology

Even during his most vitriolic denouncements of philology as German state 'barbarism' during the war, Pound was laying the seeds of a rapprochement of sorts in his poetry. While it may appear apposite to see Pound's poetry as anti-philological, it is in reality post-philological, rooted at all points in the discipline he disparaged. During the war, Pound published one of his most important poems on the troubadour theme as part of his collection, *Lustra* (1916). 'Near Perigord' (first published in *Poetry* in 1915) was a repetition of a subject that Pound had worked on for many years. Pound was fascinated by the character of the warrior-troubadour Bertran de Born. According to Thomas Connolly, Pound based the structure of the poem on Robert Browning's *The Ring and the Book*.[58] At the centre of the poem is a lyric by de Born entitled 'Dompna pois de me no'us cal', wherein the poet, spurned by his lover, the Lady Maent of Montaignac, writes a poem describing a 'composite lady' out of all of the renowned women of Provence. Even this, de Born says, does not match Lady Maent. Pound summarises this canzone in the second stanza of 'Near Perigord':

> Bertrans, En Bertrans, left a fine canzone:
> 'Maent, I love you, you have turned me out.
> The voice at Montfort, Lady Agnes' hair,
> Bel Miral's stature, the viscountess' throat,
> Set all together, are not worthy of you....'
> And all the while you sing out that canzone,
> Think you that Maent lived at Montaignac,
> One at Chalais, another at Malemort
> Hard over Brive – for every lady a castle,
> Each place strong.[59]

Pound explores a hypothesis in 'Near Perigord' that Bertran's love poem was, in fact, a calculated reflection of his military ambitions in the area. In impressing Lady Maent, Bertran would have increased his political influence in Provence, and established a greater power base in the region.

Part I of 'Near Perigord' ends with a series of questions that casts doubt on the sincerity of Bertran's intentions towards Lady Maent. Pound's list reads as a list of the questions he believed should be asked by literary scholarship:

> Is it a love poem? Did he sing of war?
> Is it an intrigue to run subtly out,
> Born of a jongleur's tongue, freely to pass
> Up and about and in and out the land,
> Mark him a craftsman and a strategist?
> (St. Leider had done as much as Polhonac,
> Singing a different stave, as closely hidden.)
> Oh, there is precedent, legal tradition,
> To sing one thing when your song means another,
> '*Et albirar ab lor bordon-*'
> Foix' count knew that. What is Sir Bertrans' singing?[60]

These questions are left unanswered. Pound's approach is certainly un-philological in its appearance. He works from speculation rather than from known facts, and he does not engage with finer linguistic points. Indeed, it is difficult to see how Pound is engaging with philology or linguistics at all in this poem, particularly as he focusses on unfounded biographical rumours. Yet, if one conceives of the kind of investigation that Pound makes in the poem, this is no celebration of Provençal aesthetic for its own sake: this is not a discussion of transmutable literary principles but rather the situating of a poem within a broader historical context. The aesthetic aspects of the work lie, of course, in the mastery of the prosody, but in terms of the poem's 'argument' it remains within the realm of literary criticism.

Later in the poem, however, Pound establishes his method against philology. He enters into the subjectivity of the poem, adorning Bertran de Born's lyrical I as a mask, creating a combination of critical geography and a psychological portrayal:

> End fact. Try fiction. Let us say we see
> En Bertrans, a tower-room at Hautefort,
> Sunset, the ribbon-like road lies, in red cross-light,
> Southward toward Montaignac, and he bends at a table
> Scribbling, swearing between his teeth; by his left hand
> Lie little strips of parchment covered over,

> Scratched and erased with *al* and *ochaisos*.
> Testing his list of rhymes, a lean man? Bilious?
> With a red straggling beard?
> And the green cat's-eye lifts towards Montaignac.[61]

The first half of the opening line, 'End fact. Try fiction', is a direct challenge to philological authority over literary figures and texts: it could
stand as an anti-philological slogan. Pound suggests, in other words, that
biographical facts and philological details have not provided an adequate
explanation of 'Dompna pois de me no'us cal', and a fictitious account of
the events surrounding the poem's composition may give a more accurate
portrayal of the meaning of the poem, as well as the 'spirit' in which it
was written. At the same time, however, this poem very much depends
on biographical and linguistic criticism, both of which serve to uphold
Pound's speculations. This poem is post-philological in that it departs
from the orthodoxies of philological criticism while simultaneously re-
maining rooted in it as subject matter. Pound's speculation here does not
emerge from an individual engagement with the poem alone, but from
over a decade's acquaintance with its place in literary history, with the
critical tradition relating to it, and with the intricacies of the language.
He was introduced to the poem by William Shepard at Hamilton College, and so his personal history with the text was facilitated by philological scholarship.[62] The Browningesque aesthetic of the poem belies
its philological foundations. What Pound founds in 'Near Perigord' is a
method of combining speculative literary criticism with poetic form, but
what this poem elides is the roots of this speculation in critical tradition.

To this end, Stuart McDougal stresses the importance of Bertran de
Born's poem in developing Pound's poetic technique. McDougal argues
that it is not simply a philological, biographical, or scholarly point that
attracts Pound to de Born's poem. Rather, he argues, Pound sources a
poetic principle of assimilation:

> For Bertran's attempt to create a 'borrowed lady' to replace the
> woman whose favour he has lost is a metaphor for the poetic activity
> of both Bertran and Pound: not only is the poet's goal the creation
> of an ideal beauty, but this beauty is composed of diverse elements
> taken from many sources. Bertran's method here is analogous to
> Pound's use of material in poems like 'Na Audiart,' 'Near Perigord,'
> and especially *The Cantos*.[63]

As Pound's hypothesis that de Born was attempting to cause political strife
is not proven, McDougal's reading is an intelligent one. It may be that
Pound was experimenting with the remnants of his training in Romance
philology and in doing so expanded upon a method between the poetry of
the *Cantos* and the method of 'luminous detail' defined three years earlier.

In his introduction to the publication of *A Walking Tour of Southern France*, Pound's account of two journeys to Provence in 1911, Richard Sieburth describes the notebook from which he drew together the text as 'recalcitrant to philology' and demonstrates Pound's struggles with his own relationship with the discipline. Sieburth describes Pound's early poetic output as a 'series of experiments in transforming romance philology into contemporary poetry', and that he saw his walking tour in Provence as a geographical culmination of much of what he had learned about the troubadours up until that point.[64] Pound wished to verify his theories and readings of the troubadours via a kind of geographical philology. As Sieburth writes, 'Pound's account of his walking tour vacillates between a confidence that the mysteries of Provençal song might be philologically or imaginatively recovered and an elegiac awareness that the world he is seeking is irrevocably lost, accessible only as trace or ruin'.[65] This concern may have been waylaid by his imagist and vorticist concerns (see the following chapter), but it was a concern to which he returned in his *Cantos*, discovering there a literary technique which would open up and transform philological language and practice into modernist poetics. We see a similar process in 'Near Perigord'.

We should be sceptical of the anti-philological mood established in Pound's early work. Philological impulses run throughout the *Cantos*, most famously announced by Pound's dramatic interruption of the account of Odysseus's descent to the underworld in Canto I, his 'Lie quiet Divus. I mean that is Andreas Divus,/In Officina Wecheli, 1538, out of Homer' (I.5). For all of Pound's recalcitrance to scholarship and philology, lines such as these (and they are numerous in the *Cantos*) give some pause. As Rebecca Beasley eloquently puts it, this line 'marks how this example of an unmediated vision is simultaneously an inevitably mediated textual translation'.[66] Beasley's line could stand for much of modernist writing, but what makes this specifically Poundian is the transparency of the process: a habit inevitable in a trained philologist, perhaps. We may also think of the 'Malatesta Cantos' (VIII–XI), in which Pound dramatises key moments in the life of Sigismundo Malatesta, a fifteenth-century warlord and patron of the arts, whom Pound conceived as an archetype of a pagan cultural intelligence continuing through the Italian Renaissance. As Lawrence Rainey's extensive research has shown, Pound's dramatisation of Sigismundo's life was not, as in Robert Browning's *Sordello*, an extended speculation, a poetic expansion of legend, but was deeply informed by intensive bibliographic and archival research.[67] Pound may have declared 'End fact. Try fiction' in 'Near Perigord', but this mantra was very much abandoned in his work on Malatesta: his poetic treatment of the subject was very much informed by his grounding in archival sources. David Ten Eyke has shown that this practice was also employed in the 'Adams Cantos', where Pound worked extensively with Adams's and Thomas Jefferson's correspondence, rooting his poetic practice, once again, in intensive research. Ten Eyke's research demonstrates the nature of Pound's 'source-based' poetics, which came to increasing prominence as the *Cantos* advanced throughout the 1920s and 1930s.[68] More recently, in an excellent article which corroborates much of what follows in the rest of this chapter, Luke McMullan has demonstrated the extent to which philological practice informs not only Pound's translations from the troubadours, but also how it informs his 1932 translation of Guido Cavalcanti's work, *Guido Cavalcanti Rime*.[69] There are grounds, then, to be deeply sceptical of Pound's wartime stances towards philology. McMullan refers to Pound's translation practice as 'counter-philology', though I would suggest that 'post-philology' is a more appropriate phrase for the ambiguity of his position. The language and history of Pound's poetry remains the material of philology: it is textual material, the manuscript. It is in this sense that we can speak of Pound's work as 'post'-philological, responding to and deriving from a subject Pound could never fully escape.

The most significant treatment of philology in the *Cantos* is one in which two philologists play a major role in the revelation of lyric poetry. In Canto XX, Pound recounts his visit to Emil Lévy to try to discover the meaning of the word *noigandres* in Arnaut Daniel's 'Er vei vermeils, vertz, blaus, blancs, gruocs'. For J. Mark Smith, Canto XX is both the 'high point' and 'limit case' of the 'interleaving of poetic and philological tradition' that he sees in modernist writing.[70] This passage of *A Draft of XXX Cantos* involves the three touchstones of Pound's engagement with linguistic ideas: the University of Pennsylvania, Arnaut Daniel, and German philology. In preparing his *Provenzalisches Supplement-Wörterbuch*, Lévy had discovered that *noigandres* was a manuscript corruption of *d'enoi gandres* ('to ward off ennui'), a combination of *noi* (ennui) and the verb *gandir* ('to ward off'), a discovery which so impressed Pound that he includes a dramatisation of its discovery in his modern epic. In terms of the narrative of the account in the *Cantos*, Pound first consults his former lecturer at the University of Pennsylvania, who advises him to seek Lévy's help and Pound then journeys to Freiburg:

> And that year I went up to Freiburg
> And Rennert had said: Nobody, no, nobody
> Knows anything about Provençal, or if there is anybody
> It's old Lévy.'
> And so I went up to Freiburg,
> And the vacation was just beginning,
> The students getting off for the summer,
> Freiburg im Breisgau,
> And everything clean, seeming clean, after Italy.

(XX.89)

Contrary to the depiction of 'philologists' in Canto XIV, here Rennert and Lévy are treated as characters in an epic adventure. Rennert is cast in a role analogous to that of Menelaus in the *Odyssey*, advising Telemachus to visit the shape-shifting god Proteus, the 'Old Man of the Sea', who will advise him on how to find his lost father. Pound treats this pursuit of a matter of philological detail as if it were a quest. While this could be ironic, the earnestness of Pound's interest in the matter is clearly revealed by the passages that follow:

> And I went to old Lévy, and it was by then 6.30
> in the evening, and he trailed half way across Freiburg
> before dinner, to see the two strips of copy,
> Arnaut's, settant'uno R. superiore (Ambrosiana)
> Not that I could sing him the music.
> And he said: 'Now is there anything I can tell you?'
> And I said: I dunno, sir, or
> 'Yes, Doctor, what do they mean by *noigandres?*'
> And he said: Noigandres! NOIgandres!
> 'You know for seex mon's of my life
> 'Effery niht when I go to bett, I say to myself:
> 'Noigandres, eh, *noi*gandres,
> 'Now what the DEFFIL can that mean!'
>
> (XX.89–90)

If we observe the role that Pound casts himself in here, the poet returned to an academic context, the dialogue reads as if a conversation between a postgraduate student and a professor. By 1912, the time of the meeting, Pound's acquaintance with Daniel's poetry was such that he could have approached the matter as an expert in his own right. It is striking, however, that as this is a linguistic matter, Pound portrays himself as a student before a master, which, as we can see by consulting the fifth volume of the *Wörterbuch* (M-O), published in 1907, was the case. We see that Lévy already offers 'ennui' as a tentative translation for *noi*.[71] In this fourth volume, we see Lévy's argument for *gandir*. He outlines seven possible meanings (all of which are my translation from the German): 'protect' or 'safeguard', 'withdraw', 'escape' or 'protect against', 'evade', 'refuse', 'save oneself', and 'elude'. There is, of course, something of all of these meanings in the passage that follows. *Noigandres* is mentioned as one of the instances which causes Lévy difficulty. He notes that it is a form not of *gandir* itself, but of the variant *gandre*. It is here that he provides that form 'd'enoi *gandres*', noting that in the text it appears as *noigandres*.[72] It is important to note, then, that Pound is collaborating in what is an authoritative speculation, an expert interpretation of a line of text, but not a fixed translation. And it is this expert speculation – the meaning of *noigandres* – which acts as a prompt,

an association, that, once revealed, opens up into a lyrical celebration
of Provence:

> Wind over the olive trees, ranunculae ordered,
> By the clear edge of the rocks
> The water runs, and the wind scented with pine
> And with hay fields under sun-swath
> Agostino, Jacopo and Boccata.
> You would be happy for the smell of that place
> And never tired of being there, either alone
> Or accompanied.
> Sound: as of the nightingale too far off to be heard.
>
> (XX.90)

In an extraordinary passage, Pound then draws out the implications of
d'enoi ganres, exploring each facet of the ways in which the sensory
encounter of Provence itself 'wards off ennui':

> The smell of that place – *d'enoi ganres*.
> Air moving under the boughs,
> The cedars there in the sun,
> Hay new cut on hill slope,
> And the water there in the cut
> Between the two lower meadows; sound,
> The sound, as I have said, a nightingale
> Too far off to be heard.
> And the light falls, *remir*,
> from her breast to thighs.
>
> (XX.90)

Here, we can see the expansion of philological practice into poetic material, a dramatisation of the very movements that Pound himself followed in the early stages of his career. The structure of this passage
is a movement of revelation: as Lévy is struck by the realisation that
noigandres is a corruption, and it is replaced by the intelligible *d'enoi
ganres*, the material becomes capable of being expanded into an aesthetic and cultural unity. This is where Pound as artist enters. As Réka
Mihálka notes in her reading of this canto, 'while Lévy's scholarship
did advance our understanding of troubadour literature, it is ultimately
poetry that can turn this knowledge into experience and thus make it
accessible'.[73] While Mihálka is clearly correct in assessing Pound's view,
would it not be better to assert the opposite? Pound uses the structure of
revelation to bring experience of Provence across. This 'luminous detail'
relies heavily on a background of intense philological research, a mass of
multitudinous details – Pound even acknowledges this, while eliding the

extent of the debt. While it is certainly the case that Pound's work lets us inhabit the vision and experience of poetic works in a way inaccessible to scholarship, by donning Daniel as a mask as the author himself did with Bertran de Born in 'Na Audiart' and 'Near Perigord', we must read this passage as a collaboration with scholarly roots. What we see in 'Canto XX', then, is a microcosm of the ways in which Pound's poetics is an aesthetic expansion of textually mediated history and culture; the way in which his poetry is an outgrowth from philology.

Lévy is symbolic of Pound's reconciliation with philology as a practice, at least on the level of the individual scholar working at the coalface of language and textual scholarship. As for philology as a discipline, as a subject, Pound continued to assail it for the rest of his career, seeing it as symptomatic of corruption in the university, the focus on extraneous and irrelevant material at the expense of the 'luminous'. Still, Pound's lyrical rapprochement with philology in Canto XX produces the following note in his *Instigations*:

> And for the rest any man who would read Arnaut and the troubadours owes great thanks to Emil Levy of Freiburg i/B for his long work and his little dictionary (Petit Dictionnaire Provençal-Français, Karl Winter's Universitätsbuchhandlung, Heidelberg) and to U. A. Canello, the first editor of Arnaut, who has shown, I think, great profundity in his arrangement of the poems in their order, and has really hit upon their sequence of composition, and the development of En Arnaut's trobar; and lastly to René Lavaud for his new Tolosan edition.[74]

Canello's *Arnaut Daniel* (1883) was the source text for most work on Daniel in the early twentieth century. Lavaud's *Les poésies d'Arnaut Daniel* (1910), contemporaneous with Pound's *The Spirit of Romance*, was an authoritative account of Daniel's poetry. *Les poésies d'Arnaut Daniel* is a union of critique and philology, and so fulfilled Pound's category of the 'luminous detail' to a requisite extent. Pound's admission of gratitude to Lévy, Canello, and Lavaud is not remotely surprising, but it does reveal the extent to which his work was not only grounded in philology, but continued to engage with it as well.

Two years later, on 8–9 July 1922, we find the following summary of his efforts with Provence in a letter sent from Pound's Paris apartment (during the early stages of his *Cantos*) to his former lecturer Felix E. Schelling, with whom Pound had an antagonistic but ultimately warm relationship:

> My assaults on Provence: 1st: using it as subject matter, trying to do as R[obert] B[rowning] had with Renaissance Italy. 2, Diagrammatic translations (those of Arnaut, now printed in *Instigations*): all part of study of verse-form (as trans. Of Cavalcanti). Note that

the English 'poet' en masse had simply said: 'these forms are *impossible* in English, they are too complicated, we haven't the rhymes'. That was bunkum, usual laziness of English, and hatred of craft. (I suppose by now I have a right to be serious about this matter, having been plugging away at it for twenty years.) Eh bien. 1. I have proved that the Provençal rhyme schemes are not *impossible* in English. They are simply *inadvisable*. The troubadour was not worried by our sense of style, our 'literary values,' he could shovel in words in any order he liked. Milton ruined his work by not understanding that the genius of English is not the genius of Latin, and that one can NOT write an uninflected language in the same way, using the same word-order that serves in an inflected language. The troubadour, fortunately perhaps, was not worried about English order; he got certain musical effects because he cd. concentrate on music without bothering about literary values. He had a kind of freedom which we no longer have.

(SL, 179)

What did Pound derive from philology, then? The answer cannot be located in the works of particular theorists. Pound's work grants us no one figure or theory of language to frame his work by. While Pound retained deep respect for certain of his lecturers, and maintained contact with some of those for whom his respect was begrudging, we cannot point to an overt lasting influence. Schelling is a significant part of Pound's correspondence. As late as 1933, Pound was writing to William P. Shepard, advising him on which contemporaneous French writers to recommend to his students, a letter which suggests that Pound's hostility towards universities and the philological method did not necessarily extend to the individuals who had taught him (*SL*, 232–233). This is not, however, an example of theoretical influence. We will also not find the answer in a particular theory of language or literature. Although William Dwight Whitney's ideas were prominent in Pound's department, his views on language provide relevance for Pound's own writings solely on the grounds that they were commonly accepted by the time Pound entered university. It is the same with various linguistic hypotheses that Pound would have studied, such as Grimm's Law, or the Neogrammarians' work; Pound was certainly aware of the regularity of sound change, but, as the letter to Schelling shows, this comparative method of linguistic analysis was imported into aesthetic judgements. Rather, what Pound gained from philology was something far more profound, more enduring, and more inextricable to his career than any one theorist or theory could grant: subject matter and practice. It was this that he was first able to 'make new'. In the letter to Schelling of July 1922, Pound also writes of how it was the 'psychological, almost physiological' elements of Arnaut Daniel and Guido Cavalcanti that came to interest him eventually

(*SL*, 180). This psychological, 'almost physiological' dynamism between mind, body, world, and language is the subject of the next chapter, and the next phase in Pound's linguistic thought, but it was grounded in a debt to philology he only ever reluctantly acknowledged.

Notes

1 Ezra Pound, '*Raphaelite Latin*', *Book News Monthly*, 25.1 (1906), 31–34 (31).
2 David Moody, *Ezra Pound: Poet* (Oxford: Oxford University Press, 2007), 16.
3 Pound, 'Raphaelite Latin', 31.
4 James Turner, *Philology: The Forgotten Origins of the Modern Humanities* (Princeton: Princeton University Press, 2014), ix.
5 See Peter Seuren, *Western Linguistics: An Historical Introduction* (Oxford: Blackwell, 1998), 89–103; for the 'manifesto', see Hermann Osthoff, and Karl Brugmann, *Morphologishe Untersuchungen auf dem Gebiete der indogermanischen Sprache* (Leipzig: Hirzel: 1878), iii–xx.
6 Gerald Graff, *Professing Literature: An Institutional History* (London: University of Chicago Press, 1987), 95. Graff, of course, mimics the pejorative descriptions of each for dramatic effect.
7 Ferdinand de Saussure, *Course in General Linguistics*, ed. Charles Bally, Albert Sechehaye, and Albert Riedlinger, trans. Wade Baskin (New York: Philosophical Library, 1959), 9–10 (1–2).
8 See Daniel Coit Gilman, *The Launching of a University and Other Papers: A Sheaf of Remembrances* (New York: Dodd, Mead & Company, 1906); Andrew Dickson White, *Autobiography* (New York: The Century Co., 1906).
9 J.M. Hart, *German Universities: A Narrative of Personal Experience* (New York: G. P. Putnam & Sons, 1874), 268–269.
10 H.C.G. Brandt, 'How Far Should Our Teaching and Text-books have a Scientific Basis', *Transactions of the Modern Language Association of America*, 1 (1884), 57–63 (58–59).
11 Ezra Pound, Letter to John Quinn, 26 August 1915, in *The Selected Letters of Ezra Pound and John Quinn, 1915–1924*, ed. Timothy Materer (Durham: Duke University Press, 1991), 41.
12 See Michael Holquist, 'Why We Should Remember Philology', *Profession* (2002), 72–79.
13 Turner, *Philology*, 253.
14 Turner, *Philology*, 380.
15 Ezra Pound, *A Visiting Card* (London: Peter Russell, 1952), 21.
16 David Moody, *Ezra Pound*, 14.
17 Stuart Y. McDougal, *Ezra Pound and the Troubadour Tradition* (Princeton: Princeton University Press, 1972), 3–4.
18 Rouben C. Cholakian, *The William P. Shepard Collection of Provençalia: A Critical Bibliography* (Hamilton: Clinton, NY, 1971), i.
19 Ezra Pound, 'Philology' [2 of 2], 21 February 1906, YCAL MSS 43, Box 87, Folder 3734, Beinecke Rare Book and Manuscript Library, Yale University.
20 Ezra Pound, 'Phonetics', 1 November 1905, YCAL MSS 43, Box 87, Folder 3735, Beinecke Rare Book and Manuscript Library, Yale University.
21 Ezra Pound, 'Philology' [2 of 2], 24 January 1906, YCAL MSS 43, Box 87, Folder 3734, Beinecke Rare Book and Manuscript Library, Yale University.
22 Walter Skeat, *An Etymological Dictionary of the English Language* (Oxford: Clarendon, 1900), vi.
23 John E. Joseph, *From Whitney to Chomsky: Essays in the History of American Linguistics* (Amsterdam: John Benjamins, 2002), 19.

24 *Catalogue of the University of Pennsylvania* (Philadelphia: University of Pennsylvania Press, 1905), 138.

25 Turner, *Philology*, 248.

26 The Platonic dialogue *Cratylus*, for example, contains a discussion on this very point.

27 William Dwight Whitney, *Language and the Study of Language: Twelve Lectures on the Principles of Linguistic Science* (London: N. Trubner & Co., 1884), 48.

28 Anne Birien, 'Pound and the Reform of Philology' in *Ezra Pound and Education*, ed. Steven G. Yao, and Michael Coyle (Orono: National Poetry Foundation, 2012), 23–46 (36–37).

29 Ezra Pound, 'Black Mirror', 1906, YCAL MSS 43, Box 86, Folder 3710, Beinecke Rare Book and Manuscript Library, Yale University.

30 Ezra Pound, 'Goal', YCAL MSS 43, Box 88, Folder 3791, Beinecke Rare Book and Manuscript Library, Yale University.

31 Ezra Pound, *Ezra Pound and 'Globe' Magazine: The Complete Correspondence*, ed. Michael T. Davis, and Cameron McWhirter (London: Bloomsbury, 2015), 299.

32 Both of these are models for Pound's career. For a comparison of Pound's and Rossetti's translation techniques and theories, see Roxana Preda, 'D.G. Rossetti and Ezra Pound as Translators of Cavalcanti: Poetic Choices and the Representation of Woman', *Translation and Literature*, 8:2 (1999), 217–234.

33 See Lucia Boldrini, *Joyce, Dante, and the Poetics of Literary Relations: Language and Meaning in* Finnegans Wake (Cambridge: Cambridge University Press, 2001).

34 Carlos Riobó, 'The Spirit of Ezra Pound's Romance Philology: Dante's Ironic Legacy of the Contingencies of Value', *Comparative Literature Studies*, 39:3 (2002), 201–222 (201).

35 Dante Alighieri, 'De Vulgari Eloquentia' in *De Vulgari Eloquentia: Dante's Book of Exile*, trans. Marianne Shapiro (Lincoln: University of Nebraska Press, 1990), 47–90 (79).

36 W.P. Ker, 'Dante, Guido Guincicelli and Arnaut Daniel', *The Modern Language Review*, 4:2 (1909), 145–152 (149).

37 Arnaut Daniel, 'Si'm fos Amors de joi donar tant larga' in *The Troubadours of Dante*, ed. H.J. Chaytor (Oxford: Clarendon, 1902), 50–51 (50).

38 Ezra Pound, *Instigations, Together with an Essay on the Chinese Written Character* (New York: Boni and Liveright, 1920), 318.

39 Ezra Pound, 'I Gather the Limbs of Osiris – IV: A Beginning', *The New Age*, 10:8 (1911), 178–80 (179).

40 Ezra Pound, 'I Gather the Limbs of Osiris – II: A Rather Dull Introduction', *The New Age*, 10:6 (1911): 130–131 (130).

41 Ezra Pound, 'I Gather the Limbs of Osiris – II', 130.

42 Pound, 'I Gather the Limbs of Osiris – IV', 179.

43 Ezra Pound, 'I Gather the Limbs of Osiris – XI: En Breu Brisaral Temps Braus', *The New Age*, 10:16 (1912), 369–370 (370).

44 Pound, 'I Gather the Limbs of Osiris – IV', 179.

45 Pound, *Hugh Selwyn Mauberley*, 13.

46 It is important to bear in mind throughout that Pound may have exaggerated his points for dramatic effect at a time of heightened anti-Germanic sentiment.

47 Vincent Sherry, *The Great War and the Language of Modernism* (Oxford: Oxford University Press, 2004), 111.

48 Ezra Pound, 'James Joyce: At Last the Novel Appears', *Egoist*, 4:2 (1917), 22.

49 Ezra Pound, *Guide to Kulchur* (New York: New Directions, 1938), 203; *A Visiting Card* (London: Peter Russell, 1952), 21.

50 Ezra Pound, "Provincialism the Enemy: I," *The New Age*, 21:11 (1917), 244–245.
51 Ford Madox Ford, *When Blood Is Their Argument: An Analysis of Prussian Culture* (London: Hodder and Stoughton, 1915), 90.
52 Peter Buitenhuis, *The Great War of Words: British, American and Canadian Propaganda and Fiction, 1914–1933* (Vancouver: University of British Columbia Press, 1987), 45.
53 Matthew Stibbe, *German Anglophobia and the Great War, 1914–1918* (Cambridge: Cambridge University Press, 2001), 74–75.
54 Ezra Pound, 'Provincialism the Enemy: I', 245.
55 Ezra Pound, 'Provincialism the Enemy: III', *The New Age*, 21:13 (26 July 1917), 288–289.
56 Pound, 'Provincialism the Enemy – III', 289.
57 Birien, 'Pound and the Reform of Philology', 36.
58 Thomas E. Connolly, 'Ezra Pound's "Near Perigord": The Background of a Poem', *Comparative Literature*, 8:2 (1956), 110–121 (110).
59 Ezra Pound, 'Near Perigord' in *Lustra* (London: Elkin Matthews, 1916), 95–103 (95).
60 Pound, 'Near Perigord', 98–99.
61 Pound, 'Near Perigord', 99.
62 See John Leigh, 'Shepard, Pound, and Bertran de Born', *Paideuma*, 14:2 (1985), 331–339.
63 McDougal, *Ezra Pound and the Troubadour Tradition*, 33.
64 Richard Sieburth, Introduction to Ezra Pound, *A Walking Tour of Southern France* (New York: New Directions, 1992), vii–xxii (ix).
65 Sieburth, *A Walking Tour of Southern France*, xv.
66 Rebecca Beasley, *Ezra Pound and the Visual Culture of Modernism* (Cambridge: Cambridge University Press, 2007), 128.
67 See Lawrence Rainey, *Ezra Pound and the Monument of Culture: Text, History, and the Malatesta Cantos* (Chicago: University of Chicago Press, 1991). An excellent account of the textual genesis of the 'Malatesta Cantos' is given in the first chapter, 25–64.
68 David Ten Eyke, *Ezra Pound's Adams Cantos* (London: Bloomsbury, 2012), 10.
69 See Luke McMullan, 'Counter-philology: Ezra Pound as Translator of Provençal and Cavalcanti, 1917–1932', in *Textual Practice* (online 10 April 2017).
70 J. Mark Smith, 'The Energy of Language(s): What Pound Made of Philology', *English Literary History*, 78 (2011), 769–800 (770).
71 Emil Lévy, *Provenzalisches Supplement-Wörterbuch: Berichtigungen und Ergaenzungen zu Raynouard's Lexique roman*: Volume 5 (Leipzig: Reisland, 1907), 402. It should be noted that the entry for *noi* is followed by a question mark, denoting Lévy's uncertainty with his supposition.
72 Emil Lévy, *Provenzalisches Supplement-Wörterbuch*: Volume 4 (Leipzig: Reisland, 1904), 33–35. Translation my own.
73 Réka Mihálka, 'Canto XX' in *Readings in the* Cantos: Volume 1, ed. Richard Parker (Clemson, SC: Clemson University Press, 2018), 187–200 (190).
74 Pound, *Instigations*, 295.

2 Reassessing *The Chinese Written Character*
Language, Consciousness, and Phenomena

If, in 1910, Pound had not found 'a language to think in', then he had by 1913. In that year, Mary Fenollosa, the widow of the sinologist, Ernest Fenollosa, contacted Pound, suggesting that her late husband's notes may be of interest to him, and he may be the person to complete certain unfinished projects. Pound met Mary McNeill Fenollosa at the house of Sarojini Naidu and dined with her on 29 September 1913, with her offering him the papers soon afterwards.[1] As Zhaoming Qian points out, Pound had been interested in the Orient before his meeting with Fenollosa, making him an unusual, but not entirely outlandish, choice.[2] Fenollosa's papers contained notes on translations from Chinese poems, lecture notes, drafts of essays on Chinese and Japanese culture, and an essay on the relationship between the Chinese written character and aesthetic theory. Pound, despite knowing no Chinese, agreed, becoming in the process Fenollosa's literary executor, and he produced three extraordinary and deeply controversial texts: *Cathay* (1915), *Noh* (1916), and *The Chinese Written Character as a Medium for Poetry* (first published in *The Little Review* in 1919, and then again in his *Instigations*, 1920). It was from these texts that Pound developed his celebrated 'ideogrammic method', a poetics based on his and Fenollosa's erroneous understanding of the Chinese written character: in Pound's 'ideogrammic writing', individual images are juxtaposed to one another and the meaning of the entire passage is not revealed discursively, but is instead worked out or discerned by the reader. Massimo Bacigalupo rightly points out that this technique was not something Pound discovered in Fenollosa, as he had found it in the work of Robert Browning over a decade earlier, but we can say definitively that it is in Fenollosa's notes that Pound found confirmation of his method.[3]

The poems in *Cathay* are among Pound's most celebrated literary achievements. They are best seen as a collaborative act of translation: out of Fenollosa's notes on individual characters, Pound created a sequence of poems combining subjective perspectives with imagist clarity. The translations are, perhaps inevitably, riddled with errors. Fenollosa even persisted with the Japanese transcriptions of Chinese names, a feature which found its way into Pound's version and his later writing. Among

Pound's poetic colleagues, however, his lack of Chinese was not seen as a bar to his poetic achievement. T.S. Eliot captured the tension between Pound's poetic innovation and *Cathay*'s status as a blind translation by describing him as the 'inventor of Chinese poetry for our time'.[4] Eliot's phrase is well chosen if only because it speaks to the ways in which the Chinese poets in *Cathay* are filtered through Pound's aesthetic prism. Ford Madox Ford apparently wrote of how 'if these are original verses, then Mr Pound is the greatest poet of the day', a valuation which relies upon a relegation of translation which Pound himself rejected.[5]

It is the essay *The Chinese Written Character as a Medium for Poetry* which has aroused the most interest in terms of Pound's theory of language. Most analyses of Fenollosa's influence on Pound have been drawn on the grounds of the linguistic sign, on a supposed claim that the Chinese character demonstrates that there is a 'natural' connection between signifier and referent, though this is a slight misreading of Fenollosa's point. Fenollosa's argument is relatively simple, though it revolves around a series of complexes: the Chinese written character is a superior vehicle for poetic expression than the alphabetic sign of Western writing systems by virtue of its 'ideogrammic' nature. That is to say, the Chinese written character is composed of what he calls 'shorthand pictures' of natural processes, whereas alphabetic scripts are merely collections of arbitrary symbols, representing abstractions, held together by nothing more than societal conventions.

> But Chinese notation is something much more than arbitrary symbols. It is based upon a vivid shorthand picture of the operations of nature. In the algebraic figure and in the spoken word there is no natural connection between thing and sign: all depends upon sheer convention. But the Chinese method follows natural succession.[6]

However, Fenollosa's central contention is, at best, a departure from linguistic realities. It relies on his base assumption that the 'picturesque' element of the Chinese character predominates. This is, of course, not the case. This, it must be said, is a slight misreading of Fenollosa's claims: his point is not that the characters are pictographs, but rather that they are ideograms: that they represent ideas, not things. The ideogram, for Fenollosa, is that which roots ideas in concrete instances, not a mere representation of nature, but a representation of the mental apprehension of nature. This is also, however, erroneous. Particular Chinese characters, like Egyptian hieroglyphs, may have started off ideogrammically, but they eventually became conventionalised representations of sounds and sound-patterns.

So what can be salvaged from this error? *Cathay*'s reputation rests on its poetic quality, rather than the validity of its translation, but how can this essay retain significance? Haun Saussy's remarkable recovery of

Fenollosa in the 2008 critical edition of *The Chinese Written Charac-ter* has allowed a fresh look at depths of the latter's arguments. Saussy refreshes a critical tradition which has forgotten that Pound is not the author of essay, and that there is a crucial sinological history behind the text's composition. The text has a long and complicated history, Saussy reminds us, of which Pound is only a part. Saussy's Fenollosa is recov-ered from the Romantic elements that many have read into the *Chinese Written Character* and is presented as a knowledgeable and authorita-tive figure in the midst of modern thought, even if he is characterised by his errors. Saussy demonstrates that Fenollosa was writing within a tradition of Japanese, Buddhist, and specifically Kegon and Tendai thought which conceived of the 'intermingling' of phenomena, of the causal structures and relations within reality, rather than static images.[7] Fenollosa's philosophy, Saussy writes, was related to a tradition of 'in-teractionism' which 'proposes, in defiance of both idealism and mate-rialism, to follow the causal relations between mind and body in both directions'.[8] 'Nature' was, for Fenollosa, 'a limitless network of causal connections, none of them self-supporting or self-elucidating'.[9] The con-siderable achievement of the 2008 edition is a twofold restoration: first, much of Fenollosa's convictions are reassessed on a transcultural level, showing the extent to which his work was an attempt at reconciling East-ern and Western traditions of thought; second, and most significantly for the present study, the 'mediated nature of "things"' is resituated 'in a causal web'. Saussy shifts the focus of *The Chinese Written Character as a Medium for Poetry* away from concerns around the sign towards a vision of reality as mediated by the interactivity between phenomena, between subject and world, between mind and body, and between lan-guage, thought, and reality.

Although the intention behind the 2008 critical edition is to assess Fenollosa beyond his Poundian context, the editors will undoubtedly permit those writing on Pound a reversal of the process. As Saussy gives us a reassessment of Fenollosa, it is essential that we reassess Pound's use of the *Chinese Written Character*. And it is here that we may note a disagreement with Saussy's claims in his excellent introduction to the text. He argues that 'whether or not he knew what he was doing, Pound cut around a specific way of thinking about reality, relation, and sym-bolization, a version of "radical empiricism" subject to the test of East Asia'. 'This', Saussy claims, 'he removed from the essay'.[10] It is my con-tention that he did not, and indeed the argument of this chapter is that it was precisely the 'specific way of thinking about reality, relation, and symbolization' that attracted Pound to the essay in the first place. The editors of the 2008 edition of *The Chinese Written Character* recovered key aspects of Fenollosa's thought from a critical tradition which had misunderstood him, and so I, similarly, hope to situate the essay into a revisionist account of Pound's engagement with it. Pound, I argue, was drawn by precisely those features which Saussy believes he ignored (with some notable exceptions, of course). It was the dynamic relationship between language and the interactive web of phenomena that drew Pound to the essay. Saussy makes a convincing case that, for Fenollosa, the etymology of certain Chinese characters, immensely flawed though it is, was not the central contention of the essay. I argue that it was not for Pound, either.

It is in the dynamic interaction of consciousness, language, and the world that we can preserve certain aspects of what Pound took from Fenollosa, while recognising their basis in grave error. First, I will argue that Pound's interest in Fenollosa was due to a number of pre-existing convictions which he held about the relationship between language and consciousness. Then, I explore the interactivity between language, consciousness, and nature in Pound's/Fenollosa's argument. I then compare this to the phenomenology of Husserl, whose work revolves around similar questions asked at a similar period of time, and shares similar philosophical roots to Fenollosa's. I end by exploring the ways in which Pound adapted Fenollosa's writing for his own key linguistic principles.

The Poundian Context

Before coming to Fenollosa, it is worth pausing on another text beyond the usual fringes of twentieth-century philosophies of language which came to influence Pound. Hudson Maxim, whose *The Science of Poetry and the Philosophy of Language* Pound reviewed in 1910, provides an interesting insight into early twentieth-century poetic thought. Rebecca Beasley and Ian Bell both argue that Maxim's book laid the foundation for Pound's encounter with Fenollosa by outlining a theory of poetry which privileges its relation to visualisation.[11] Maxim argues, at all points, against a separation of thought and language: the verbal dimension of verse is one designed to 'stimulate and qualify the mind of the hearer for the perception of thought, by inducing a mood in harmony with the thought exprest [*sic*]'.[12] Maxim's views about language are of a piece with his era. He argues that 'speech is an instrument for conveying ideas of experience from one individual to another by means of symbols of sensuous impressions' and that, in terms of writing, 'a written letter is an arbitrary sign used to symbolize a sound, which in turn is used as the sign of an idea'.[13] In terms of his affinities with Pound, we can also look to his writing on abstraction. For Maxim, all abstract thought must be grounded in sensory impressions: 'poetry transforms the abstract to the concrete, the intangible to the tangible'. The movement here is interesting (from the abstract to the concrete) and, as we shall see, it is one that Pound reverses, preferring to discern the abstract solely by means of the concrete. The difference from Maxim is subtle, but significant. As Beasley and others have pointed out, the sentence in the book that must have drawn Pound's attention the most is one that he could have written himself: 'Poetry obeys the law of conservation of energy. By poetry a thought is presented with the utmost economy of word symbols'.[14] This sentence not only echoes, as Vincent Sherry has argued, in Pound's 'I Gather the Limbs of Osiris', but in his later definition that 'poetry is simply language charged with meaning to the utmost possible degree' in *How to Read* (1928) (*LE*, 23). What is most striking about Maxim's account is that although it draws on the Social Darwinist account of Herbert Spencer for a lot of its treatment of the development of language, it is constantly inflected by the arbitrariness of language. Alongside Herbert Spencer, we also find contemporaneous psychological arguments by William James. Maxim's account is not essentialist about language and, by stressing the importance of thought in relating the concrete to the abstract, offers a way to conceive of Pound doing the same.

Maxim's account of language is, however, static: it focusses on the individual relations of signs and phenomena without making the necessary movement which Saussure, for example, does in stressing his interrelation of signs to one another. As a model for a poetics of the individual image, it does indeed hold in its account of language as an act of visualisation, as a concretisation of the abstract, and as a means of tying language to sensuous impressions of an apprehended object, itself rooted in physical phenomena. By 1913, Pound had begun the search for principles which would allow him to move beyond the formulaic image towards a more dynamic language. As Herbert N. Schneidau writes in his account of Pound's movement towards Vorticist aesthetics, an intentional paradox lies at the heart of the programme: 'it is dynamic and yet static: fixity in flux'.[15] Pound encountered Fenollosa's work at the outset of his Vorticist period, and his editorship of Fenollosa's writing and his translations of *Cathay* are contemporary with the two issues of *BLAST* (1914, 1915), Wyndham Lewis's Vorticist journal for which Pound provided bombastic and provocative manifestos. Where Pound had emphasised the nature of the image alone in his theorisation of Imagism, often in static terms, Vorticism expresses the dynamism and movement of the image as it appears in our consciousness. It makes more sense to conceive of the difference between Vorticism and Imagism in Pound's career as a conceptual shift in his aesthetics, rather than in his poetic praxis: many of Pound's imagist poems qualify as Vorticist by virtue of their movement. Pound's writing in his Vorticist phase is undoubtedly more aggressive, more dynamic, and it moves away from the fine, sensual qualities of his earlier poetry, though the movement is more of an evolution than the revolution it seems.

What is striking about Pound's manifesto 'Vortex' (1914) is that it begins, after a paean to mechanics, with a reflection on the nature of human thought and its relationship with the world. Where one might expect a purely formalist manifesto, and Pound's vitriolic style can certainly serve to give this impression, one finds a number of revealing meditations hidden behind a largely satirical aesthetic. See, for example, how Pound conceives of the Vorticist:

> You may think of man as that toward which perception moves. You may think of him as the TOY of circumstance, as the plastic substance RECEIVING impressions.
>
> OR you may think of him as DIRECTING a certain fluid force against circumstance, as CONCEIVING instead of merely observing and reflecting.[16]

Vorticist man is one who grasps that consciousness is not merely a receptacle for reality but a creative space which can affect and frame it; the artist masters his or her situation, bending material to his or her will or vision. The Vorticist artist is not necessarily one who adheres to a particular school of painting nor to a fixed set of dogmas, but one who holds to the creative rather than reflective power of art. There are reasons to be sceptical of such a claim, however. The overt aggression of Vorticism, Julian Murphet shows, developed according to an ideological opposition between what Pound saw as masculine creativity and female receptivity. Such writing, Murphet argues, relies on a 'gendered division of labour at the level of sense perception in modernist aesthetics'.[17] This is reflected not only in the pages of *Blast*, but also in Pound's translation of Remy de Gourmont's *The Natural Philosophy of Love* (1922).

In 'Vortex', Pound vacillates between the aggressive masculinity of Vorticist aesthetics and the reflective tone of a theorist, attempting to bring the two together with mixed results. The only fundamental unit the Vorticist requires is what Pound calls the 'primary pigment', which he explains in the following terms: 'every conception, every emotion presents itself to the vivid consciousness in some primary form'. For a poet, for example, this appears as 'the most highly energized statement, the statement that has not yet SPENT itself it [sic] expression, but which is the most capable of expressing'; that is to say, it is an interior conception which the poet must bound through in the *mot juste*. He further elaborates in starker, more definite terms:

> EVERY CONCEPT, EVERY EMOTION PRESENTS ITSELF TO THE VIVID CONSCIOUSNESS IN SOME PRIMARY FORM. IT BELONGS TO THE ART OF THIS FORM. IF SOUND, TO MUSIC; IF FORMED WORDS, TO LITERATURE; THE IMAGE, TO POETRY; FORM, TO DESIGN; COLOUR IN POSITION, TO PAINTING; FORM OR DESIGN IN THREE PLANES, TO SCULPTURE; MOVEMENT TO THE DANCE OR TO THE RHYTHM OF MUSIC OR OF VERSES.[18]

Note how the fundamental meaningful unit of poetry remains the image, demonstrating that, for Pound, Vorticism absorbs, rather than replaces, the principles of Imagism. What Pound presents here is a kind of transcendental, conscious basis for all aesthetics, one which lies behind all art forms and is then differentiated in the nature of the individual experiences, becoming music, prose, poetry, design, sculpture, dance, or painting depending on the nature of experience or the object described. The true artist recognises that the nature of the individual concept, of the individual emotion, or of the image, dictates the form it will take, but this relativity is bound together by an *a priori*, universal capability on the part of artists to discern the 'primary form'. What Pound gestures towards here is a location of aesthetics in the nature and structure of 'vivid consciousness' itself. Later in the manifesto, he argues that the Vorticist artist is not concerned with art as likeness or 'mimicry', but rather is concerned with 'art before it has spread itself into a state of flaccidity, of elaboration, of secondary applications'.[19] The absolute relation, following Pound's suggestion here, is not to be understood as the accuracy or precision of an art form relative to things as they appear in the world but to things as they appear in the mind. In what is a quintessentially modern movement, Pound seems to suggest that artistic reality, and the language which attends it, must be located in consciousness.

What is somewhat perplexing here is that Pound, who dedicated considerable energy to disparaging the legacies of Romanticism in his pre-Raphelite and Symbolist forebears, in particular the vagueness of their language and the 'softness' of their sensibilities, seems to be arguing for an understanding of art in relation to the individual genius. It is helpful here to consider the linguistic explanations Pound provides in *Gaudier-Brzeska*, written two years later, particularly in the ways in which he attempts to distinguish his work from Symbolism. Pound rejects the notion that his work merely continues Symbolism by claiming that the Symbolist poets of the nineteenth century 'degraded the image to the status of a word'; that is, he argues that the images in symbolist poetry operate as a kind of second language, and the words of the poetry itself, for example, become then symbols of a second order. Imagistic and Vorticist poetry, by contrast, stops with the image itself: the thing described is the thing intended, as opposed to a symbol of another object at an even further remove. The question, of course, is where the 'image' is located. Pound's 'image' is not a symbol of external reality, but it is instead a meaningful unit located in the mind in its apprehension of external reality, and it is both the starting foundation and terminal point of poetic symbolisation:

> The image is the poet's pigment. The painter should use his colour because he sees or feels it. I don't much care whether he is representative or non-representative. He should *depend*, of course, on the creative, not upon the mimetic or representational part in his work.

It is the same in writing poems, the author must use his *image* because he sees it or feels it, *not* because he thinks he can use it to back up some creed or some system of ethics or economics.

An *image*, in our sense, is real because we know it directly. If it have an age-old traditional meaning this may serve as proof to the professional student of symbology that we have stood in the deathless light, or that we have walked in some particular arbour of his traditional paradiso, but that is not our affair. It is our affair to render the *image* as we have perceived or conceived it.[20]

Where Pound calls for a 'precision of language' in his manifestos, it is not solely a refinement of language qua language, but language as bound to images in human consciousness. The 'precision of language' is a precision of language as an instrument of thought, as the form in which a creative consciousness had imbedded itself. Language is, for Pound, a multifaceted, creative process, always with the capacity to extend beyond itself. According to Pound, poetic language is, then, not an extension of ordinary speech, nor a privileged metalanguage intended to draw our attention to the function or disfunction of signs, but the ordering and patterning of images and melodies; its fundamental unit is not the word, but the image and mood to which the words refer. By the time Pound came to approach Fenollosa's work, he had developed an intense focus on the image in consciousness, and an understanding of language's absolute relation as being with 'vivid consciousness' itself. It is in this framework that we may now proceed to read his collaboration with Fenollosa.

Fenollosa's Argument

The place held by Fenollosa in Pound's thinking about language and aesthetics has long been known, not least because of the insistence of the latter himself. Fenollosa is often considered a misguided scholar on the periphery of twentieth-century aesthetics, but in his *Composition*, his former student Arthur Wesley Dow offers a picture of a profound and influential thinker. Written before Fenollosa's death, Dow's *Composition* stands with Pound's work as one of two contemporaneous instances of his legacy. Dow had met Fenollosa during his time at the Boston Museum of Fine Art. He describes Fenollosa as 'a philosopher and logician gifted with a brilliant mind and great analytic power'. 'This', he claims, 'gave him an insight into the nature of fine art such as few ever attain'.[21] It would be remiss to suggest that Fenollosa was an international driving force for modern art, but he had at the very least a profound grasp of its central principles. Although poetry is not Dow's central concern, the term does recur with relative frequency in the early parts of his text. Like his former teacher, Dow attempts to outline the 'fundamentals of all aesthetics'. Dow's inheritance of Fenollosa's ideas and their importance for his pedagogic practice as delineated in *Composition* is evidence of his importance beyond his influence on Pound alone. Language does not play a major role in Dow's thinking, but in his chapter on Notan, a concept involving the juxtaposition of dark and light elements in Japanese design composition, he outlines a possible extension of his artistic principles to general linguistic ones:

> Line, Notan, Color – the elements by which the whole visible world is apprehended – may or may not be used as the language of art. Like speech, this three-fold language may voice noble emotions in poetic style, or may subserve the vulgar and the humdrum. Art-language must be an art-form; a number of facts, or an incident, accurately described in paint and color may have no more connection with art than a similar set of written statements – just plain prose. There is no art unless the statements are bound together in certain subtle relations which we call beauty. When beauty enters, the parts cease to have a separate existence, but are melted together in a unit.[22]

The significant aspect of Dow's thought is his use of the phrase 'apprehended' and, subtle though its implications may be, this notion requires some elucidation. It is the process of apprehending the world, existing in a state of perception, that forms the structure of the human consciousness in its relation to art. What Dow means by 'apprehension' here is a kind of transcendental state, a structure of perception. Art conforms to 'line, Notan, Color' not just because these are the elements that make up the world but because they are the elements that make up our apprehension of the world; art conforms not to structures of external reality, but to internal reality, to the structures of consciousness. The visible world is, thus, an apprehended world.

In terms of the linguistics of his work, Fenollosa's claim is not, as has sometimes been thought, a refutation of our understanding of language as a semiotic system based on arbitrary abstraction, but rather it is a claim for the exceptionalism of the Chinese writing system (indeed, as for the phonetic components of the Chinese language, Fenollosa is more conspicuously reserved than he is dismissive). This separation is not a curious feature of Fenollosa's thought alone, but is instead based on what was a commonplace assumption in the linguistics of the period. In his *Language*, for example, Otto Jespersen asserts – in terms which raise questions treated in Chapter 3 – that 'primitive picture-writing' is the origin of the Chinese written character.[23] Leonard Bloomfield offers a summary of Western thought on Chinese writing in the early twentieth century:

> Our oldest texts are inscriptions, some of which may date as far back as 2000 B.C., but since Chinese writing uses a separate symbol for each word, with little indication of sound, even an intelligible

document may tell us little or nothing about the language; our knowledge of Chinese speech, therefore, does not set in before about 600 A.D.[24]

While this does not excuse the errors made by Fenollosa and Pound, it does explain and contextualise them, and it does give some justification to the intense focus on the written character at the expense of the phonetic elements. It is clear that Pound and Fenollosa's error in understanding Chinese writing was common to early twentieth-century linguistic thought.

In his *Language (1933)*, Bloomfield – one of the preeminent linguists of the first half of the twentieth century – gives us an insight into the state of knowledge about Chinese writing among Western scholars during the 1920s and 1930s. Bloomfield challenges the division of writing systems into alphabetic and ideographic systems. 'Writing is an outgrowth of drawing', he claims, arguing that all writing systems have their origin in paintings, depictions of certain things or events.[25] Eventually, a speech community, having developed a system of drawing comes up against the limits of the system, as it cannot represent abstract thought nor does it correspond to the individual phonemes and parts of speech as language is used. The speech community then 'develop[s] a convention of representing every part – say, every word – of the spoken utterance by some character'. This, Bloomfield says, is presupposed by what he calls 'real *writing*' (emphasis in text), by which he means writing which makes use of 'picturable object' and 'a phonetic or linguistic form'.[26] Eventually, the phonetic/linguistic element predominates, and the characters become increasingly conventionalised and lose their pictorial quality, representing sounds. The written mark thus becomes a symbol (or 'written sign' in Saussurian terms), conventionally determined to stand for certain words – Bloomfield stresses that at this 'stage' in language development, writing represents words, and not individual phonemes (as alphabetic script does). It is here we can see the difference between the two kinds of writing that Saussure outlines; Bloomfield, however, takes issue with the label *ideographic* or *ideogrammic* writing. This, he argues, implies that the individual characters of such writing systems represent ideas, the 'practical world' of the writer, whereas he insists that these characters represent features of the writer's language and should, therefore, be called *logographic* (or *word-writing*) systems. Thus, we get Bloomfield's account of the relations between the elements of abstract compound characters in Chinese writing, which stands in stark contrast with Fenollosa's:

In the device of representing unpicturable words by phonetically similar picturable words, we see the emergence of the phonetic factor in writing. Once a symbol is associated with a particular word, the phonetic features of this word may suffice to bring about the writing of the symbol. In Chinese, where the words are of uniform structure, this transference has been made only from word to word, and the compound characters, in accordance with this structure, are written as units and held down to uniform size.[27]

Here Bloomfield, otherwise a staunch defender of Saussurian linguistics, departs from a distinction in the latter's work. In the sixth chapter of his *Cours*, Ferdinand de Saussure makes the following claim, remarkably similar to Fenollosa's and Pound's thoughts.

There are only two systems of writing

1   In an ideographic system, each word is represented by a single sign that is unrelated to the sounds of the word itself. Each written sign stands for a whole word and, consequently, for the idea expressed by the word. The classic example of an ideographic system of writing is Chinese.

2   The system commonly known as 'phonetic' tries to reproduce the succession of sounds that make up a word. Phonetic systems are sometimes syllabic, sometimes alphabetic, that is, based on the irreducible elements used in speaking.

Moreover, ideographic systems freely become mixtures when certain ideograms lose their original value and become symbols of isolated sounds.

The statement that the written word tends to replace the spoken one in our minds is true of both systems of writing, but the tendency is stronger in the ideographic system. To a Chinese, an ideogram and a spoken word are both symbols of an idea; to him writing is a second language, and if two words that have the same sound are used in conversation, he may resort to writing in order to express his thought. But in Chinese the mental substitution of the written word for the spoken word does not have the annoying consequences that it has in a phonetic system, for the substitution is absolute; the same graphic symbol can stand for words from different Chinese dialects.[28]

Saussure's interests are naturally different to Fenollosa's, as the latter is concerned with the universal application of the aesthetic impulses that lie behind the Chinese character, rather than its practical use in a speech act, a linguistic community, or in a semiotic system. Nevertheless, Saussure begins his study of writing with a radical separation of two different kinds, the one emphasising a system of arbitrariness, a further degree of remove from the material basis of the spoken word; the other performing, pragmatically at least, its task with a greater degree of precision.

We find a similar movement in Pound's *ABC of Reading* (1934), in a passage based on Fenollosa's ideas:

> Spoken language is noise divided up into a system of grunts, hisses, etc. They call it 'articulate' speech.
>
> 'Articulate' means that it is zoned, and that a number of people are agreed on the categories.
>
> That is to say, we have a more or less approximate agreement about the different noises represented by
>
> a, b, c, d, etc.
>
> Written language, as I said in the opening chapter, can consist (as in Europe etc.) of signs representing these various noises.
>
> There is a more or less approximate agreement that groups of these noises or signs shall more or less correspond with some object, action or condition.
>
> cat, motion, pink.
>
> The other kind of language starts by being a picture of the cat, or of something moving, or being, or of a group of things which occur under certain circumstances, or which participate a common quality.
>
> (*ABC/R*, 28–29)

Contrary to Pound and Fenollosa, Saussure does not, of course, believe that this link is due to the embodiment of 'natural succession', and his separation is on practical, rather than theoretical grounds (for Saussure, the Chinese character is distinct because of its lack of dependence on sound). As a practising philologist, Saussure is on firmer linguistic ground in discussing the relative qualities of Chinese and 'phonetic' scripts, even if his assumptions show their age: his awareness of the phonetic foundation of Chinese characters is greater than that of Fenollosa, who admits it only reluctantly. What this does show, however, is that Fenollosa's radical separation of ideograms and 'alphabetic' writing, his assumptions based on this separation, and his concern with the permutations of adopting the inbuilt ideas of other systems for thought and art had much in common with linguistic figures now far more renowned. If it does not lend his work linguistic legitimacy, and Saussure certainly does not lend Fenollosa and Pound sinologistic legitimacy, it does at least grant some contextual grace to his wider assumptions.

When reading Fenollosa, one must begin with aesthetics and then move to language. This is the movement that Fenollosa himself makes, and the subject which the essay explores: to separate the linguistic from the aesthetic, or vice versa, in the context of Fenollosa's discussion is to have already misunderstood him. 'My subject is poetry, not language', he writes, though he caveats this immediately with the admission that 'the roots of poetry are in language' (*CWC*, 360). Here Fenollosa's claims are unremarkable, and we must remember that the special claim of his argument is 'the *Chinese* method follows natural succession' (emphasis mine). It is on these grounds that Fenollosa can be easily misinterpreted. 'Poetry', Fenollosa argues, is 'like music…a *time art*'; that is to say, it not only takes place in time, but is also constituted by temporal sequences and temporal forms (*CWC*, 360). The fundamental law that this expresses is the order of cause and effect, a sequence that we watch unfold whenever we observe natural phenomena, and, because Fenollosa conceives of poetry as a record of our experience, this order is the structure of the poetic. And the poetic, is, in turn, the structure of thought: 'The transferences of force from agent to object, which constitute natural phenomena, occupy time', Fenollosa argues, concluding that 'therefore, a reproduction of them in imagination requires the same temporal order' (*CWC*, 361). This leads Fenollosa to conclude that the form of the sentence is not a result of social convention, but rather the 'reflection of the temporal order of causation' (*CWC*, 366). Though it is framed in Romantic terminology, the contention at the root of it, that the universality of the sentence has a biological, rather than a social, cause, is not too far from contemporary assumptions in Chomskyean Universal Grammar.[29] What should be stressed about Fenollosa's argument about the sentence is that it should be taken as microcosm of the ways in which the structures of language as a whole reflect both the structures of human consciousness and how these, in turn, reflect the transferences of power embedded in the laws of physics: in short, his argument is that they are part of the same interactive superstructure.

Where Fenollosa differs from linguists, aside from the nature and depth of his expertise, is that his task is aesthetic recovery and an apologia for a particular approach to poetry, rather than the description of linguistic phenomena. What concerns Fenollosa is that an apparent overreliance on abstraction in alphabetic writing has led to a loss of concrete imagery, which he – like Pound – believes to be the meaningful unit of poetry. A good example of this is his claim about the prevalence of intransitive verbs in English writing. 'Grammarians', he claims, have long held that transitive verbs derive from intransitive verbs: we first have the abstract notion 'to run', and from there, we derive the notion 'to run a race' (*CWC*, 368). Fenollosa overturns this order. He argues that a transitive verbal phrase, such as 'farmer pounds rice', corresponds to the transference of energy in nature, the natural order of temporal succession, by reflecting what he takes to be the universal sentence structure of agent-verb-object. The theory that intransitive verbs are primary proposes that verbs denote states rather than actions, whereas his understanding of the primacy of transitive verbs argues that all human thought begins with action in the world. In a phrase that must have caught Pound's attention, he argues that the privileging of intransitive verbs has created a linguistic situation in which 'we get weak and incomplete sentences which suspend the picture' (*CWC*, 368). Fenollosa, contemporaneous with Imagism, was arguing for a theory of poetic writing which would reassert the primacy of experience, of visions seen, heard, felt, tasted, or smelled, over abstract thought. This is not to dismiss abstraction entirely, but quite simply to overturn the order of thought, to begin with phenomena and then move to the general; to derive the abstract from the concrete – a modernist movement.

There is a tendency to forget that Fenollosa conceives of the Chinese written character as a symbolic structure. He draws a distinction between the purely arbitrary signs of alphabetic languages and the poetic Symbolism of the Chinese character, but symbolic representation remains at the centre of his understanding of language. The difference lies in the extent to which the arbitrariness of linguistic signs affects the metaphorical structure of language as it is written down. In Western phonetic scripts of writing, he argues, words retain little of the original creative spirit that lies behind language. As Fenollosa writes,

> Only scholars and poets feel painfully back along the thread of our etymologies and piece together our diction, as best they may, from forgotten fragments. This anemia of modern speech is only too well encouraged by the feeble cohesive force of our phonetic symbols. There is little or nothing in a phonetic word to exhibit the embryonic stages of its growth. It does not bear its metaphor on its face.
>
> (CWC, 379)

The 'cohesive force' holding Chinese written characters together, Fenollosa believes, is that of a poetic method which retains enough of the vital force of man's natural propensity for metaphor. According to Fenollosa, relying more on contention than on scholarship, the 'ideogram' of the Chinese character works by combining a series of concrete images. See, for example, his infamous claim that the verb *to see* was composed of the signs for 'eye' and 'to run': the eye in motion. Fenollosa does not explain why this should be read as 'to see', rather than as a representation of the literal movement of the eye, but Fenollosa's point is rather subtler. What Fenollosa reads into the characters is not so much the literal interpretation of the images depicted, but rather the relations that they symbolise. The conceptual relation between the characters 'eye' and 'run' is one of motion: the representation of an eye in motion is valued for its metaphoric, not its literal content. As he writes, 'the more concretely and vividly we express the interactions of things the better the poetry' (CWC, 382–383); the stress here should be on the word 'interactions'.

That Fenollosa's stress is on the metaphorical structure of the ideogram, its representation of the structural interactions of phenomena, rather than its literal depictions of nature, is seen in the conclusion to his essay. It is here that Fenollosa approaches the question that is of most relevance to Pound's work, though he does not answer it: what is the aesthetic lesson that can be learned from such an interpretation of another language's writing system? According to Fenollosa, 'if we attempt to follow [the suggestion of the Chinese character] in English we must use words highly charged, words whose vital suggestion shall interplay as nature interplays' (*CWC*, 386). He does not provide an explanation of what such words would be, how this 'charging' is to be achieved, nor what this means for the epistemological notions that he has introduced, yet it is here that we can see where Pound takes up the challenge laid down by Fenollosa's essay. Before we come to a discussion of how Pound takes Fenollosa's ideas forward, however, it is first necessary to situate those ideas in relation to certain philosophical debates in the early twentieth century. It is not my claim in the following that Fenollosa and Pound actively take part in those debates, but rather that there is a philosophical counterpart to much of the conceptual shifts in their aesthetics: phenomenology.

A Poetic Phenomenology?

One figure who took Fenollosa's influence on Pound to have been of philosophical significance is Jacques Derrida, as noted in the introduction. In his *Of Grammatology*, he allots Fenollosa and Pound a canonical role in the development of a grammatological approach to language, that is, one which reverses the long-held privileging of speech over writing, one which overturns Western metaphysics.

> The necessary decentering cannot be a philosophical or scientific act as such, since it is a question of dislocating, through access to another system linking speech and writing, the founding categories of language and the grammar of the *episteme*....This is the meaning of Fenollosa whose influence upon Ezra Pound and his poetics is well-known: this irreducibly graphic poetics was, with that Mallarmé, the first break in the most entrenched Western tradition. The fascination that the Chinese ideogram exercised on Pound's writing may thus be given all its historical significance.[30]

According to Derrida, the proper subject of *The Chinese Written Character as a Medium for Poetry* is ontology. He sees Pound and Fenollosa (and Mallarmé) as belonging to a list of figures such as Nietzsche, Freud, and Heidegger, who sought to destroy the metaphysical privileges of Western philosophy by asserting the primacy of the written word, the fundamental unknowability of linguistic signs, and the fragility of the concept of being. This Derrida sees in his 'irreducibly graphic poetics', by which he means a theory of aesthetic founded on the primacy of the visual, on the written.

While Derrida's statement does much to assert the significance of Fenollosa, this action is performed on shaky ground. Derrida seems to misread Fenollosa. Close reading of *The Chinese Written Character as a Medium for Poetry* would suggest its topic is not ontology but epistemology; Fenollosa is concerned by the ways in which we think and know reality, rather than our own place within it. We have similar reason to be sceptical of the claim that poetics outlined in his *ars poetica* are 'irreducibly graphic'. This can be seen in the very notion of an 'ideogram'. Fenollosa's conception of the Chinese written character has often been assumed to be based on the idea that the ideograms are, in fact, pictograms, that is, that they are images, or depictions of natural objects: that each sign is a representation of a natural object alone. Accordingly, to understand the profundity of Fenollosa's ideas, we need to ground our understanding in an interpretation of the graphic. In truth, however, Fenollosa's understanding of the ideogram is one in which the Chinese characters refer not necessarily to things themselves, but to our mental apprehension of them and the relations between them. An ideogram is, for Fenollosa, not an essentialist depiction of an object, but a representation of our interpretation of phenomena as they appear in consciousness. In this way, the ideogram cannot be 'irreducibly graphic', as it is a representation of an intractably complex set of relations, graphic, linguistic, aesthetic, and mental. It is for this reason that Fenollosa stresses the structure of metaphor in his conclusion to the essay.

It is this very set of relations, and their location in the human imagination, in the mind, that leads us to a philosophical approach with which Fenollosa and Pound never seem to have engaged, but which Derrida did. Strange as it may seem, phenomenology offers a way to understand the philosophical implications of Fenollosa's writing. Where Fenollosa writes of 'phenomena', his work engages in a philosophical tradition which provides the essential context for his broader aesthetic claims. In many ways, Fenollosa's arguments around the loss of energy in a supposed shift from transitive to intransitive verbs recalls the work of Franz Brentano, the father of phenomenology as a discipline, who argued that Western philosophy has gone awry since the late middle ages through a loss of what he calls 'intentionality'. Intentionality is the conscious act of perceiving, representing, or considering objects. As Brentano explains,

> Every mental phenomenon is characterized by what the Scholastics of the Middle Ages called the intentional (or mental) inexistence of an object, and what we might call, though not wholly unambiguously, reference to a content, direction towards an object (which is not to be understood here as meaning a thing), or immanent objectivity. Every mental phenomenon includes something as object within itself, although they do not all do so in the same way. In presentation something is presented, in judgement something is affirmed or denied, in love loved, in hate hated, in desire desired and so on. This intentional in-existence is characteristic exclusively of

mental phenomena. No physical phenomenon exhibits anything like it. We could, therefore, define mental phenomena by saying that they are those phenomena which contain an object intentionally within themselves.[31]

Brentano's return to mediaeval thought is analogous to movements made not only by inheritors of his work like Heidegger, but also by Pound later in his middle period. Intentionality is a state of relation between subject and object, conceiving the object as a phenomenon in the conscious act of perception. The concept of intentionality allows us to understand the full series of relations between the mind of an observer and a thing observed, between the thinker and the thing thought; it is, in short, the directionality of consciousness. Returning to Fenollosa's notion of the transitive verb, and his example of a farmer pounding rice, intentionality allows us to follow his argument a little easier. Were we to speak of a 'farmer pounding', we would have an abstraction, the intransitive verb demonstrating a loss of intentionality in our description. In discarding intransitive in favour of transitive verbs, the poet of Fenollosa's idealisation recovers not only a lost grammatical force, but also the intentional in-existence of phenomena in conscious states. Seen this way, Fenollosa's poetics calls not for poetry based on a naïve understanding of external reality, but for aesthetics of internal reality, which sits well alongside the work of his philosophical contemporaries.

It is in the work of Brentano's famous student, Edmund Husserl, that we see the most fruitful intellectual companion to the kind of thinking that Fenollosa approaches in *The Chinese Written Character*. Husserl's 1900 text *Logical Investigations* (*Logische Untersuchungen*) contains the most systemic outline of phenomenology as a discipline. In terms of its range of subjects, influences, dimensions, and effect on later thought, it is perhaps most comparable to Saussure's *Cours* in linguistics. Were Husserl to have a slogan associated with him (in the vein of the Poundian 'make it new'), it is 'we must go back to the things themselves' (*die Sachen selbst*), the modernist, aesthetic correlative of which may be found in William Carlos Williams's dictum that the poet seeks 'no ideas but in things' as declaimed in his *Patterson*.[32] We find a similar logic in Fenollosa's claim that in reading Chinese, one seems 'to be watching *things* work out their own fate', as opposed to a language composed solely of abstract, mental concepts (*CWC*, 363).[33] This return to 'the things themselves' should be understood in the context of a Kantian distinction between *Phenomena*, the appearances of things in our minds, and *Noumena*, their actual essences. As opposed to a systemic, idealistic metaphysics, which seeks to frame the essences of things in terms of conceptual schemata, Husserl attempts to schematise the ways in which *Phenomena*, or the appearances of things, appear to us in consciousness. Husserl, following Kant's lead (albeit with significant distinctions), conceives of reality as the framework of consciousness in relation to the world: in other words, the structure of consciousness is the structure of reality according to the individual subject, and our interaction with things, with *Phenomena*, is always part of a consciousness conditioned by intentionality. The analyses of *Phenomena* are located, thus, not in a purely external reality, but in the mental apparatuses with which we engage with reality; 'the things' of Husserl's philosophy are mental objects, and what the phenomenologist studies is the relationship between subjects and *Phenomena* within the framework of consciousness. Where Fenollosa writes of the ways in which the Chinese character reproduces the sequences of natural 'phenomena' in the imagination, he may err grossly in terms of linguistic detail, but he speaks to contemporaneous concerns about the relationship between language and thought.

It is in Husserl's remarks on the fundamental 'unity' of scientific enquiry that we find the most affinity with Fenollosa, however. Husserl defines science as 'an *interconnection of things* to which our thought-experiences (actual or possible) are intentionally directed, or, on the other hand, as an *interconnection of truths*, in which this unity of things comes to count objectively as being what it is' (emphases in text).[34] We may compare this with Fenollosa's claim that 'all processes in nature are interrelated', that 'the more concretely and vividly we express the interactions of things the better the poetry', and his insistence that poets in English should 'use words highly charged, words whose vital suggestion shall interplay as nature interplays'. If we stress the notions of interrelation, interaction, and interplay as the underlying structure of both reality and our conscious experience of it (should we recognise such a separation), then Fenollosa's project and Husserl's seem nearer than one would assume. The interconnection of things and the interconnection of truths about them are, according to Husserl, *a priori* and inseparable. Husserl here refers not only to the observation of nature, as Fenollosa does, but also to abstract thought, mathematical formulae, or concepts. His notion of interconnection is significantly broader, more detailed and more profound, than Fenollosa's, but the emphasis on the intersubjectivity of consciousness, on the structural interconnectedness of things, and on the way in which the unity of scientific truth is built out of a conscious observation of the 'interconnection of things' plunges to similar psychological depths as Fenollosa's *Chinese Written Character*. This is not to suggest, of course, that Fenollosa and Husserl share a discipline, project, or philosophy, but it does at the very least demonstrate the philosophical and modernist validity of Fenollosa's argumentation. It also, more significantly, allows us – through analogy – to view the *Chinese Character as a Medium for Poetry* as a study concerned with the relationship between language and phenomena (a movement of philosophical modernity) and not one between language and essences.

The comparison between Fenollosa's thought and that of the turn of the century phenomenologists is licenced not only by certain similarities in their thought, but also by shared roots in German idealism. Husserl's work grew, as he acknowledges in *Logical Investigations*, out of a tradition with its origins in Kant, before turning away from the speculative nature of idealism in favour of a 'concrete' engagement with consciousness.[35] We may observe a similar sequence of movements in Fenollosa's thought. Fenollosa's academic background was rich in German Idealism and it is important to see his work in relation to this philosophical tradition.[36] In many ways, *The Chinese Written Character as a Medium for Poetry* is a response to the place held by oriental culture and language in a tradition of Western thought: it is an argument for the significance of an overlooked aspect of human thought to a tradition which claims transcendental universality. Fenollosa may not have quite intended the revolution in philosophy to which Derrida assigns him a role, but he certainly sought to overturn a number of long-held assumptions. A good example of the tradition to which Fenollosa responds can be seen in Hegel's interpretation of Chinese characters in *The Subjective Spirit* (the following is taken from a contemporaneous translation):

> Alphabetic writing is on all accounts the more intelligent: in it the *word* – the mode, peculiar to the intellect, of uttering its ideas most worthily – is brought to consciousness and made an object of reflection. Engaging the attention of intelligence, as it does, it is analysed; the work of sign-making is reduced to its few simple elements (the primary postures of articulation) in which the sense-factor in speech is brought to the form of universality, at the same time that in this elementary phase it acquires complete precision and purity. Thus alphabetic writing retains at the same time the advantage of vocal language, that the ideas have names strictly so called: the name is the simple sign for the exact idea, i.e. the simple plain idea, not decomposed into its features and compounded out of them. Hieroglyphics, instead of springing from the direct analysis of sensible signs, like alphabetic writing, arise from an antecedent analysis of ideas. Thus a theory readily arises that all ideas may be reduced to their elements, or simple logical terms, so that from the elementary signs chosen to express these (as, in the case of the Chinese *Koua*, the simple straight stroke, and the stroke broken into two parts) a hieroglyphic system would be generated by their composition. This feature of hieroglyphic – the analytical designations of ideas – which misled Leibniz to regard it as preferable to alphabetic writing is rather in antagonism with the fundamental desideratum of language – the name.[37]

For Hegel, the superiority of alphabetic writing to 'hieroglyphs' lies in its similarity to spoken language, in that its signs stand for concepts, rather than things, and that the material aspect of the language stands in for abstraction. Pound and Fenollosa grant this truism, but for them it is the source of the language's inferiority, in that languages based on alphabetic signs lose the vital forces of nature. While Fenollosa similarly locates the nature of written characters in the nature of thought, he overturns Hegel's formulation. Fenollosa argues, for example, that it is not alphabetic writing which 'spring[s] from the direct analysis of sensible signs', but rather the ideograph, composed as it is out of the structural nature of reality. It is also interesting that Hegel argues that the 'fundamental desideratum of language' is the 'name' or noun. Fenollosa, by contrast, stresses scepticism towards nouns, the 'name' of which Hegel writes, arguing that 'in nature, the isolated noun does not exist' (*CWC*, 364), taking the dynamic transitive verb as his fundamental unit of meaning. Were we to follow Derrida's line of thought and see Fenollosa's work as part of a radical break with epistemology, an overturning of the history of metaphysics, it lies in the overturning of Hegel's hierarchies, not necessarily of his entire programme. We must be careful to distinguish between shifts of form and shifts of content. Fenollosa's work radically disagrees with a tradition of thought with regard to the Chinese written character, and explicitly overturns a series of assumptions about language, but it does not necessarily follow that Fenollosa affects a philosophical revolution in Pound's work. Fenollosa's work remains idealist in that it is concerned with the transcendental nature of human consciousness and its relation to a theoretically external reality. In many ways, Fenollosa, like Pound, seeks a relocation and a renewal of certain ways of thinking, rather than a total revolution. Derrida seeks to read Fenollosa as a radical anti-foundationalist, affecting a shift from epistemology to a kind of sceptical ontology, but this reading is difficult to reconcile with the latter's stress of a 'scientific' methodology, of the relation of consciousness to the world, and of the nature of language.

Cathay

It would be remiss to explore Fenollosa's relation to Pound's thought without commenting on translation. Pound was able to wrest out of Fenollosa's, Ariga's, and Mori's notes two translations, celebrated and controversial in equal measure. Pound has long been considered to be at the forefront of modern thought on translation. In his hugely influential *The Translator's Invisibility* (1995), Lawrence Venuti celebrates Pound's 'foreignizing' translation technique, one which focusses 'on the signifier, creating an opacity that calls attention to itself and distinguishes the translation both from the foreign text and from prevailing values in the target-language culture'.[38] It is for this reason, Venuti argues, that Pound's translations abound in archaism, as they seek to maintain the cultural distance and 'foreignness' between reader and text. While Venuti provides perceptive readings of Pound's translation of Arnaut Daniel's canzone, 'The Seafarer', and Guido Cavalcanti, *Cathay* is not a major consideration in his understanding of Pound's translator technique. Venuti's work has long since established Pound as a major figure in twentieth-century translation studies.

What we see in Pound's translation of *Cathay* is perhaps counterintuitive to the image of Pound as an assertive theorist of the material aspects of translation. The critical reaction to *Cathay* has largely been one of wonder at Pound's development of the psychological aspects of the poems. Wim Lip, for example, writes that while one can easily 'excommunicate Pound from the forbidden city of Chinese studies' on account of the numerous errors he makes, 'it seems clear that in his dealing with *Cathay,* even when he is given only the barest details, he is able to get into the central consciousness of the original author by what we may perhaps call a kind of clairvoyance'.[39] Such a reading is problematic as we know that Pound's clairvoyance was misdirected at best, conflating two poems into one in 'The River-Song' and even in the case of the most famous poem of the sequence, 'The River-Merchant Wife: A Letter', changing the aspects of not only the mood, but the subject as well.[40] Yet 'clairvoyance' is a well-chosen term as the subject matter of these poems remains the expressions of mood, emotion, and consciousness mediated by particular speakers with regard to particular phenomena.

Perhaps one reason why Venuti little comments on Pound's Chinese works in *The Translator's Invisibility* is that the poems in *Cathay* are not translations in the same way that Pound's versions of Arnaut Daniel, Guido Cavalcanti or even his later work on Confucius are translations, and so they cannot be judged by the same standards. In each of those cases, Pound had a strong grasp of (or at least a decent enough acquaintance with) the original language and so was able to make judgements as to the meanings of words, the context of certain phrases, and the tone of the poetry. In the case of *Cathay*, he was dependent upon Fenollosa's notes. To say that Pound 'translates' the poetry of Li Bai is to elide the curious nature of the translations' production. Venuti is quite correct that we cannot judge Pound's translations by means of their fidelity to the original poems, but not necessarily for the reasons he suggests. Pound was entirely bounded by the limits of his language and, for this reason, we have to shift the burden of qualitative assessment from the poetic input to the poem's output, to its effects. Pound's poetic practice in *Cathay* is the development of an aesthetic principle which revolves around the dynamic interaction of speaking subject and phenomenal world. There is a duality of movement in each poem in *Cathay* which constitutes the lyrical passages of the collection: we move from state of mind to concrete object and from concrete object to state of mind, each constituting the other. Between these two poles, subjective mood and apprehended phenomena, Pound limits, constrains, and controls his language, a limitation which reflects the constraints under which he worked. In this, I argue, he discovered an affirmation of his linguistic dispositions.

Leaving aside (momentarily at least) the question of whether to treat these poems as originals or translations, and moving beyond the conditions of *Cathay*'s production, Pound's poetic achievement can be seen in the ways in which the poems alternate between the foreign and the familiar. In contrast to Venuti's stress on the opacity of the foreign, Daniel Katz writes that 'the most impressive achievement of the poems is Pound's invention of a language and a tone that walks the tightrope between supple familiarity and the uncanny alterity which a translation of texts so distant geographically, temporally, and linguistically would seem to require'.[41] Katz's summary here quite movingly captures the vacillation between alienation and familiarity which the reader feels on any encounter with *Cathay*. Pound's aesthetic is grounded in 'alterity', but the emotions and the psychological dimensions of the poem are undoubtedly grounded in the familiar. To begin with the title alone, *Cathay*, the volume announces that this is not a China of our acquaintance but an orientalist, archaic China of the literary imagination, 'Cathay'. The first poem, Qu Yuan's ('Kutsugen') 'Song of the Bowmen of Shu', however, undoubtedly speaks to an audience which, in 1915, was all too aware of the psychological strain of war:

> Here we are, picking the first fern shoots
> And saying: When shall we get back to our country?
> Here we are because we have the Ken-nin for our foemen
> We have no comfort because of these Mongols
> We grub the soft fern-shoots,
> When anyone says 'Return', the others are full of sorrow.
> Sorrowful minds, sorrow is strong, we are hungry and thirsty.
>
> (C, 5)

The passage is both familiar in terms of its subjective mood and its spoken lament, the opening two lines granting expression to a universally accessible (and, indeed, universally poignant) feeling before this is located in a foreign phrase: 'Ken-nin'. The spoken phrase in the poem, 'Ken-nin', K.K. Ruthven writes in her gloss of this poem, comes from the Japanese *Ken-in*, meaning 'wild tribes' or 'Huns'.[42] In leaving the phrase untranslated, Pound introduces alterity into the poem, the effect of which is not lessened by translating the phrase the line after. But this technique is not Pound's invention, nor is it a feature of modernist poetry alone. If we compare this passage with James Legge's 1871 translation, we can see that this technique of grounding the poem in proper names was a feature of previous Chinese translation.

Let us gather the thorn-ferns, let us gather the thorn-ferns;
The thorn-ferns are now springing up.
When shall we return? When shall we return?
It will be late in the [next] year.
Husband and wife will be separated,
Because of the Hëen yun.
We shall have no leisure to rest,
Because of the Hëen yun.[43]

What sets Pound's translation apart is the language and the imagery. Where Legge has the Bowmen gathering the ferns, Pound has them 'picking' and 'grubbing'. In Pound's case, the concrete image of the Bowmen forlornly picking at the fern shoots is a subtle extension of their state of mind, whereas, in Legge, the conventionalised image serves solely to emphasise the setting. As Legge was working from the original poem – as his extensive accompanying notes show – there can be little doubt that his is a more informed rendering, but Pound's is clearly the more masterful performance, and the reason for this lies less in the accuracy of the transfer from one language to another than it does in the intensification of language as such.

In terms of the development of his own aesthetic, Pound's achievement in *Cathay* is best revealed by the one poem for which he provides an explanation, 'The Jewel Stairs' Grievance' by Li Bai ('Rihaku'). The poem is short enough to quote entire:

The jewelled steps are already quite white with dew,
It is so late that the dew soaks my gauze stockings,
And I let down the crystal curtain
And I watch the moon through the clear autumn.

(C, 13)

In this poem, four interrelated descriptions of phenomena are layered next to one another. In his discussion of Pound's translation of this poem in relation to the prejudices of a Confucian paternalistic system, Zhaoming Qian comments that 'remarkably, Pound seems aware of some psychic energy in the lone woman's muteness', and that he 'recaptures both the reticence and its biting force'.[44] The reason for this, I would like to suggest, is that Pound draws on a psychological reading of the poem, rather than on accuracy of translation. This is outlined in his note:

Jewel stairs, therefore a palace. Grievance, therefore there is something to complain of. Gauze stockings, therefore a court lady, not a servant who complains. Clear autumn, therefore he has no excuse on account of weather. Also she has come early, for the dew has not merely whitened the stairs, but has soaked her stockings. The poem is especially prized because she utters no direct reproach.

(C, 13)

Pound's note provides an overt interpretation that is required to support the imputed meaning of the poem. It assumes a smoothness of relation between mood and image, however. Much like his 'In a Station of the Metro', the poem relies upon the title to make sense of the whole. From the poetry itself, it is unlikely that most readers would discern a grievance. Nor is it immediately apparent that each description Pound picks out reveals the exact meaning his note implies. Nevertheless, what we see here is the operational logic of Pound's aesthetic: it is an aesthetic of imputed mood, the language itself drawing out the duality of subjective emotion and phenomena, each constituting and limiting the other. The images in this poem are thus extensions of mood, a crystallisation of the unexpressed into concrete form.

Although *Cathay* and its permutations for modernism are well known, the *Noh Plays* are a relatively understudied aspect of Pound's corpus and they demand revisiting. Not only is the language of the plays beautiful poetry in its own right, but also Pound's notes and commentaries on the plays provide key insight into his own poetics. The *Noh Plays* were assembled and translated from Fenollosa's collections, meaning that the errors of the translations are not entirely his own. The collection itself is a combination of short plays and fragments, notes, commentaries, extracts from Fenollosa's diary, and an extended extract from Fenollosa's own commentary on the *Noh*, creating a collaborative effort, working much like the ideogrammic quality Pound reads into the plays to build a single work out of a series of complex relations. The significance of the masks, the ghostly characters, and their attendant spectral imagery provide ample metaphors for Pound's own poetic project. Indeed, by tracing Pound's remarks on the *Noh Plays*, we can see the germinal seeds of the *Cantos'* poetics. In his introduction to the plays, Pound celebrates the ways in which Noh is an holistic art, comprising dance, music, performance, and the poetry of the spoken word. Consider, for example, his argument for the beauty of the plays:

> In the Noh we find an art built upon the god dance, or upon some local legend of spiritual apparition, or, later, on the gestes of war and feats of history; an art of splendid posture, of dancing and chanting and acting that is not mimetic. It is, of course, impossible to give much idea of the whole of this art on paper. One can only trace out the words of the text and say that they are spoken, or half-sung and chanted, to a fitting and traditional accompaniment of movement and colour, and they are themselves but half shadows. Yet, despite the difficulties of presentation, I find these words very wonderful, and they become intelligible if, as a friend says, 'you read them all the time as though you were listening to music'.
>
> (N, 21)

According to Pound, Noh operates at the intersection of intellectual, musical, and visual arts, drawing on both human spirituality and human artisanal abilities. There is a tenderness in Pound's appreciation of the Noh, one that reveals a deep affinity with the artwork. On the dramaturgy of the plays, he writes that it is a 'stage where every subsidiary art is bent precisely upon holding the faintest shade of a difference', a quality we would ordinarily associate with the linguistic logic of the *Cantos* (N, 6).

We need not base the claim that the Noh is one of Pound's models for the *Cantos* on an extension of its aesthetic principles, however. In a revealing note to his translation of the 'Suma Genji', Pound hints at the significance of the Noh for his poetics. In the 'Suma Genji', a folklorist priest, Fujiwara is in search of information about the folk hero, Genji, when he encounters an old woodcutter. Enquiring after Genji, the old man reveals that he had been in that place, before disappearing into the elements, reappearing as the spirit of Genji in a supernatural form of waves, moonlight, and air. Pound's translation of his moment of transformation is thus:

> How beautiful the sea is! When I trod the grass here I was called 'Genji the gleaming', and now from the vaulting heaven I reach down to set a magic on mortals. I sing of the moon in this shadow, here on this sea-merge of Suma. Here I will dance Sei-kai-ha, the blue dance of the sea waves.
>
> (N, 42–43)

Genji then becomes one with the elements. Pound's commentary helps us to read this play, or at the very least to discern a lasting interpretation: If this play seems unsatisfactory in terms of its dramatic tension, Pound explains, it is because a Western audience must make the conceptual leap the Noh demands, remembering that these lines are completed in the movements of the dance, bearing in mind that 'the Noh has its unity in emotion'. Pound then claims that Noh 'has also what we may call Unity of Image' (N, 45). This last line is Pound's emendation to Fenollosa's notes and it should be considered as much a commentary on the ideals of his poetics as it is an outline of the poetics of Noh theatre. Indeed, in an accompanying footnote, Pound contextualises his treatment of Noh within the intentions of Imagism:

> The intensification of the Image, this manner of construction, is very interesting to me personally, as an Imagiste, for we Imagistes knew nothing of these plays when we set out in our own manner. These plays are also an answer to a question that has several times been put to me: 'Could one do a long Imagiste poem, or even a long poem in vers libre?'
>
> (N, 45n)

Pound would, of course, answer this question in the affirmative and it would appear that Noh showed him the way. However, Pound's phrasing here, the 'unity in emotion', 'unity of Image', and 'intensification of the Image', requires some clarification. He seems to imply that unity and intensification are the same 'manner of construction', and his use of the word 'unity' itself seems to take the place of 'meaning' in more popular forms of literary criticism. He further elaborates in the second part of *Noh Plays*, writing:

> One must build out of [the plays'] indefiniteness a definite image. The plays are at their best, I think, an image; that is to say, their unity lies in the image – they are built up about it as the Greek plays are built up about a single moral conviction.
>
> (N, 79)

If we take the imagist definition of image, as Pound implies we should, as 'an emotional complex in an instant of time', then the 'image' of a particular Noh lies in the ways in which it unifies various emotional strands within particular natural symbols. Its 'meaning' is therefore not an abstract principle which is explored in various ways, but is an abstracted image which is built up out of the particulars of the play. What the Noh play does, according to Pound, is layer image upon image. It would be remiss to claim that this was the origin of Pound's famous ideogrammic method, but we can certainly see the Noh drama as part of the affirmation of his changing poetics.

The theoretical framework for this realisation comes not from Pound's commentary but from Fenollosa's, whose comments on Noh drama were the source of Pound's own impressions (indeed, Fenollosa, it must be remembered, was quite literally the only source for the material Pound uses here). Fenollosa describes the principle of composition which lies behind the Noh drama as one which derives from a 'primary' emotion or drive, bound through in an ideal symbol:

> The beauty and power of Noh lie in the concentration. All elements – costume, motion, verse, and music – unite to produce a single clarified impression. Each drama embodies some primary human relation or emotion; and the poetic sweetness or poignancy of this is carried to its highest degree by carefully excluding all such obtrusive elements as a mimetic realism or vulgar sensation might demand. The emotion is always fixed upon idea, not upon personality.
>
> (N, 120)

While this may seem to place Noh drama in an abstract realm anathema to Pound, it is precisely the kind of emotion of which Fenollosa writes that grounds Noh in the real: the plays, Fenollosa argues, derive from human character, from the primal emotions of brotherly or filial love, of jealousy, of anger, of specific types of haunting, of spirituality, and of unrequited love. 'Some one of these intense emotions is chosen', Fenollosa writes on the same page, 'and in it elevated to the plane of universality by the intensity and purity of treatment'. Noh drama, Pound and Fenollosa suggest, is an art bound to the realities of human existence, much like the Chinese character is (allegedly) bound to natural processes, not because of some mimetic quality, but because it embodies the foundational structures of human consciousness and the foundational emotions and spirituality of human existence. It is for this reason that Fenollosa refers to the Noh dramatists, whose work is so far removed from the detailed naturalism of Emile Zola or Guy de Maupassant, as 'great psychologists'.

It is in this light that we can return to *Cathay* and its numerous inaccuracies. What Pound reproduces is the unities of emotion expressed, rooted as they are in the image as bound through the various speaking personae. It is this that he sought to translate, the operational logic of the poetry, which he mistakenly believed to be the relationship between the language of the original and the mental states that it represented. Although Fenollosa's and Pound's errors are well known, the beauty and unity of *Cathay* in and of itself endures, in great part because this operational logic was adopted by the translator. The real test of the 'unity of Image' that Pound read into the Noh plays as a principle for an extended poem lies not in his translations, but in his own long poem.

What *Cathay* and Pound's and Fenollosa's commentaries on the Noh plays show us is the significance of the speaking subjects mediating the images. This is a methodology which is adapted in the *Cantos*. In each canto, individual images (in the Poundian sense), quotations, symbols, phrases, and citations are juxtaposed against one another, layered one over the other, to create a pattern of seemingly disjointed fragments. The poem by and large rejects ordinary syntax, relying on the combinations and patterns of images to create an overall meaning, without syntactic or abstract logic drawing them together. Instead, the reader must discern the ways in which the particulars of the poem form a general meaning. It is here that we can see the 'unity' or 'intensification' of the 'Image' in the *Cantos* as well as in Noh drama. The patterns and sequences of Pound's poem serve to intensify the image at root: to speak of 'meaning' in the *Cantos* is to speak of the image, or ideogram, that the individual instances in each poem create; to speak of meaning in the *Cantos* is thus as intractable as speaking of the meaning of phenomena and perception.

A Phenomenology of Reading?

In terms of language, Pound's most extended post-Fenollosan treatment of the subject is his *How to Read* (1928). Published 15 years after his encounter with Fenollosa's work, *How to Read* marks Pound's most ambitious attempt at systematising his view of language and, like

The Chinese Written Character as a Medium for Poetry, it concerns the interrelation of language, mind, and reality. Pound outlines his crucial distinction between different types of poetry, all of which form the basis for his poetics in different ways. These different ways refer to the ways in which language is 'charged' with meaning, a phrase which he borrows from Fenollosa's concluding demand at the end of *The Chinese Written Character as a Medium for Poetry*, namely that poets 'use words highly charged'. What we must first establish, however, is precisely what is meant by 'meaning'. By the late 1920s, this phrase had become philosophically fraught. In the philosophy of language, particularly in the work of G.E. Moore, Bertrand Russell, and Ludwig Wittgenstein, meaning became central to philosophical investigation. For Russell, for example, the 'meaning' of a phrase was a shorthand description of the objects, persons, and states of mind that it described. Wittgenstein and the Ordinary Language Philosophers moved towards a pragmatic definition of meaning as use: the meaning of a word is the use to which it is put in any given language situation. In all of these cases, however, the meaning of a word is understood in terms of the *objective correlate*, of the thing which it described: in other words, meaning is identified with referents. Here, it is useful again to turn to Husserl. In *Logical Investigations*, Husserl criticises precisely this perspective as a category error, pointing out that we have a tendency to see meaning as either a property of words themselves, or as a commentary on the ontological status of an object: a word has meaning if and only if the object it signifies exists. Both cases are false, Husserl argues, as it makes much more sense to think of meaning as a process of intentionality in the mind of a speaker or hearer: 'the function of a word...is to awaken a sense-conferring act in ourselves, to point to what is intended, or perhaps given intuitive fulfilment in this act, and to guide our interest exclusively in this direction'.[45] Meaning thus emerges as a conscious process, or a series of processes, activated by language. Following Husserl, it is a mistake to speak of the meaning of words; instead, we should speak of the meanings that words invoke in speaking or listening subjects; meaning is, in other words, a property of subjects, not of language.

Where we speak of the meaning of a word or phrase, we thus speak of the intentional process it evokes. Where Pound writes of 'charging' language with meaning, we should think of this in terms of an enhancement of a series of mental processes and associations. In *How to Read*, Pound distinguishes between three different poetic modes, each one corresponding to a mental process: first, 'melopoeia', in which the sound of the language, and its cadences, rhythms, and music are used to enhance the meaning or to suggest some nuance; 'phanopoeia', in which the imagery that the words evoke in the mind of the reader or hearer adds certain shades of meaning, or is the main force of the poetry as in Imagism; and 'logopoeia', the vaguest of Pound's categories, which relies on the conceptual associations a reader or hearer forms in response to a certain word or phrase. In each of Pound's categories, the meaning-making property of the mode is not one belonging to language in and of itself, but one bound to the poetic, aesthetic use of language, and in particular to the effect that this produces in the mind of the reader. While the audience of Pound's categories of poetry rarely extends beyond that of his poetry, they do merit renewed attention in the light of Pound's broader thought on language and his contributions to modern poetry.

Pound dedicates the most time to melopoeia, which he defines as 'words...charged, over and above their plain meaning, with some musical property, which directs the bearing or trend of that meaning' (*LE*, 25). He further defines three kinds of melopoeia: '(1) that made to be sung to a tune; (2) that made to be intoned or sung to a sort of chant; (3) that made to be spoken' (*LE*, 28). He further describes melopoeia as 'a force tending to lull, or to distract the reader from the exact sense of the language. It is poetry on the borders of music and music is perhaps the bridge between consciousness and the unthinking sentient or even insentient universe' (*LE*, 26). The reason for this is the materiality of its aesthetic: music, according to Pound's line of thought, is an art form which relies on the physical properties of its media and the sensory reception it achieves in its audience. Music, though it may have a symbolic structure as well, achieves its primary aesthetic significance in the fact that it is itself a phenomenon. Its artistic significance lies in its phenomenal structure. *Melopoeia* is the type of poetry that makes most use of the material nature of language, its *signifiers* in Saussurian terms, themselves a part of the insentient universe of objects.

The limitations of melopoeia lie in its translatability. Precisely that from which this kind of poetry derives its strength, the sounds, and features of specific languages is that which limits it. Although, Pound admits, a 'foreigner with a sensitive ear' can appreciate the poetic force of melopoeia, they cannot necessarily grasp the nuances of its meanings, nor the full potency of the mode. 'It is practically impossible to transfer or translate it from one language to another', Pound argues, 'save perhaps by divine accident, and half a line at a time' (*LE*, 25). This is because melopoeia is always bound to the specificity of a language; to reproduce the sound of writing in translation, one must in nearly all cases sacrifice sense, as in Louis Zukofsky's late translations of Catullus, for example. Zukosfky's translation of Catullus's 'Nulli se dicit mulier mea nubere malle' reads 'Newly say dickered my love air my own would marry me all'.[46] Although the work is masterful in its own right, and offers a fascinating commentary on the nature of the classics in translation, it is not a full reproduction of the melopoeia of the original for one simple reason: melopoeia, as Pound suggests, directs the bearing or trend of a 'plain' or ordinary meaning. In Zukofsky's case, the candences do not direct so much as diverge. The distinct quality of melopoeia lies in its unification of the sound of a word and its meaning, of the material and the conceptual; to translate one means some sacrifice in the other.

This is not necessarily the case, however, with the second of Pound's categories, *phanopoeia*. It is here that Pound's distinctions become the most useful for understanding the details of his linguistic theories. Although phanopoeia predates Fenollosa's work as Pound's privileged concept, it found its strongest affirmation in *The Chinese Written Character*. Phanopoeia is, Pound claims, 'a casting of images upon the visual imagination' (*LE, 25*). It is this kind of poetry towards which his writing on *le mot juste*, his imagistic and Vorticist periods, and his engagement with Fenollosa drives. He writes that 'in *phanopoeia* we find the greatest drive toward utter precision of word; this art exists almost exclusively by it' (*LE, 26*), a notion which recalls the thrust of his career to that point. It is curious that Pound dedicates the least amount of space to outlining *phanopoeia* in 'How to Read'. One reason for this could be that readers familiar with his work should recognise the concept from his other writing – he may also have thought it the most self-explanatory. Regardless, it is worth stressing the conceptual nature of *phanopoeia*: Pound emphasises that the images are cast 'upon the visual imagination', that is, they are phenomena located in consciousness and they require, to paraphrase Pound's notion in other terms, a high degree of intentionality – it is a notion of this kind to which the 'precision of word' refers.

In terms of examples, he claims that 'the Chinese (more particularly Rihaku and Omakitsu) attained the known maximum of *phanopoeia* due perhaps to the nature of their written character' (*LE, 27*). Pound's caution in asserting the centrality of the Chinese character itself is somewhat revealing, demonstrating that Pound prioritised certain aspects of Fenollosa over others (namely, a criticism of abstraction, and a poetry of concrete images, rather than actual etymologies). In terms of Pound's contemporaries, a good example of *phanopoeic* writing is H.D.'s work. The poems of H.D.'s first collection, *Sea Garden* (1916), are prime examples of imagistic writing, the poetry deriving its force primarily from the pattern of images that H.D. arranges around a theme. The second stanza of 'Evening' is a good example:

> The cornel buds are white
> But shadows dart
> from the cornel-roots –
> black creeps from root to root,
> each leaf
> cuts another leaf on the grass
> shadow seeks shadow,
> then both leaf
> and leaf-shadow are lost.[47]

H.D. structures her imagery in a temporal sequence, following the fading of the light as night draws near. What occurs is a lyrical evocation of the mood that such a scene provokes. H.D. achieves this by carefully and precisely 'presenting in an instant of time' a depiction of the event itself. It is here that one may note the critical distinction between Symbolism and the 'modern poets' of Pound's circle: according to Pound, were this poem symbolist, the images themselves would operate as a kind of second language, standing as signs and representations of something else. In the *phanopoeia* of H.D.'s writing, however, the meaning of the poem is as intractable as the scene itself. In theoretical terms, at least, to ask what the 'meaning' of the poem 'Evening' is to is ask of the meaning of our experience of evening itself. In terms of language, *phanopoeia* enhances our visual consciousness: the poetic craft lies in bounding this through in words.

The final of Pound's categories is the most difficult to grasp: it also seems to have been the concept to which Pound came last. Where *melopoeia* and *phanopoeia* can be ascribed to quite definite aesthetic experiences on the part of the reader, *logopoeia* is much more intractable. In Pound's words, it is

> the 'dance of the intellect among words', that is to say, it employs words not only for their direct meaning, but it takes count in a special way of habits of usage, of the context we *expect* to find with the word, its usual concomitants, of its known acceptances, and of ironical play. It holds the aesthetic content which is peculiarly the domain of verbal manifestation, and cannot possibly be contained in plastic and music. It is the latest come, and perhaps most tricky and undependable mode.
>
> (*LE*, 25)

If the *melopoeia* and *phanopoeia* speak the language of the senses, then, *logopoeia* speaks the language of the intellect, but certain questions remain. What role, for example, does the intellect play in the former two categories? Is Pound drawing too strongly an age-old distinction between the intellect and the imagination, a distinction his work otherwise seems to blur? And if *logopoeia* holds the 'aesthetic content which is peculiarly the domain of verbal manifestation', then surely it is that mode upon which poetry most strongly defends? For which reason, it is curious that Pound does not spend more time considering its nature. *Melopoeia* and *phanopoeia* are transcendental aesthetic modes: they make use of music and the visual arts, respectively, and while their ability to be translated varies, they are not the sole preserve of the literary in the same way that *logopoeia* must be. The literary form of *logopoeia par excellence* is, for Pound, satire. In particular, he locates the discovery of *logopoeic* writing in the work of Sextus Propertius and Jules Laforgue. To Laforgue,

Pound ascribes a definite discovery, while he admits that the discovery of *logopoeia* in Propertius is based on his own conjecture. He also sees elements of the *logopoeic* in the satires of the eighteenth century and the work of Heinrich Heine.

Pound's privileged example of *logopoeia* was Laforgue. According to Peter Nicholls, Pound discovered Laforgue's work in 1914 in discussion with T.S. Eliot.[48] Laforgue led a full and short life, ending in 1887. What Pound and Eliot prized in Laforgue was the way in which he forged a poetic language out of the idioms of speech. In a 1917 commentary on Laforgue, Pound stresses that the qualities of his work lay in his use of 'delicate irony', which Pound describes as the 'citadel of the intellect'.[49] Pound, celebrating Laforgue as 'a purge and a critic', writes that he 'deal[s] for the most part with literary poses and *clichés*, taking them as his subject matter', and thus 'making them a vehicle for the expression of his own very personal emotions, of his own unperturbed sincerity'. He quotes a passage of Laforgue's 'Pierrots' (1886) as an illustration of Laforgue's craft:

> Je ne suis pas « ce gaillard-là! » ni Le Superbe!
> Mais mon âme, qu'un cri un peu cru exacerbe,
> Est au fond distinguée et franche comme une herbe.[50]

In *Pavannes & Divigations* (1918), Pound translates this stanza as follows:

> I am not 'that chap there' nor yet 'The Superb'
> But my soul, the sort which harsh sounds disturb,
> Is, at bottom, distinguished and fresh as a March herb.[51]

Pound's translation is an attempt to capture the original's end rhymes, cadences, its syllabic structure, and the combination of *mot juste* wit and casual speech which forms its idiom. The latter is the location of *logopoeia*: the force of the poem is derived from the ironic use of 'Le Superbe', the audacity of rhyming it with 'exacerbe' and 'comme une herbe', all of which reflect the overall tone of the piece. To find a modernist example, we might look at T.S. Eliot's 'The Love Song of J. Alfred Prufrock', the opening lines with their sardonic wit, beginning with a simplistic invitation – 'let us go then, you and I/when the evening is spread out against the sky' – which is then brought to a dead stop with 'like a patient etherised upon a table'. Or perhaps the weariness of the lines 'in the room the women come and go/talking of Michelangelo' which transmutes the weariness of two lines of ordinary speech into a refrain at once haunting, amusing, and dull.[52]

The three ways in which language is 'charged with meaning' are not essentialist properties of words themselves, nor are they natural impressions brought about by objects in the world, they are principles of poetic use which derive their force from either emotional or conceptual complexes of human psychology. In each case, they embody an aspect of the ways in which Pound tried to extend the principle of the *mot juste* to a language of poetry. The differentiation of the poetic *mot juste* into these three forms is one of Pound's most significant contributions to the poetic aspects of language. What is perhaps most important about the three is that they are all drawn from literary sources, and are an extension of aesthetic principles. The movement from aesthetic principle to linguistic form is precisely what Pound valued in Fenollosa's essay. Though Pound would continue to compound Fenollosa's errors, and to draw his own conclusions from them, at the root of their coming together is not a shared interest in erroneous semiotics, but rather a shared approach to the interrelationship of language, phenomena, and the structures of reality. Fenollosa is, in many ways, a point of departure for Pound, and, following his interest in the primary conscious structures of humanity and their relationship to language, Pound would become increasingly interested in anthropology, as we shall see in the following chapter. If Fenollosa demonstrated to Pound what was possible in translation, Lucien Lévy-Bruhl and Leo Frobenius would demonstrate limits and relativities drawn up around different mentalities, languages, and, most troubling for our reading of Pound, cultures.

Notes

1 Ezra Pound, Letter to Dorothy Shakespear, 2 October 1913, *Ezra Pound and Dorothy Shakespear: Their Letters* (New York: New Directions, 1984), 264.
2 Zhaoming Qian, 'The Orient', *Ezra Pound in Context*, ed. Ira B. Nadel (Cambridge: Cambridge University Press, 2010), 335–344 (336).
3 Massimo Bacigalupo, *The Forméd Trace: The Later Poetry of Ezra Pound* (New York: Columbia University Press, 1980), 12.
4 T.S. Eliot, 'Introduction' in *Selected Poems* by Ezra Pound (London: Faber & Faber, 1928), 14.
5 Ford Madox Ford, quoted in T.S. Eliot, *Ezra Pound: His Metric and Poetry* (New York: Knopf, 1917), 26.
6 Ernest Fenollosa, 'The Chinese Written Character as a Medium for Poetry' in *Instigations* by Ezra Pound (New York: Boni and Liveright, 1920), 357–388 (362–363). Subsequent textual references are to this edition, and will be designated with the abbreviation *CWC*.
7 See Haun Saussy, 'Fenollosa Compounded: A Discrimination' in Ernest Fenollosa and Ezra Pound, *The Chinese Written Character as a Medium for Poetry: A Critical Edition,* ed. Haun Saussy, Jonathan Stalling, and Lucas Klein (New York: Fordham University Press, 2008), 1–40.
8 Saussy, 'Fenollosa Compounded', 31.
9 Saussy, 'Fenollosa Compounded', 39.
10 Saussy, 'Fenollosa Compounded', 40.
11 Rebecca Beasley, *Ezra Pound and the Visual Culture of Modernism* (Cambridge: Cambridge University Press, 2007), 52–53; Ian F.A. Bell, *Critic as Scientist: The Modernist Poetics of Ezra Pound* (New York: Methuen, 1987), 27.

12 Hudson Maxim, *The Science of Poetry and the Philosophy of Language* (London: Funk & Wagnalls, 1910), 35.

13 Maxim, *The Science of Poetry*, 113–114.

14 Maxim, *The Science of Poetry*, 36, 37.

15 Herbert N. Schneidau, 'Vorticism and the Career of Ezra Pound', *Modern Philology*, 65:3 (1968), 214–227 (222).

16 Ezra Pound, 'Vortex', *Blast*, 1:1 (1914), 153–154 (153).

17 Julian Murphet, 'Towards a Gendered Media Ecology', in *Modernism and Masculinity*, ed. Natalya Lusty, and Julian Murphet (Cambridge: Cambridge University Press, 2014), 53–67 (57).

18 Pound, 'Vortex', 153–154.

19 Pound, 'Vortex', 154.

20 Pound, *Gaudier-Brzeska*, 86–87.

21 Arthur Wesley Dow, *Composition: A Series of Exercises in Art Structure for the Use of Students and Teachers* (New York: Doubleday, Page & Company, 1913), 4.

22 Dow, *Composition*, 89.

23 Otto Jespersen, *Language: Its Nature, Development and Origin* (London: George Allen & Unwin, 1922), 437.

24 Leonard Bloomfield, *Language* (London: George Allen & Unwin, 1933), 69.

25 Bloomfield, *Language*, 283.

26 Bloomfield, *Language*, 285.

27 Bloomfield, *Language*, 287.

28 Ferdinand de Saussure, *Course in General Linguistics*, 25–26.

29 Hugh Kenner also makes this point in *The Pound Era*; see 163.

30 Derrida, *Of Grammatology*, 92.

31 Franz Brentano, *Psychology from an Empirical Standpoint*, ed. Oskar Kraus, and Linda McAlister, trans. Antos C. Rancurello, D.B. Terrell, and Linda McAlister (London: Routledge, 1973), 68.

32 Edmund Husserl, *Logical Investigations*, trans J.N. Findley (London: Routledge, 1970), 168.

33 Fenollosa, *The Chinese Written Character as a Medium for Poetry*, 45.

34 Husserl, *Logical Investigations*, 144.

35 See Husserl, *Logical Investigations*, 135–136.

36 See Saussy, 'Fenollosa Compounded', 11.

37 Georg Wilhelm Friedrich Hegel, *Philosophy of Mind: Translated from the Encyclopedia of the Philosophical Sciences*, trans. William Wallace (Oxford: Clarendon, 1894), 81–82.

38 Lawrence Venuti, *The Translator's Invisibility: A History of Translation* (London: Routledge, 1995), 34.

39 Wim Lip, *Ezra Pound's* Cathay (Princeton: Princeton University Press, 88.

40 Ron Bush, 'Pound and Li Po: What Becomes a Man' in *Ezra Pound Amongst the Poets*, ed. George Bornstein (Chicago: University of Chicago Press, 1985), 35–62 (40).

41 Daniel Katz, *American Modernism's Expatriate Scene* (Edinburgh: Edinburgh University Press, 2007), 78.

42 K.K. Ruthven, *A Guide to Ezra Pound's* Personae *(1926)* (Berkeley: University of California Press, 1969), 223.

43 James Legge, *The Chinese Classics,* Vol. 4, Part II (London: Trubner & Co., 1871), 258.

44 Zhaoming Qian, *The Modernist Response to Chinese Art: Pound, Moore, Stevens* (Charlottesville: University of Virginia Press, 2003), 58.

45 Husserl, *Logical Investigations*, 193.

46 Louis Zukofsky, *Selected Poems*, ed. Charles Bernstein (New York: Library of America, 2006), 51; Daisy Dunn's recent translation renders the line 'My lady says she would rather marry no one'. Catallus, 'LXX', *The Poems*, trans. Daisy Dunn (London: William Collins, 2016), 108.

47 H.D., *Selected Poems* (London: Carcanet, 1989), 5.

48 Peter Nicholls, '"Deeps in Him": Ezra Pound and the Persistent Attraction of Laforgue', 9–19 (10).

49 Ezra Pound, 'Irony, Laforgue, and Some Satire', *Poetry*, XI:2 (1917), 93–98 (95).

50 Jules Laforgue, *Poems*, trans. Patricia Terry (Berkeley: University of California Press, 1958), 92. Terry's translation, on page 93, is far more streamlined than Pound's:

> I'm not at all 'that gay blade!' nor 'Superb!'
> But my soul which a raspy cry can disturb
> Is candid and distinguished, like an herb.

51 Ezra Pound, *Pavannes & Divigations* (New York: Knopf, 1918), 43.

52 T.S. Eliot, *Selected Poems* (London: Faber & Faber, 1954), 3, 4.

3   'Words So Full of Detail'
Paideuma and Linguistic Relativity

If Pound's engagement with Fenollosa opened his mind further to the possibilities of poetic translation, then his interest in anthropology in the 1920s and 1930s seemed to have the opposite effect. 'The sum of human wisdom is not contained in any one language, and no single language is CAPABLE of expressing all forms and degrees of human comprehension', Pound argues with a tone of regret in the *ABC of Reading*. 'This is', he argues, 'a very unpalatable and bitter doctrine', but it is one which he apparently 'cannot omit' (*ABC/R*, 35). The *Cantos* abound with translation (see Pound's beautiful rendering of Cavalcanti's 'Donna mi pregha' in Canto XXXVI, for example), but they also rely heavily on a variety of different languages. The *Cantos* are fundamentally plurilingual, shifting not only between languages but holding them all together in one poetic lexicon. On the variety of languages, Pound wrote to Sarah Perkins Cope on 15 January 1934 to explain that 'the quotes are all either explained at once by repeat or they are definitely *of* the things indicated', with Pound later concluding that he 'can't conceal the fact that the Greek language existed' (*SL*, 251–252). Five years later, Pound wrote to Hubert Creekmore that 'literature rises in racial process', indicating that the racial and anti-Semitic turns in his economic and political writing had inevitably affected his aesthetic and linguistic writing. Pound then further explains that 'when finished, *all* foreign words in the Cantos, Gk [Greek], etc., will be underlinings, not necessary to the sense'. A complete sense, Pound claims, 'will exist without them' and the 'Greek, ideograms, etc. will indicate a *duration* from whence or since when' (*SL*, 322). The plurilingualism of the *Cantos* thus serves a symbolic function, one which is bound up with Pound's increasingly disturbing views on race. Michael North has written of Pound's 'racial masquerade' in *The Dialect of Modernism* (1994), writing that Pound uses dialect in the *Cantos* to 'carry the social and cultural dislocations of the period', suggesting that passages in which Pound mimics African-American voices, for example, really serve to reinforce a sense of cultural superiority.[1] Indeed, there is an argument to be made that Pound's use of various languages in the *Cantos* is not really plurilingual, but is rather a reinforcement of central passages in English: we might beg the question of the extent to which the various passages in different languages in the *Cantos* are really indexical; to what extent do they really use linguistic differences 'enregister', to borrow a phrase from Asif Agha, cultural differences? By exploring the linguistic elements of Pound's interest in anthropology, we can see just how far the language of the *Cantos* goes down into the relativistic cultural, linguistic, and racial theories of the day.

Reading Pound's notion that human knowledge cannot be contained in one language against the backdrop of early twentieth-century anthropology, it is difficult to see it as anything other than a resigned statement of linguistic relativity, the argument that differences in language not only express real differences in psychology and culture, but constitute them as well. In terms of the modernist period, the most famous expression of a linguistic relativist theory is ascribed to the linguist Edward Sapir and his student, Benjamin Lee Whorf, a theory which is largely erroneously described as the 'Sapir-Whorf Hypothesis'.[2] According to Sapir, 'no two languages are ever sufficiently similar to be considered as representing the same social reality. The worlds in which different societies live are distinct worlds, not merely the same world with different labels attached'.[3] Sapir's statement has long been interpreted in two different strands: a weak thesis, linguistic relativism, an outgrowth of cultural relativism, which sees language as being embedded and thus inextricably bound to the different worldviews of different cultures; and a strong thesis, known as linguistic determinism, which argues that the language one speaks, the construction and structure of the grammar, and the nature of the lexicon, determines one's understanding of reality. If Sapir adopted either position, he was closer to a moderate version of the former. The latter we may associate with the work of Benjamin Lee Whorf on the Hopi tribe. Whorf argued that the nature of their language demonstrated that they had a radically different conception of time to speakers of Indo-European languages.[4]

Was Pound a linguistic relativist? Looking across the whole of Pound's career, at his insistence that certain poetic forms, such as the Canzone, are limited by the contours of their language, or his use of archaisms to stress linguistic and cultural distances, his distinctions between the literary forms of certain cultures and language, and the polylingual nature of his *Cantos*, mediating as they do between the translatable and the untranslatable, the answer seems to be 'yes'. The truth, however, is rather more complex. We must be careful not to overstate the agency of language in most cases of linguistic relativism. Even Sapir's thought, as I have argued elsewhere, cannot be so easily reduced to a formula of linguistic relativism: if one takes a close look at his theory of language as a whole, we see that while language may be relative in Sapir's thought, he conceived of human psychology in far more universal terms.[5]

There was a hardening of Pound's theories of language in response to a burgeoning interest not only in economics, as Peter Nicholls and

Richard Sieburth have consummately demonstrated, but also in anthropology.[6] His interest in the latter grew out of his long-term interest in
the nature of thought, his work on Chinese culture, and, perhaps rather
surprisingly, his 1920s forays into music. In the 1920s, he dedicated a
considerable amount of time to the practice and study of music, taking it
as the centre point of his discussions of a wider variety of topics.[7] Pound
outlined a number of his linguistic tenets in a 1924 article on the music
of George Antheil in *The Criterion*, while also expressing an interest in
anthropology. Reflecting on the elements of his own art, he writes 'the
medium of poetry is words, i.e. human symbols, conventions; they are
capable of including things in nature, that is, sound quality, timbre, up
to a point'. Here, poetry has affinity with music (in terms of *melopoeia*,
at least) as both rely upon cadence and an 'interior rhythm, there can be
rhythm in their arrangement, even tone leadings, and these with increasing precision'. However, as words are dependent upon linguistic structures that are founded upon convention and arbitrary meaning, '[one]
can not get a word back into the non-human'.[8] As a poet so invested in
human states of consciousness, and human interaction with the natural
and divine, Pound's attempt to create a poetics best able to represent that
investment comes to rely upon a medium (language) that is ultimately
'superfluous' or 'wholly inadequate'. What the 'good' artist searches for,
Pound argues, is an 'ideograph of admirable compound-of-qualities that
make any work of art permanent', but such an 'ideograph' is, in his
view, accessible only in turning away from the contemporary culture of
the West.[9] Pound's argument led him to suggest that such 'permanence'
draws inspiration from other cultures.

> I mean that from such fragmentary and confused writing the in-
> telligent observer will induce the fact that the artist is very gravely
> concerned with the bases of his art, and with the relations of that art
> to *everything else*. This is very different from preciosity; emollients;
> trimmings; connoisseurship; traditions regarding superfices, or the
> customs or fashions of the moment.
>
> Hence the permanent resemblances of masterwork, the 'revo-
> lutionary' nature of genius, the returns to the primitives, and so
> forth.[10]

Pound's notion of a return to 'the primitives' sits alongside 'primitivist' aesthetics developed in the visual arts by Paul Gauguin and Pablo Picasso, as
well as Pound's acquaintances Jacob Epstein and Henri Gaudier-Brzeska.
The notion of a 'primitive' state is, however, fraught with assumption
and prejudice, and draws on underlying racial, linguistic, and cultural
notions, even if Pound is partially attempting to undermine them. Gill
Perry has noted in her discussion of modernist notions of the 'primitive' that the term 'primitivism' itself was at that time 'generally used to

refer to the discourses on "the primitive"', thus becoming more part of a Western, introspective conversation.[11] It is, in other words, a Western comment on itself, and not a manifestation of otherness. For many of Pound's generation, the word 'primitive' has a shifting meaning. It is at once both the 'primordial' state of their own culture, leaving traces in the present, and it is a descriptor for the 'state' of culture in other peoples. What is most troubling, of course, is that for Pound and others, this links to an intellectual milieu which viewed these two meanings as one and the same.

At the beginning of the 1930s, Nancy Cunard's Black Hours press published the first complete section of Pound's long poem, *A Draft of XXX Cantos* (1930). The title itself makes it clear that Pound's project was a work in progress, but it nevertheless marks an important moment in Pound's middle period as it is the first division of *The Cantos*. The next eleven cantos, *Eleven New Cantos* (1934), would be devoted increasingly to contemporary economics and the history of the early American republic and considerably less to myth and Renaissance European history. Thus, 1930 is a year of departure. It is also in this year in which Pound met the German ethnographer Leo Frobenius, following an excursion to Frankfurt from Vienna, an event recounted in Canto XXXVIII. Frobenius's work, which Pound read between 1929 and 1930, explores the particularities of African culture, describing the habits, languages, and myths of various tribes and relating them to a general theory of *kulturmophologie*. Pound's interest in Frobenius's research must be read alongside his interest in the work of Lucien Lévy-Bruhl, the French philosopher who proposed that there are two kinds of mentality: a 'logical mentality' which is found in the 'civilised' west, and a 'prelogical mentality' found among groups described as 'primitive'. These differences, Lévy-Bruhl argues, are manifest in language. It is on this very point that Pound brings his interest in Frobenius and Lévy-Bruhl together in Canto XXXVIII.

> The ragged arab spoke with Frobenius and told him
> The names of 3000 plants.
>   Bruhl found some languages full of detail
> Words that half mimic action; but
> generalization is beyond them, a white dog is
> not, let us say, a dog like a black dog.
>
>   (XXXVIII.189)

I shall explore this canto in greater detail below, but Pound's premise is that the language of so-called 'primitive' peoples is better able to register details, and is closer to a 'primordial vitality' than Western, Indo-European languages. While this is, of course, a disturbing position, it does require further explanation in the context of 1920s and

1930s linguistic anthropology. In looking at the textual genesis of this poem alongside Pound's reading in anthropology, however, we can see that the label 'linguistic' relativity is an oversimplification. To borrow a phrase from Bernd Weiler, Pound's position was one of 'axiological relativism', which saw the world divided into two (in Pound's case, gleaned from his reading, three) different mentalities.[12] This, as Pound writes in *ABC of Reading*, leaves trace in the language and was for him, entirely bound up with race.[13]

Evolutionary Anthropology

Early twentieth-century anthropology can be characterised by two opposing positions: evolutionism and cultural relativism. Evolutionism depends upon a universal understanding of human mental functions, which holds that the physiological, mental, and social aspects of all human cultures are fundamentally similar and differ only in detail and gradation. Combining this with evolutionary theory, advocates of this view held that the indigenous people of Africa, Australasia, and North America (the three most common areas of study) existed in a 'primitive' state of mankind. The universalist and evolutionist standpoints were articulated most fully by Edward Burnett Tylor. In his most famous works, *Primitive Culture* (1871) and *Anthropology* (1881), Tylor laid the foundations for the discipline by establishing a relatively objective and scientific methodology. His evolutionism eschews the Social Darwinism of Herbert Spencer, arguing that 'it appears both possible and desirable to eliminate considerations of hereditary varieties or races of man, and to treat mankind as homogenous in nature, though placed at different grades of civilization'.[14] By considering different groups according to cultural and historical factors rather than purely racial distinctions, Tylor was able to provide a focus for the new discipline of anthropology.

According to the evolutionist stance, language is also seen on a scale of values, with Indo-European languages seen as inherently 'civilised' and the languages of the indigenous people of North America and Australasia placed as naturally 'primitive'. Tylor compared the linguistic and psychological operations of his subjects with those of children in Western society, sharing in the popular belief that the languages of these peoples are far simpler and less advanced than Indo-European languages such as English or Latin.

> The theory that the original forms of language are to be referred to a low or savage condition of culture among the remotely ancient human race, stands in general consistency with the known facts of philology. The causes which have produced language, so far as they are understood, are notable for that childlike simplicity of operation which befits the infancy of human civilization...Such a state of

things agrees with the opinion that such rudimentary speech had its origin among men while in a childlike intellectual condition, and thus the self-expressive branch of savage language affords valuable materials for the problem of primitive speech.[15]

Tylor applies etymological techniques in speculating on the origin of language, an approach that draws on the legacy of nineteenth-century historical linguistics. Stephen G. Alter, for example, notes the close connection between Darwinist evolutionary thought and the structural models of philology.[16] Tylor's work expands the connection to the anthropological. He uses a kind of etymological teleology to suggest that the languages of certain tribes whose speech is of non-Indo-European origin, and who make extensive use of non-verbal systems such as gesture, are less developed. Their languages, therefore, are seen as living and 'organic' evidence of mankind's ancient past. According to Robert Ackermann, Tylor's work was the main inspiration for the comparative religious studies of J.G. Frazer, whose *Golden Bough* was an important influence on modernist anthropological and religious theories.[17]

Shortly after the turn of the century, the cultural relativist school of anthropological thought grew out of, and significantly departed from, Tylor's approach under the guidance of the German-American anthropologist Franz Boas. Rather than seeing cultures as more or less civilised according to an ethnocentric scale of values, Boas argued that culture is not the variable, but the common standard of humanity: all groups, according to Boas, have 'culture' equally and must be studied on their own terms. Like Tylor, he believed that racial distinction was both irrelevant and spurious, relying on historical factors as the main determinant of cultural differences. It was these differences, however, that Boas took to be of fundamental interest in disparate cultures, and not any underlying similarities with Western culture. Explicitly rejecting the idea of evolution within culture, particularly according to the standards of Western society, Boas reformulated the remit of anthropological and ethnographic research, insisting that only objective anthropological study of cultures was their relation to historical contexts. Boas exerted great influence in the development of the field over the next four decades from his position as head of the Department of Anthropology at Columbia University, as well as in his guiding role in the American Anthropological Association. Many of Boas's students became eminent anthropologists and linguists, and those working under his direct influence included Ruth Benedict, Alfred L. Kroeber, Robert H. Lowie, and Edward Sapir.

In contradistinction to Tylor, Boas explicitly argued that language cannot be taken as an example of cultural value. Rejecting the idea that so-called 'primitive' languages are more simplistic than Indo-European ones, Boas used evidence from his fieldwork to demonstrate that they are merely different in construction:

Many primitive languages are complex. Minute differences in point of view are given expression by means of grammatical forms; and the grammatical categories of Latin, and still more so those of modern English, seem crude when compared with the complexity of psychological or logical forms which primitive languages recognize, but which in our speech are disregarded. On the whole, the development of languages seems to be such, that the nicer distinctions are eliminated, and that it begins with complex and ends with simpler forms, although it must be acknowledged that opposite tendencies are not by any means absent.[18]

This position was to become extremely influential. Susan Hegeman warns against seeing Boas as the originator of an American 'culture concept', as he wrote little on the topic itself until 1930, but the influence of Boas's cultural and linguistic anthropology which emphasised civilisation as a relative, not absolute, concept was felt extensively in anthropological circles during the modernist period.[19] The legacy of Boas's outline of linguistic research can be seen particularly in Sapir's work. Sapir was a published poet, a connoisseur of Romantic and modern literature, and an accomplished essayist. He saw thought, language, and culture in permanent states of dynamic interrelation, and spent much of his later career concerned with the psychological question of how individuals situate themselves in relation to the matrices of culture and language. An outstanding linguist, Sapir applied Boas's methods to his study of language, with a particular focus on the indigenous languages of North America. Sapir published poetry and literary reviews in addition to his extensive work on North American languages, with his work appearing in *The Nation*, *The Dial*, and *Poetry*, journals ingrained in modernist culture. As a result, he is an important figure in measuring the relationship between language as a science and language as an art form. He is an interesting comparison point for Pound's work. Although they had numerous nodes in the modernist nexus in common, they do not seem to have had much contact with each other. Sapir, in fact, defined language as 'a symbolic guide to culture' in a significant essay of 1929, entitled 'The Status of Linguistics as a Science'.[20] The final three words of the phrase were similarly selected by Pound for the title of his volume on anthropology, culture, philosophy, and literature: *Guide to Kulchur*.

Sapir suggests a more contemporary precedent for Pound's literary approach to language, and the relativism inherent in his approach. Sapir, who had written that 'single Algonkin words are like tiny Imagist poems', balanced poetic sensibility with linguistic science in developing his definition of language as the 'symbolic guide to culture'.[21] Each literature, according to Sapir, is inextricably bound to the 'genius' of the language (or perhaps more accurately the culture) in which it is written.

Language is the medium of literature as marble or bronze or clay are the materials of the sculptor. Since every language has its distinctive peculiarities, the innate formal limitations – and possibilities – of one literature are never quite the same as those of another. The literature fashioned out of the form and substance of a language has the color and the texture of its matrix. The literary artist may never be conscious of just how he is hindered or helped or otherwise guided by the matrix, but when it is a question of translating his work into another language, the nature of the original matrix manifests itself at once. All his effects have been calculated, or intuitively felt, with reference to the formal 'genius' of his own language; they cannot be carried over without loss or modification.[22]

The failure to translate fully from one language or culture to another, the expression of a national 'genius' in literature, and the sculptural analogy are all points that Pound himself could have made. Although Sapir's definition of 'culture' is far more in line with traditional discourses, and he was a professor in American university departments of the kind that Pound so often criticised, there is a correspondence between their work that requires further exploration.

Sapir's interest in crossing the boundaries of literary and linguistic circles makes his work a useful vantage point for scholarship looking at the relationship between the two disciplines in the modernist period. Sapir explored his understanding of the relationship between an individual writer and the cultural and linguistic matrices within which they write in a 1925 review of H.D.'s poetry in *The Nation*. Answering apparent claims that her poetry is un-American due to its Hellenism, Sapir's review, though brief, is a passionate defence of her work, insightfully writing that in H.D.'s poetry, 'each world is symbol and nostalgia'. He sees the spirit of her work to be particularly American in temperament, in fact, and that 'the impatience of the rhythms and the voluptuous harshness and bleakness of the sea and shore and woodland images manifest [that temperament]'. Sapir concludes, on the subject of the non-American subject matter of the poems, that 'H.D. is of those highly characteristic and most subtly moving American temperaments that long for an emotional wealth of expression...that they cannot wholeheartedly desire – and must not, if they are to be true to themselves'.[23] It would appear that Pound did not read Sapir's work, but there are undoubted connections in their work that could have proven fruitful; in the modernist nexus, theirs is one of the more regrettable missed connections.

The two positions of universalism or evolutionism and cultural relativism are, of course, not dogmatic and absolute, and many of the key figures on either side of the debate adapted elements of both into their research. Nonetheless, the two positions provide a spectrum against which to measure Pound's views, as well as those of the figures who influenced him. Pound was extremely interested in both Frobenius's and Lévy-Bruhl's treatments of language, and refers to their work in the *Cantos*, the *ABC of Reading*, and *Guide to Kulchur*. In reassessing the relativistic aspects of their work, however, we can see once more that Pound was interested in the complex interactivity of language, reality, and, above all, mentality.

Axiological Relativism in the Work of Lucien Lévy-Bruhl

It is not known when Pound encountered Lévy-Bruhl's work but, given his fame, it is likely that he would have been known in intellectual circles. Lévy-Bruhl was not strictly speaking an anthropologist. Leon Surette and, more recently, Susanna Pavloska, both describe Lévy-Bruhl as an anthropologist in their discussions of the idea of 'the primitive' in the modernist period, but he was in fact a professor of Philosophy at the Sorbonne from 1899 to 1927, and he did not undertake any fieldwork during his career.[24] According to Surette, Lévy-Bruhl 'relativized the "past" through an ahistorical perception characteristic of modernism'. While this 'ahistorical perception' may be true of modernist works such as T.S. Eliot's *The Waste Land* or, indeed, Pound's *Cantos*, Lévy-Bruhl's work is not necessarily characteristic of anthropological research in the modernist period. His acquaintance with much of his material was second-hand, and he is best seen as a conceptual starting point for Pound's interest in anthropology.

Lévy-Bruhl's position with regard to linguistics is outlined in his 1911 book *How Natives Think*. He surmises that due to alleged differences in mental habit and construction, the languages spoken by different peoples must register (rather than merely reflect) that difference.

> In the long run the mental habits of the group cannot fail to leave some trace upon their modes of expression since these are also social phenomena, upon which the individual has little, if any, influence. With differing types of mentality, therefore, there should be languages which differ in their construction.[25]

Lévy-Bruhl states that due to a relative lack of knowledge of the linguistic material (as of 1911) and the difficulty in attaching a particular language to a particular ethnic group due to migratory, historical, and political reasons, 'we can therefore safely establish nothing more than a very general correspondence between the characteristics of a language and those of the mentality of the social group'.[26] As a result, this is not a position of linguistic determinism, and Lévy-Bruhl, like Pound and Sapir, operates on the principle that language is primarily influenced by thought, rather than the other way around.

Lévy-Bruhl supports his argument by exploring the wealth of detail expressed in languages across the world, with the native North American language families as his primary example. He writes that the descriptive qualities of the Klamath language (from Southern Oregon and Northern California), for example, demonstrate an entirely different mental capacity, and a linguistic function that 'express[es] concrete details which our languages leave understood or unexpressed'.[27] The reason for Lévy-Bruhl's choice of North American languages is as much practical as it is ideological, and it is not least due to the fact that American anthropology, for one, was producing more detailed accounts of those languages than any others. Other examples, mainly from Australasia and Africa, are also cited as evidence. A major source for Lévy-Bruhl's discussion is A.S. Gatschet's *The Klamath Indians of Southwestern Oregon* (1890), an extensive account of the Klamath people and their language. Using Gatschet as evidence, Lévy-Bruhl focusses his enquiry through two main aspects of thought: generalisation and pluralisation. 'The primitive's mentality needs to differentiate between two, three, a few, or many subjects or objects, to indicate whether they are together or separate', Lévy-Bruhl claims, and as a result '[the mentality] has no general terms for "tree" or "fish" but special terms for every variety of tree or of fish'.[28] This is not to say that Lévy-Bruhl argues that people of non-Indo-European languages cannot pluralise (as Pound suggests in Canto XXXVIII), but merely that they do it in a radically different way. Taking Klamath as his example, and quoting Gatschet, he suggests that the 'distributive reduplication' employed in the Klamath performs a function analogous to Western concepts of pluralisation. Distributive reduplication indicates plurality by duplicating a word or part of a word (the base). To give an example of partial reduplication, Gatschet argues that the word *Pá'dsha* refers to the state of being blind in one eye, whereas total blindness is given by *papá'dsha*, or blindness in two eyes.[29] The phoneme *pa* is the reduplicant. According to Lévy-Bruhl's interpretation, this does not represent the plural as the student of an Indo-European language would understand it, but instead represents the kind of plurality necessitated by an apparently different mentality.

While focussing on Klamath, Lévy-Bruhl characterises the wealth of detail available to the languages he refers to as 'primitive'. Klamath suffixes alone, for example, are said to be able to denote a variety of meaning that would be impossible for single words in English:

> 'to begin, continue, cease, to be accustomed to do...to move in a zigzag or in a straight line, to go up, along the ground, or below, to describe circles in the air, to come towards or to go away from (the subject or object being visible or invisible)', and a number of other details besides.[30]

Lévy-Bruhl's general thesis, then, is that the intense detail of languages such as Klamath (and the various other language families he amalgamates) reflects an essential need for detail in daily life that is alien to the logical, abstract world of Europe and the United States. The languages he describes thus denote a mentality in which logical and grammatical categories are aligned, and which is held in opposition to the mentality of Lévy-Bruhl's own society.

I suggest that Pound agrees with this principle on the whole, as his citation of Lévy-Bruhl in Canto XXXVIII demonstrates. In fact, the exact passage to which Pound refers is to be found in Lévy-Bruhl's chapter on language. Lévy-Bruhl quotes Brough Smyth's *The Aborigines of Virginia* to effect that 'in Western Australia, the natives "have names for all the conspicuous stars, for every natural feature of the ground, every hill, swamp, bend of a river, etc., but not for the river itself"'.[31] Pound underlines his faith in Lévy-Bruhl's argument that such languages register precise details but cannot generalise by paraphrasing Brough Smyth's quotation in his posthumously published 'How to Write' (written in 1930). First, Pound summarises the argument, writing that 'Lévy-Bruhl points out the savage's lack of power to generalise', and claiming that 'he has forty verbs where we have two or three verbs and some adverbs'. The result of this, Pound writes, is that 'the savage language grades down into pantomime and mimicry'. Aside from the unpalatable phrasing, notice Pound's use of '*the* savage language' (emphasis mine), conflating many unrelated languages into one (a pitfall of Lévy-Bruhl's approach as well). Pound continues, claiming that this 'savage language' contains a kind of natural vitality that all good writers should aspire to rediscover in their own language:

> What Lévy-Bruhl says about the verbs of savages, what Fenollosa says about verbs in Chinese, what I had written about Dante's verbs before I had heard of Fenollosa all joins up. The good writer need not throw over anything humanity has acquired but he will in the measure of his genius try to recover the vividness of Dante, Li Po and the bushman. The savage to whom the wood or the bend in the river is not a wood or a bend but one particular stretch of wood, one particular bend in that river.[32]

Pound's poetics of concretion and precision of language lead him to a position whereby he celebrates the 'vividness' of so-called 'primitive' languages at the expense of the languages of societies he believes to be more advanced. Here Pound connects the aesthetic aspects of his own project with twentieth-century anthropology (at least as he encountered it). He connects his *The Spirit of Romance* and Fenollosa's *The Chinese Written Character as a Medium for Poetry* with Lévy-Bruhl's ethnological studies, and the nature of this connection is drawn on the linguistic-aesthetic axis of his own project. What drives Pound at all points in his engagement with Lévy-Bruhl is the same as that which drove him in his engagement with Fenollosa, an attempt at aesthetic restitution through linguistic 'vividness'.

Interestingly, Pound does not specify which languages Lévy-Bruhl refers to in particular. This is perhaps due to the nature of Lévy-Bruhl's thesis and the agenda behind his practice. *How Natives Think* suggests that the distinction between 'logical' and 'prelogical' mentality is such that it readily divides the people of the world (and their languages) into two distinct camps. Any one member of Lévy-Bruhl's categories can be taken for the whole, and differences between groups are either ignored or taken to be an anomaly in relation to a fixed, general rule. Thereby, wholly distinct languages (with little in common) are amalgamated into one mentality. Native American, Australasian, and African languages, all of which are unrelated (and, are indeed composed of various families themselves), are taken to be evidence of the same social reality and opposed to 'logical' mentalities in Europe and America. The terms 'prelogical' and 'logical' are drawn on an axis both evolutionist and relative. A similar axis is employed in the work of Leo Frobenius.

Leo Frobenius's Theory of Culture: Language and *Paideuma*

The exact details of Pound's first engagement with Frobenius's work are difficult to determine. According to Noel Stock, Pound first encountered Frobenius's work in 1929, through reading the works of Oswald Spengler, who relied heavily of Frobenius's research. Alternatively, Pound suggests in an undated fragment of a manuscript at the Beinecke entitled 'Frobenius', that it was Jo Bard who first recommended Frobenius to him, but Pound's phrasing is unclear.[33] Regardless, by 1930, he had bought the fourth volume of Frobenius's, *Erlebte Erdteile,* which had been published separately in 1921 as *Paideuma*, and which contains the longest theoretical treatment of his ideas.[34] What is clear is that Pound's first significant engagement with Frobenius's work is in late 1929 or early 1930. On 3 March 1930, Pound wrote to the Director of the Frobenius Institute asking for the translation rights for Frobenius's *Paideuma*.[35] Later in 1930, Pound travelled to Frankfurt to see George Antheil in concert. There he met Frobenius and invited him to the concert, and began a long correspondence with the Frankfurt Institute of *Kulturmophologie*. By the mid-1930s, this took place primarily in English with Frobenius's assistant, Douglas Fox. Fox was of vital importance to Pound for a number of reasons: first, as an American, he enabled Pound to engage with Frobenius's ideas in English; second, he was enthusiastic about the correspondence and was thus keen to discuss anthropological theories in detail; third, he was aware of Pound's standing in artistic circles and encouraged Pound to view Frobenius's work from a literary (and linguistic) standpoint.

Frobenius's reputation outside Germany depended more upon the detail contained in his ethnography than on his theories. In a 1909 review, Frobenius's *The Childhood of Man*, Barbara Freire-Marecco, an English anthropologist and folklorist, argued that the book was more useful as 'a selection to illustrate certain theories' than as a comprehensive explanation of mankind's origins. Freire-Marecco notes Frobenius's popularity in Germany, but argues that *The Childhood of Man* is difficult to place in relation to English anthropology due to a number of structural and theoretical problems.[36] Franz Boas refers to Frobenius's work a number of times in his 1914 essay, 'Mythology and Folk-Tales of the North American Indians'. He praises Frobenius's contribution to the study of cultural dissemination, but casts doubt on the validity of his evidence of actual connections between cultures.[37] A decade later, the Boasian anthropologist Melville Herskovits, who worked primarily on African influences in African-American culture, examined Frobenius's position in ethnological research. Herskovits used Frobenius's research for the value of his details and descriptions, but not as a theoretical force, making use of instances of ethnographic information, but only to illustrate his own arguments.[38] A.R. Radcliffe-Brown summarised the academic attitude to Frobenius in the 1920s, arguing that while he shows 'a much keener appreciation of what does and does not constitute evidence than many of the writings of similar schools of ethnology', his work comes to rest upon a theoretical scheme that is too simple for the complex processes that he describes.[39] By the time Pound became interested in Frobenius's work at the end of the 1920s, then, he was not representative of current debates in anthropology.

That is not to say, however, that Frobenius remains an insignificant or obscure figure. Suzanne Marchand has argued that Frobenius's work, in fact, marks an important engagement with, and disavowal of, the cultural and colonial assumptions of the West.[40] Marchand sees Frobenius as composing a sustained critique of Eurocentric values, and argues that his ethnography was motivated by a great admiration of African culture, using it as a counterpoint to the decadence of the West, and Frobenius's own discomfort with the *fin de siècle* values he encountered in his home country. This aspect of his work, combined with his general theory of culture as Pound encountered it in the late 1920s, explains why Frobenius's ideas become a central thread in the *Cantos'* tapestry.

The idea that Pound prized most was Frobenius's concept of *Paideuma*, which Pound defines as 'the tangle or complex of the inrooted ideas of any period' (*GK*, 57), a definition which leaves much to be desired in terms of clarity. Indeed, Pound seems to be trying too hard to combine *Paideuma* with the 'complex' of his Image. If we look to Frobenius's eponymous text, we find a working definition that is much easier to grasp. For Frobenius, *Paideuma* is a kind of *Erziehung*, a phrase which encompasses a combination of the English phrases 'nurture' and 'upbringing'. In many ways, it is an attempt to replace *Kultur* ('culture' – a concept Pound referred to as a 'damned word', *GK*, 183). In *Paideuma*, Frobenius explores personal and social elements of the concept. As he is primarily an ethnologist, it is naturally the social aspects of *Paideuma* that are of most interest. Frobenius sees the culture of an individual civilisation not as the sum total of its achievements, technological and artistic, but instead as a unique interaction of mentality and environment. Each civilisation has a distinct 'spirit', an individuating element which he designates by the term *Paideuma*. Frobenius conceives of Paideuma as an 'organic' function, and this manifests itself in the personal and social elements in his thought. On the one hand, *Paideuma* is not an abstract concept, nor is 'organic' meant entirely metaphorically, but it is the individuating cultural element within each person; it is a part of their biological development. On the other hand, 'organic' does function in Frobenius's work as a kind of shorthand way of understanding the unique direction that each culture takes. What is perhaps most striking about Frobenius's approach is that stark separation he draws between people and cultures:

> There are neither better humans here nor there. The question of the superior quality of humans comes from a false starting point; this is because humans are, apart from a small number of qualities inherited from culture, the same here as there – the same, apart from the cultural form. And this I have to stress, even more so in the year 1920 than in Anno 1895, is an independent organism. In its great organicity, culture appears to me today even more independent of people than before.[41]

Here one sees a way in which Frobenius occupies a middle point between evolutionism and cultural relativism: human nature is universal; culture is relative. Furthermore, the intention of his work is to provide a way of reading other cultures from the perspective of their *Paideuma*, a position which speaks to the significance of cultural relativism:

> The following undertaking should in no way be understood as a description of individual cultures, it should rather be seen as an attempt to allow the reader to empathise with the soul-like element or, as I have called it in the main term of this book, the *Paideuma* of the essence of a culture.[42]

It is perhaps best to define *Paideuma* as the genius of a culture in time and place: it is not the individual cultural forms or artefacts of a culture, but rather that which constitutes them, the element which grants them a certain cultural form over another. Frobenius often describes *Paideuma* as a kind of *Seelenhafte*, a word which best translates as 'soul-like', a slight distinction from 'soul' with its metaphysical and religious dimensions. This soul-like element of culture is, by definition, essentialist. *Paideuma* is, then, the essence of a culture in a given time and place. His work ultimately concerns 'the problem of which force – at the end – determines the historical development of a folk culture'.[43]

Frobenius's understanding of culture as organism led him to see its development as analogous to that of a human being. He outlines two different kinds of *Paideuma*: an individual one and a cultural-social one. The '*Paideuma* of the individual' moves from a 'daemonic' childhood phase characterised by the power of creativity to an 'ideal' phase of adolescence, which centres around conceptual understanding, before reaching a period of the 'real' or 'actual' (*Tatsachen*), itself marked by a directed consciousness of purpose. Just as the human being, he argues, goes through the three stages of childhood, adolescence, and adulthood, so too culture (as organism) goes through three phases of *Paideuma*. The first of these is what Frobenius terms *Barbarei* ('barbarism'). This phase is marked by what he refers to as a 'primitive' creativity, an artistic and spiritual engagement between subjects and the environment. The next phase of *Paideuma*, *Kulturei* (a rather rare word in German science, it is roughly approximate to something like 'culturedness') is characterised by *Gestaltung* ('design' or 'form'), by a process of composition or structuring of the world. The final phase, *Mechanei* (mechanistic), which is intended to describe the 'level' of culture in which Frobenius and Pound lived, is characterised by cultural fulfilment (by which he means a bringing about of harmony between the cultural aspects of the previous cultural levels). Frobenius thus maps the histories of cultures according to a series of movements from daemonic creativity to monumental structuring to a harmonising of all previous phenomena. Frobenius's thought is axiological in the sense that he does not conceive of these cultural 'levels' as phases in human history, but phases that all cultures will go through at some point, but do not go through at the same level.[44]

Frobenius's tripartite structure would have been attractive to Pound, if solely on the grounds that it represented a rationalising of the intuitive structures which he had used to analyse human civilisation. One final aspect of the foundations of Frobenius's thought that corresponds well with Pound's own writing is the relationship of each level of *Paideuma* to time and history. According to Frobenius, in the *Barbarei* phase of *Paideuma*, a group or tribe experiences the world in a series of a pretemporal and unhistorical relations; in the *Kulturei* phase, a *Volk* (a 'people') has an 'episodic' relation to time; and in the *Mechanei* phase, culture is characterised by supratemporal and transhistorical features. In searching for correlatives, we may think of the harmonies provided by Pound's poetry when writing in Canto III of how 'Gods float in the azure air/ Bright gods and Tuscan, back before dew was spread' (III.11), or in his appropriation of the line 'time is not. Time is the evil' in Canto LXXIV (464).

Most significant for our discussion, of course, is Frobenius's discussion of language. This Pound recognised early in his reading, as 'Date Line' (1934) makes clear: 'however much you accept of Frobenius' theory of *paideuma* as general and overreaching…the spoken idiom is not only a prime factor, but certainly one of the most potent, progressively so as any modality of civilisation ages'. 'As language becomes the sole instrument of perfidy, so language alone can riddle and cut through the meshes' (*LE*, 77), he writes. A principle, I argue, he draws directly from Frobenius's *Paideuma*. Unlike many of his contemporaries, Frobenius does not get drawn into debates around linguistic determinism. From the outset, he asserts a theoretical separation of culture and language. Language is, for Frobenius, the handmaiden of cultural differences and levels of *Paideuma*. The best way to understand Frobenius's thought on language is to consider the linguistic as a manifestation of the cultural, a position which maintains an exalted privilege for language but which still relegates it to a secondary role behind culture. In terms of concrete linguistic discussions, Frobenius is more concerned with the nature of language in the 'mechanistic' phase of *Paideuma*, and it is here that his ethnography becomes self-reflexive, offering a critique of the culture of his own society. In particular, he was concerned by the ways in which a culture which had 'developed' to the mechanistic stage adversely affected the natural development of children. Despite the 'level' of their national or social culture, a child is still in the 'daemonic' phase, according to Frobenius's categories, and yet, through standardised and abstract learning strategies used at school, they are forced to understand the world through the strictures of further developed, adult mechanistic, factual frameworks.

> An example of this is a child who, instead of discovering things gradually on his own, encounters them in the forms of names based on involuntary sounds and signs. Language thus emerges as an inorganic element, a medium, a tool, a help. If I make the child break a sentence down into object, subject, and predicate, I demand from him an expedient use of language, which in the infantile *Paideuma* becomes a not only superfluous, but also damaging strain, because it is against his nature – it is an extraordinarily dangerous measure, insofar as it inhibits the natural growth of the infantile soul.[45]

Language is what Frobenius calls a 'purely external convenience' (82) deriving from 'echoing repetitions of tone…. Springing from an emotional level'. It was 'not languages, but rather sound-conventions which were the first inherited facts of the use of voice'. In this sense, Frobenius argues, the act of speaking is in 'no way a conscious…process', but rather a tool in the service of consciousness itself indicative of a stage of *Paideuma*.

The childlike-genius Paideuma, the daemonic creativity, therefore develops independently from language, and speech, just as every other form of meaningfully structured communication is, accordingly, a newly acquired cultural item that, like any other, undergoes development through three periods: spontaneous & sporadic variability, harmonic organicity, and inorganic mechanics. These three stages run through all languages.

At a mature age, however, consciousness shifts in *Paideuma* from being bound to the object of language to the linguistic mode of expression itself, and thus language and culture become inextricable. This 'linguistic consciousness', that is, consciousness as bound through the linguistic system, creates a separation between the human mind and nature, which the *Paideuma* must work to reconstitute, becoming an 'adhesive' between language and objects in the world. Language is thus a problematic stage in conscious development: 'Language is therefore something externally given, something externally "inherited", that must be laboriously brought into harmony with the internal *paideumic* being and with what was previously experienced and yet now is only conscious, existing solely in knowledge'.[46] As each new stage of *Paideuma* contains traces of the previous ones, however, this daemonic creativity, Frobenius posits, remains in the form of artistic impulses. These impulses then transcend the linguistic mode of expression. As all artists know, Frobenius claims, 'each new creativity arises beyond the border of speaking'. The problem with art, and here he chimes with both Sapir and Pound, is that it is immensely difficult 'to bring creativity into a linguistic form, that is, to make communicable for others what is inwardly clear and known to him'.[47] Poetry thus revolves around the attempt to bound daemonic creativity through a 'mechanical' language, a language which has become the mode of expression for a *Paideuma* which inheres against this creativity.

In the poetry of tribes such as the Hottentots or in the children's poetry of Nordic peoples, Frobenius argues, we see 'a great amount of images ordered side by side, or facts lined up, behind which a meaning, a living force germinates, which, however, lives solely in the mind of the poet or singer, and not in the spoken works'. Frobenius is here interested in the 'Sinn an sich', the meaning in and of itself; the content, in other words, which he conceives as incidental to the form. Frobenius's work is essentialist about culture and entirely unessentialist about language, drawing a radical separation between the two. For Frobenius, 'tone painting' is simply the conclusion to an 'infantile life of sound', and it is only later rendered intelligible and artistic by means of literary convention, such as rhyme and alliteration.

Significantly, and perhaps most usefully in terms of reading Pound, Frobenius seeks a radical difference in 'modern' poetry (we should understand this as meaning poetry from the late nineteenth century, more than 'modernism'), itself not a reflection of a 'childlike' or, perhaps better said, primordial soulfulness but rather of a 'mechanistic' civilisation. Exceptions to this, Frobenius claims, are 'atavistic relapses' in the form of transcendent experiences or Dadaistic expressions, which attain the qualities of daemonic consciousness. On the whole, however, Frobenius's account of 'mechanical' poetry chimes with Pound's castigations of the prevalence of abstraction in his literary forebears (and many of his contemporaries), and the two men share a conviction that as language has created major cultural problems, the solution must begin with language. Frobenius's tone is, however, more pessimistic than Pound's:

> Westerners can no longer be aware of the high meaning of language, because their language has now become an almost a purely mechanistic item. That means, however, that language once, just as it remains today in each real artwork, was an end in itself, that there were once exalted formations and artforms of language, which were to the people then as a verse of Aeschylus, a painting by Raphael, a Bach Fugue meant to the people of their time. Once language and the act of speaking were something holy; divinity was within; and now they have become solely mechanical media, meaning that the children of highly civilised peoples only encounter them in this [mechanical] form.[48]

In such a passage, we can see how Pound's concern for decadence in language finds confirmation in the theories of Frobenius. Here also we can see that Pound's interest in Frobenius was not a new departure, but rather a logical continuation of his broader aim of finding a 'language to think in', a way of speaking and writing and thinking, which would restore the vitality of conscious existence lost in the 'mechanical' world.

Axiological Relativism in *The Cantos*: Reading 'Canto XXXVIII'

I will now look at the ways in which Lévy-Bruhl's and Frobenius's axiological accounts of human consciousness and its relations can be seen in the *Cantos*, particularly in Canto XXXVIII. The latter demonstrates Pound's account of the corruption of a 'mechanistic' society, and its juxtaposition to the 'daemonic creativity' of other cultures. Canto XXXVIII, written in 1933, largely concerns Pound's presentation of corrupt arms dealerships juxtaposed to the Douglasite theories that Pound felt would serve to produce a kind of economic rectitude in Western society. It may seem odd, then, that Pound introduces his readers to Lévy-Bruhl and Frobenius in a canto dedicated to an exploration of economic theory. However, Peter Nicholls and Richard Sieburth have both demonstrated the extent to which Pound conceived economics and language as analogous systems, both networks of semiotic practice that require a functional rectitude which would bring them more in line with natural process. As Sieburth shows, Pound's interruption of his economic passages with commentaries on language and the natural world is consistent with his writing during the middle period of his career:

> Pound's economic writing of the thirties and forties combine a prophetic denunciation of the golden idols of the marketplace with a rather eighteenth-century (and typically physiocratic) concern for the analytical classification and representation of natural wealth and order....Pound's economic writings, which return again and again to the problem of the 'monetary representation' or 'money picture' of extant goods in the context of what he terms economic 'orthography' or Confucian 'rectification of names,' are shaped by similar Enlightenment assumptions concerning the twin semiologies of language and money.[49]

It is clear, then, that Pound draws a kind of analytical equivalence between his theories of language and of economics. Sieburth draws out the contingencies between the twin theories and argues that there is a kind of semiotic superstructure that lies behind Pound's conception of both. It must be pointed out that Pound did not himself amalgamate the two, however, closely related scholars have later shown them to be. Pound's solution for linguistic problems and his solution to economic issues have the same root as they are both part of a paradigm shift that he hopes his poetry will affect in *Paideuma*.

Economics is thus the subject matter of Canto XXXVIII, but it is the individual instance of a problem that is rooted in wider cultural concerns. The primary example is a character named Matevsky, an arms dealer who exploits war for financial gain. Pound highlights how language, and particularly conversation, is used to manipulate economic dealings and to encourage corruption:

> Don't buy until you can get ours.
> And he went over the border
> and he said to the other side:
> The *other* side has more munitions. Don't buy
> until you can get ours.
> And Akers made a large profit and imported gold into England
> Thus increasing gold imports.
> The gentle reader has heard this before.
>
> (XXXVIII.187)

Pound clearly makes the point that language is the medium by which corruption is transmitted. Usurious and corrupt political activity is upheld by conversation, discourse, and argument. Thus, in response, Pound formulates a different mode of presentation in order to reveal the corruption inherent in the language of business, politics, and economics.

Canto XXXVIII is saturated in economic detail, and the flashes of lyrical beauty that often penetrate Pound's denser Cantos are absent. This canto is notable for articulating a theory that Pound would repeat consistently throughout the decade: that corrupt and usurious activity is inextricably bound to a language system that does not take care to fix its meanings and limit the power of its generalisations. This can be seen in the central episode of the canto, which refers to Pound's visit to Vienna and Frankfurt in 1930, the trip in which he met Frobenius for the first time:

> And Schlossmann
> suggested that I stay there in Vienna
> As stool-pigeon against the Anschluss
> > Because the Ausstrians needed a Buddha
> (Seay, brother, I leev et tuh yew!)
> The white man who made the tempest in Baluba
> Der im Baluba das Gewitter gemacht hat...
> > they spell words with a drum beat,
> 'The country is overbrained' said the hungarian nobleman
> in 1923. Kosouth (Ku' shoot) used, I understand
> To sit in a café – all done by conversation –
> It was all done by conversation,
> > possibly because one repeats the point when conversing:
> 'Vienna contains a mixture of races.'
> wd. I stay and be Bhudd-ha?
>
> > > > (XXXVIII.189)

Pound's portrayal of Austrian and Austro-Hungarian culture belies the seriousness of the point he makes. The 'overbrained' nature of this society is contrasted disconcertingly with the 'ragged Arab' who 'spoke with Frobenius and told him/the names of 3000 plants'. As Pound met Frobenius in person in the period he recounts, it is likely that this was an anecdote. The comparison between central European culture, in the years preceding the war felt to be one of the bastions of Western civilisation, and what was, relatively, a less well-known culture is not simply anecdotal. Pound's critique of Western discourse, and even, to a great extent, its language, implies that there are in other languages and cultures, the ability to register specifics and details that make ambiguity and disagreement less likely, and thus bring about a cultural unity.

This idea is linked not only to Frobenius's research, but also to Lévy-Bruhl's notion of 'collective representations', which he hypothesises govern the cultural activities of the civilisations he discusses. Indeed, it is Lévy-Bruhl's research that is then evoked in response to the 'over-brained' and corrupt culture of the Western world:

> Bruhl found some languages full of detail
> Words that half mimic action; but
> generalization is beyond them, a white dog is
> not, let us say, a dog like a black dog.

This reference to Lévy-Bruhl, though short, is of great significance, and requires explanation. It is, in fact, the only explicit reference to his work in *The Cantos*. On first reading, the references to Lévy-Bruhl and Frobenius seem somewhat disjointed from the rest of the poetic sequence. Victor Li argues that the disjunction between the economic passages and this linguistic anecdote is a vital component in the 'ideogrammic' structure of Canto XXXVIII:

> To the lies and gossip of Western capitalist society, Pound opposes, in almost Rousseauistic fashion, the verbal precision and rectitude of primitive societies whose languages are so close to natural objects and actions that they are incapable of deceits built on hollow generalizations or empty locutions. Leaving aside the question of the fallaciousness of a linguistic theory which believes in 'a natural connection between thing and sign,' what is important to note is that Pound sees in the linguistic researches of anthropologists like Frobenius and Lévy-Bruhl, an opportunity for moral intervention, a way of combatting social diseases as verbal ones, and by prescribing a linguistic cure, Pound makes of the writer a medicine-man and regains for him the importance and authority he had lost.[50]

This is, I believe, an accurate account of this passage's place in the canto. It is undoubtedly meant to be read in opposition to the misleading terminology of Pound's financiers and armaments manufacturers. Due to the alleged impossibility of verbal infamy, the speakers of these tribes are, Pound would seem to imply, incapable of deceit. It must be stressed that Pound nowhere argues for a return to a previous linguistic state. Rather, language is a symptom of a usurious culture. Words are used to mislead people, and in a language like English which has many abstract categories, such disingenuous argument is more readily possible than in a language near-solely comprised of concrete detail (as Pound and Lévy-Bruhl believe Klamath and its related languages to be). In response to the obfuscation of meaning that Pound believes to have taken root in English, he offers up the idea of a culture whose very language resists the acts of generalisation and logical analysis, which result in an overflow of abstraction.

The drafts of Canto XXXVIII, and the traces of the editorial process behind the production of the final version, reveal the importance that

Pound attached to the juxtaposition of 'logical' and 'prelogical' mentalities, and the ways in which he amalgamates different cultures into categories of *Paideuma*. The earliest handwritten drafts of the poem echo presentations of twentieth-century Central European society in Canto XXXV ('So this is (we may take it) Mitteleuropa', XXXV.172), but by the time of the second typescript, Pound had added references to Frobenius and Lévy-Bruhl and the poem began to take on a completed shape:

> The ragged arab spoke with Frobenius, and told him
> the names of 3000 plants,
>> Bruhl found the language full of details
> of words that half mimic an action, but
>> systhesis [*sic*] is beyond them. a white dog is
> not, let us say
>> a dog like a black dog.
> such things do not happen, Romeo and Juliet, do not
>> happen
> Unhappily I have lost the cutting of that fait divers
> but apparently such things do still happen,
> he suicided outside the door while they were
> preparing the funeral.[51]

'Systhesis' is obviously a mistyping of 'synthesis' (or 'sinthesis' as Pound spells in the later typescripts).[52] Indeed, by the time of the fifth typescript, Pound changed 'synthesis' to 'analysis', which he clearly felt to be a term that encompassed the logical practices that he believed lay behind Western culture's philosophical and linguistic divisions.[53] It was finally changed to 'generalisations are beyond them' in the final typescript for the American edition.[54] The change from 'language full of details' to 'languages so full of detail' may have been for aesthetic and rhythmic reasons, but the plurality in the latter suggests a more widespread phenomenon than an individual example would. It does, however, reveal that the basis of this line referred to one language (Lévy-Bruhl's treatment of Klamath) which is then taken to stand not only for the mentality of an entire people, but of a section of humanity. Pound, following Lévy-Bruhl's and Frobenius's suggestions, loses his specificity here, fading into a general point about 'primitive' society. Despite its myriad references, the poem very clearly divides cultures into a modernised, Western camp and a 'primitive', non-Western camp. The second typescript also contains more information on the reference to 'Romeo and Juliet', which was clearly a contemporary event which resembled the plot of Shakespeare's play. Although Pound's contention is unclear, by using this event immediately after referring to the detail and clarity of individual words in the languages detailed in Lévy-Bruhl's work, it would seem that he is suggesting that the nature of abstraction and generalisation in

Indo-European languages leads to fundamental (and fatal) misunderstandings. As opposed to the rigour and detail of the languages explored in Frobenius's and Lévy-Bruhl's accounts of non-Western societies, Western culture's dependence on 'synthesis' and abstraction is reflected in its language. Pound's task, then, is to recover the sense of detailed clarity he assumes the languages of non-Western cultures reflect. In Frobenius's terms, it is the role of the poet to recover the lost languages of particularity – indicative of the 'daemonic' early *Paideuma* – in order to guard against the infelicities and abstractions of the modern 'mechanical' *Paideuma*. Pound implies that the power of 'synthesising' and abstracting, useful as these practices may be for philosophical and scientific analysis, has come at a price.

The drafts for the sequence itself also contain more material on Frobenius, but it is unclear to which canto Pound intended to add the passages, and they do not find their way into the published edition of the poem. The pages are an elaboration of the anecdote that lies behind the line 'the white man that made the tempest in Baluba':

> that made the tempest in baluba
> and in … Kashan walking over the hump of the ruin
> and a bundle of rags walked towards him
> and these rags had no outer possessions;
> but the mind full of the names of plants
> //
> and here in ////
>   have they a manner of drummin
> to each day and ea[c]h hour its motiv[e]
> to each hill and each plant its name
> a name called on the flute   do la do la,
> so do fa la, la si mi do; that the call the frond
> of the palm tree;
>
> and when /// forgot his paper,
> wa ban beat on a tree trunk, and over ten miles and twenty
> came the answer,
> we have found the box of the zinc sheet behind the door
> in his cabin, and we are bringing the paper;
> so la do la, do la so fa;
>
> and they have a word for a fat man walking and
>   shaking his rump up and down and they have a
> word for a thin man walking like that jackass Woodrow Wilson
> and they have a word for a/the way a man
> talkis [*sic*] when he looks like a lemon, kiskibashija.
>
> //The poetry is the
>   workings.[55]

Frobenius describes this 'drum language' in *The Childhood of Man*, a text translated into English by A.H. Keane in 1909. 'The language', he explains, 'is introduced and specialized by beats on different parts of the drum. There are four distinct notes, which may be imitated with the mouth, and then produce a language which differs absolutely from that in daily use'.[56] This allows communication and interpretation over a great distance. Frobenius explains its cultural spread:

> And this language, an independently developed form of speech, indicates a very great treasure in the hands of the not very numerous primitive peoples who possess it. It would appear to be most highly developed in the western parts of equatorial Africa, although scarcely less widespread in Oceania, that is, in the insular lands lying north-west and north-east of New Guinea. In New Pomerania itself the different villages communicate over wide areas by means of the drum-telegraph, which has also a wide range in the Amazons valley and in Mexico. The North-west Americans, too, possess similar instruments.[57]

Frobenius implies that the ubiquity of the drum telegraph as a means for communication indicates that it is a key moment in the 'development' of more 'advanced' linguistic practices. It is the similarity of various groups that is emphasised here, not the differences and nuances in the use of drum telegraphy.

Where Frobenius departs from Lévy-Bruhl's implicit evolutionism is in his cyclical approach to history. Frobenius's account of culture draws on Oswald Spengler's famous account of individual cultures as organisms, as opposed to the wholly abstract concept of 'Mankind'. Spengler describes human culture in the following terms: 'each Culture has its own new possibilities of self-expression which arise, ripen, decay, and never return'.[58] Frobenius's treatment of history as a series of cycles revolving around the rise and fall of civilisations was attractive to Pound, and it particularly allowed him to promote the idea of his *Cantos* as an attempt to diagnose the state of contemporary European and American culture (with regard to a potential collapse). Ruins are, after all, a recurring image throughout the poem (Canto IV opens, for example, with the image of Troy as a 'heap of smouldering boundary stones', IV.13) and serve, like the 'falling towers' or the injunction to 'consider Phlebas' of Eliot's *The Waste Land*, as a forewarning against modern civilisations' own ruinations.[59] Pound's primary use of Frobenius, then, is to measure the health and state of an individual culture. Moreover, the notions of 'advanced' and 'less advanced' civilisations can be considered as much stages in the organic life cycle of individual cultures as they can a means of cross-cultural comparison (as in the work of Tyler, for example). Ruins are traces of the collapses in past *Paideuma*. On 26 February 1934,

Pound wrote to Douglas Fox with a summary of his interpretation of Frobenius's theories. He wrote of his intention to produce 'an ideogram of the ESSENTIALS of Frob/'s thought...in condensed CONCRETE cases illustrative' for which Fox would provide the introduction.[60] In it, he included the following poetic extract:

> traces of high civilization (as in drum
> telegraph
> and language of (not exactly
> melody   but at lea[s]t thematic material
> as vocabulary.
> 'nothing is without efficient cause'.[61]

Although only a few lines long and vague with regard to details, this segment is both curious and telling. Pound's use of 'traces' is the most fascinating from a cultural perspective. As Frobenius's conceptions of history and the mutability of culture's organic nature allow for rise and fall, or growth and decay, but it is not clear whether these 'traces' are of a lost 'high civilization' or one to come. While this is, of course, an erroneous and deeply problematic understanding of culture, it is slightly more nuanced than the history of civilisations being a progression from 'low' to 'high' culture. Drum telegraphy in Pound's view may not be indicative of the equivalence of non-Western cultures to Western ones, nor is it necessarily an example of the development of communicative practice, but it may be a remnant from a collapsed civilisation. It may, along with language, be part of a civilisation's *paideumic* structure: that which is fundamental and immutable; recoverable even after the civilisation itself has decayed or even disappeared. In the case of language, poets such as Pound are analogous to ethnologists like Frobenius, reading into words the *Paideuma* of the culture or civilisation from which they came. The 'words so full of detail' bear traces of *Paideumic* structure more clearly than the 'generalisation' or 'synthesis' of Western culture, and may be evidence of the persistence of cultural values even after civilisational decay. While Pound's conception of culture is bound up with an erroneous vision of anthropological thought at best – and disturbing racialist tendencies at worst – it is more nuanced than his use of terms such as 'primitives' and 'savages' would suggest. It is all the more surprising, then, that Pound does not include examples of Lévy-Bruhl's language(s), an oversight which suggests that Pound is really offering a commentary on the language of his own culture.

Towards a Totalitarian Conception

Pound's planned 'ideogram' of Frobenius's ideas did not come to fruition, though it undoubtedly formed the foundation of the *ABC of*

Reading and *Guide to Kulchur*. Both texts are, however, disappointing in light of the depth and gravity that Pound claims Frobenius's theories represent. The 'ideogram' of Frobenius's thought is thus dispersed as a kind of ghost text across a variety of articles and books from 1934 onwards. It was Pound's intention to use Frobenius's thought to conduct a thorough analysis of his own, supposedly 'advanced', culture. The next stage in Pound's use of Frobenius is revealed in an article in the *North American Review*, a year before Faber & Faber brought out the book. In what is a largely tangential discussion of the period of European history from the middle ages to the Renaissance and the Enlightenment, Pound delineates what he believes to be an 'anthropological dissociation' of the European *paideuma*. Specifically, Pound is interested in what he refers to as a 'Mediterranean' dedication to order. This he traces from Sparta, through Byzantium and the Holy Roman Empire, before reaching its fullest expression in Dante's *Commedia*, and its 'sense of gradations': its concept of a stratified and hierarchical cosmological order. Here, Pound explains his rationale behind the adoption of Frobenius's phrase over more traditional discursive terminology. 'I have found it helpful and clarifying to adopt the word *paideuma*', he explains, 'a term resurrected from the Greek by the German anthropologist Leo Frobenius to denote "mental formation and inherited habits of thought" as opposed to a statal *weltanshauung*'.[62] This he then advances in *Guide to Kulchur*.

As *Guide to Kulchur* is not fully coherent with any one particular theory of culture or language, it is difficult to draw conclusions on the book as a whole. However, the most dominant aspect of the book is the extent to which Pound outlines his cultural theory in Frobenius's terms. This is a faith in a particular kind of ethnography that interprets culture according to two facets: the value of the culture at any one time in relation to its own history, and what is unique about the sensibility of each individual culture. In addition to this, though far more implicit than explicit, is the comparison made between cultures, which, like Lévy-Bruhl's unintentional hierarchy of values, unavoidably asserts the superiority of some cultures over others. Despite this, Pound makes no claims towards an explicitly racist outlook, and argues that a hostile attitude towards people who are simply different is not only pointless, but incorrect. The following passage has often been used to defend Pound against the charges that his anti-Semitic writings and broadcasts have necessarily brought him:

> Race prejudice is red herring. The tool of the man defeated intellectually, and of the cheap politician. No one will deny that the jews have racial characteristics, better or worse ones. 'Every Polish nobleman had his jew.'
>
> The use, and more than use, the NEED of Frobenius' dissociations shows at this juncture. Whatever one thinks of his lists of

symptoms, Hammite, Shemite, etc. he rhymes with Dante 'che'l giu-
deo fra voi di voi no ride'. It is nonsense for the anglo-saxon to revile
the jew for beating him at his own game. The nomad in search of
cattle, the romantic tradition. Happy is the man who inherits a rich
field and a strong house and can take up a classis 'Anschauung' with
no inconvenience (to himself).

$$(GK, 242)^{63}$$

As a letter to Langston Hughes, speaking out against the Scotsboro trial,
makes clear, Pound's view of race is complex and nuanced, but there is a vast
difference between denouncing individual instances of racial prejudice and
distancing oneself from racialism.[64] This passage is in fact among Pound's
most explicit arguments in favour of racial distinction and classification. It
is not a great step to expand this to a totalitarian world view which catego-
rises and separates the world and its languages according to racial features.

Following the *ABC of Reading and Guide to Kulchur*, Pound continued
his use of organic metaphors in his discussion of culture and language in an
article entitled 'Significato di Leo Frobenius', which appeared in the Italian
periodical Indice (1938). It was later reproduced in Siegfried de Rachwiltz's
translation of Frobenius's 'The Lute of Gassir' into Italian (1976). The most
consistent in this essay is the discussion of history and culture (and language, by extension) in terms of the causes and symptoms of disease. This,
he states clearly, is the direct influence of Frobenius, and the most significant aspect of his research. 'The importance of Leo Frobenius', Pound
writes, 'consists in his having demonstrated that when art is sick, the evil
is not art alone. Art can be a symptom', an argument that he maintains
consistently.[65] Thus, he believes, the role of the modern critic is to use
the symptom to trace the cause. Pound then argues that a crucial mistake
is misdiagnosis based on reading symptoms for causes, as 'attacking the
symptom without first seeking the cause is the procedure of the savage. The
symptoms are studied. The basic causes of a disease are cured by fighting
or repairing'. Frobenius's methods and theories are thus posited as hygienic
and diagnostic. The separation between 'primitive' and 'civilised' mentalities, undoubtedly drawn from his earlier interest in Lévy-Bruhl as much
as his continued engagement with Frobenius, is here maintained. By identifying a 'primitive' mentality with misdiagnosis, Pound clearly asserts the
superiority of what he assumes to be 'civilised' society.

As his preface demonstrates, Pound is not interested in ethnography
as mere curiosity, nor does he seem to read Frobenius's work on its own
terms, preferring to recontextualise it within economic, political, and
artistic domains. Pound sees precedence for methodologies of study in
other fields, and links this explicitly to the example set by Frobenius's
field work and later academic career.

> Frobenius truly represents the crisis *of* and not *in* the system. And to
> us, who do not have the benefit of his direct instruction, he provides

collateral for the new totalitarian philosophy. The totalitarian state creates, but in the state are active elements or idle elements or those just passive (bromides).[66]

Pound's insistence on the relevance of anthropology and archaeology to the totalitarian state is unsettling, particularly in light of Pound's allegiance to Mussolini, his casual acceptance of Hitler, and the growing ferocity of his anti-Semitism. Frobenius's notion of *paideuma*, that which denotes the persistence of certain cultural traits, inclusive as it is of a myriad of artistic and practical attributes, is also by its nature exclusive. The ethnologist, according to such a method, must decide upon the genuine and valuable aspects of a culture, and dismiss those undesirable elements.

Nevertheless, the remark that Frobenius 'represents the crises *of* and not *in* the system' goes some way to explaining Pound's lack of interest in more reputable anthropologists such as Boas or Sapir, both of whose work would have been readily available to him should he have required it. If, as Pound believed, Frobenius's work is incompatible with the perceived failures of his contemporaries, and if his theories are to be accepted, he seems to have seen little gain in investigating the field further. This paves the way for further criticism of nameless anthropological positions, with Pound declaring that Frobenius's 'archaeology does not anatomise death and the past'. Presumably, Pound is referring as much to the treatment of history as to anthropology or archaeology (he refers to the two disciplines interchangeably). Furthermore, Pound argues, Frobenius's approach is not 'affected by savagery. He studies the primitive races with the same method by which Koch studied his guinea pigs'. Such lines demonstrate a disturbing trend in Pound's writing, though they undoubtedly also spoke to disturbing trends in his audiences.

Frobenius, Pound argues, is in fact quintessentially modern, and responds precisely to the needs of his contemporary society. Pound uses the preface as another platform to address his particular concerns with regard to history and, most significantly, language.

> However, in much higher degrees, Frobenius' practical purpose agrees profoundly with today's needs, the needs of totalitarian perception. He offers us the tools for totalitarian research and in a large part a *method* for the intelligent study of history. Beginning with primitives, who alone today hold the keys of the distant past that serve to open up cultural elements of more advanced civilizations, his system would serve to study the whole of history. In China, for example, over twenty centuries ago, a healthy and constructive dynasty can be seen as founded upon the basis of Confucius' philosophy.
>
> The decline of the European visual arts coincided with a rise in the tolerance of usury. With obscurantism and obfuscation of the significance of words, of terminology, so too decayed the perception

of borders and the limits of plastic form. The moral domain declined, too. The dissociation of ideas weakened, and this weakness of spirit infected all human manifestations.[67]

There are two major points that Pound makes in this passage, and both of them need to be fully drawn out. First, the reason for Pound's interest in Lévy-Bruhl's and Frobenius's works becomes clear from this passage: Pound clearly has an evolutionist tendency to see civilisations that his contemporaries deemed 'primitive' as less advanced than Western civilisations, conceiving of them as evidence of an less developed stage of humanity. This is a more developed version of Pound's commentary in *Guide to Kulchur*. The 'primitive' subjects of Lévy-Bruhl's and Frobenius's research have value, according to Pound, because they are to be read as a living and vital embodiment of what is immediate in human experience. Their languages, 'bound up with mimicry and gesture', are seen to be closer to the original linguistic discoveries of mankind, and are not studied as developed languages in their own right, as Sapir and Bloomfield have done so notably.

Second, and in light of the fact that this is one of Pound's most repeated points, the exact relationship between *Paideuma* and language is explained. Language, made as it is to 'serve thought', is only ever studied by Pound in relation to something else. He does not study language as language itself, but always alongside culture, literary expression, or economics. Language is not, in other words, a cause but a symptom, but it is the prime symptom, and where diagnosis and healing must begin. Just as Pound believed it to be possible in the future for the economic health of a culture to be discernible in its art forms, language is seen to be the relative expression of a culture. This relativity, however, is axiological, reliant upon a hierarchy of cultures, measured according to the values Pound attaches to certain cultures. What is clear from his reading of Lévy-Bruhl and Frobenius from 1928 to 1938 is that Pound's understanding of language is more complex than the opposition of Fenollosa's sinology to Western alphabets, and that it is expressly linked to debates around Pound's interest in fascism, his racial views, and the cultures explored in his *Cantos*.

As late as 1940, Pound still had ambitions to produce a book adapting Frobenius's work. On 1 February 1940, nearly half a year into the Second World War, Pound wrote to T.S. Eliot with his plans to produce a work on culture: 'Gittin down to thet book', he writes. 'There is, so far as I know, no English work on Kulturmorphologie, transformation of cultures. Can't use a German term at the moment. Morphology of cultures. Historic process taken in the larger'. Pound's letter makes troubling reading, as he continues to assuage Eliot's doubts about Frobenius (compared to J.G. Frazer, for example) by writing that 'neither of us likes savages, black habits, etc. However, for yr. enlightenment, Frazer worked largely from documents. Frob went to *things*, memories still in the spoken tradition, etc.' Pound's project would 'get on from where Frobenius left off', he claims, noting a difference in their approaches: 'his Morphology was applied to savages and my interest is in civilizations at their *most*' (*SL*, 336). Quite what Pound intended to do with his interest in civilisations at their *most* is the subject of the next chapter, and is explored in relation to an unlikely figure: C.K. Ogden.

Notes

1 Michael North, *The Dialect of Modernism: Race, Language, and Twentieth Century Modernism* (Oxford: Oxford University Press, 1994), 99.
2 As infamous as this theory is, Sapir and Whorf never worked together on formulating a hypothesis of this kind, and Sapir's work offers as many tools to criticise the theory as to support it.
3 Edward Sapir, 'The Status of Linguistics as a Science', *Language*, 5:4 (1929), 207–214 (209).
4 See Benjamin Lee Whorf, 'Science and Linguistics' in *Language, Thought, and Reality: Selected Writings of Benjamin Lee Whorf*, ed. J.B. Carroll (Cambridge, MA: MIT Press, 1956), 230–232. First published in 1940.
5 See James Dowthwaite, 'Edward Sapir and Modernist Poetry: Amy Lowell, H.D., Ezra Pound, and the Development of Sapir's Literary Theory', *Modernist Cultures*, 13:2 (2018), 255–277.
6 See Peter Nicholls, *Politics, Economics and Writing* (Basingstoke: Macmillan, 1984); Richard Sieburth, 'In Pound We Trust: The Economy of Poetry/The Poetry of Economics', *Critical Inquiry*, 14:1 (1987), 142–172.
7 See Michael Ingham, 'Pound and Music', in *The Cambridge Companion to Ezra Pound*, ed. Ira B. Nadel (Cambridge: Cambridge University Press, 1999), 236–248.
8 Ezra Pound, 'George Antheil', *The Criterion*, 2:7 (1924), 321–331 (325).
9 Pound, 'George Antheil', 326–327.
10 Pound, 'George Antheil', 327.
11 Gill Perry, 'Primitivism and "The Modern"', in *Primitivism, Cubism, Abstraction: The Early Twentieth Century*, ed. Francis Frascina, Charles Harrison, and Gill Perry (New Haven: Yale University Press, 1993), 3–85 (5).
12 Bernd Weiler, 'Cultural Relativism', in *The Blackwell Encyclopedia of Sociology*, Volume 2, ed. George Ritzer (Malden, MA: Blackwell, 2007), 908–910 (909).
13 Ezra Pound, *ABC of Reading* (New York: New Directions, 1934), 36.
14 E.B. Tylor, *Primitive Culture: Researches into the Development of Mythology, Philosophy, Religion, Language, Art and Custom* (London: John Murray, 1871), 7.
15 Tylor, *Primitive Culture*, 236–237.
16 Stephen G. Alter, *Darwinism and the Linguistic Image: Language, Race and Natural Theology in the Nineteenth Century* (London: Johns Hopkins University Press, 1999), 17–18.
17 Robert Ackermann, *The Myth and Ritual School: J.G. Frazer and the Cambridge Ritualists* (London: Routledge, 2002), 45; for a thorough account of Frazer's influence on modernist literature, see John B. Vickery, *The Literary Impact of The Golden Bough* (Princeton: Princeton University Press, 1973).
18 Franz Boas, *The Mind of Primitive Man* (New York: Macmillan, 1911), 172.
19 Susan Hegeman, *Patterns for America: Modernism and the Concept of Culture* (Princeton: Princeton University Press, 1999), 39.

20 Edward Sapir, 'The Status of Linguistics as a Science', *Language*, 5:4 (1929), 207–214 (210).
21 Sapir, *Language*, 244.
22 Sapir, *Language*, 237.
23 Edward Sapir, 'An American Poet', *The Nation*, 121 (1925), 211–212 (211–212).
24 Leon Surette, *The Birth of Modernism: Ezra Pound, T.S. Eliot, W.B. Yeats and the Occult* (Montreal: McGill-Queen's University Press, 1993), 59; Susanna Pavlovska, *Modern Primitives: Race and Language in Gertrude Stein, Ernest Hemingway, and Zora Neale Hurston* (Abingdon: Routledge, 2013), 63.
25 Lucien Lévy-Bruhl, *How Natives Think (Les Fonctions mentales dans les sociétés inférieures)*, trans. Lilian A. Clare (London: George Allen & Unwin, 1926), 147.
26 Lévy-Bruhl, *How Natives Think*, 139.
27 Lévy-Bruhl, *How Natives Think*, 140.
28 Lévy-Bruhl, *How Natives Think*, 142.
29 Albert Samuel Gatschet, *The Klamath Indians of Southwestern Oregon* (Washington: Government Printing Office, 1890), 253.
30 Lévy-Bruhl, *How Natives Think*, 155.
31 Lévy-Bruhl, *How Natives Think*, 174
32 Ezra Pound, 'How to Write', in *Machine Art: The Lost Thought of the Italian Years*, ed. Maria Luisa Ardizzone (Durham: Duke University Press, 1996), 97–109 (90).
33 Ezra Pound, 'Frobenius', Undated, YCAL MSS 43, Box 104, Folder 4336, Beinecke Rare Book and Manuscript Library, Yale University.
34 Noel Stock, *The Life of Ezra Pound* (London: Routledge, 1970), 284.
35 Ezra Pound, Letter to the Director of the Frobenius Institute, 3 March 1930, YCAL MSS 43, Box 17, Folder 774, Beinecke Rare Book and Manuscript Library, Yale University.
36 Barbara Freire-Marecco, 'Review – Culture: The Childhood of Man: A Popular Account of the Superstitions, Manners, Games, Arts, Occupations, and Folklore, &c., &c., of Primitive Man', *Man*, 9 (1909), 125–126 (125–126).
37 Franz Boas, 'Mythology and Folk-Tales of the North American Indians', *The Journal of American Folklore*, 27:106 (1914), 374–410, (384).
38 Melville Herskovits, 'A Preliminary Consideration of the Culture Areas of Africa', *American Anthropologist*, 26:1 (1924), 50–64 (62).
39 A.R. Radcliffe-Brown, 'Review: *Atlas Africanus. Belege zur Morphologie der afrikanischen Kulturen herausgegeben im Auftrage des. Forshcungs-Institut für Kulturmorphologie* by Leo Frobenius, Ritter V. Wilm; *Das Unbekannte Afrika; Aufhellung der Schicksale eines Erdteils* by Leo Frobenius; *Hadschra Maktuba; Urzeitliche Felsbilder Kleinafrikas* by Leo Frobenius, Hugo Obermaier', *American Anthropologist*, 27:2 (April 1925), 325–329 (327, 329).
40 Suzanne Marchand, 'Leo Frobenius and the Revolt Against the West', *Journal of Contemporary History*, 32:2 (1997), 153–170 (p. 165).
41 Leo Frobenius, *Paideuma; Umrisse einer Kultur- und Seelenlehre* (Munich: C.H. Beck'sche Verlagsbuchhandlung, 1921), 11. Translation my own.
42 Frobenius, *Paideuma*, 12.
43 Frobenius, *Paideuma*, 29.
44 Frobenius provides a good summary of these 'levels' of *Paideuma* in table form on p. 117.
45 Frobenius, *Paideuma*, 75.
46 Frobenius, *Paideuma*, 84.

47 Frobenius, *Paideuma*, 80.

48 Frobenius, *Paideuma*, 84.

49 Richard Sieburth, 'In Pound We Trust', 155.

50 Victor P. H. Li, 'Philology and Power: Ezra Pound and the Regulation of Language', *boundary 2*, 15:1 (1986–1987), 187–210 (202).

51 Ezra Pound, Canto XXXVIII autograph ms. and typescript/n.d., YCAL MSS 43, Box 73, Folder 3268, Beinecke Rare Book and Manuscript Library, Yale University.

52 Ezra Pound, Canto XXXVIII autograph ms. and typescript/n.d., YCAL MSS 43, Box 73, Folder 3271, Beinecke Rare Book and Manuscript Library, Yale University.

53 Ezra Pound, Canto XXXVIII autograph ms. and typescript /n.d., YCAL MSS 43, Box 73, Folder 3271, Beinecke Rare Book and Manuscript Library, Yale University.

54 Ezra Pound, Canto XXXVIII autograph ms. and typescript/ n.d., YCAL MSS 43, Box 73, Folder 3284, Beinecke Rare Book and Manuscript Library, Yale University.

55 Ezra Pound, Cantos 35–39: notes and drafts; autograph ms. and typescript, with four clippings, YCAL MSS 43, Box 73, Folder 3258, Beinecke Rare Book and Manuscript Library, Yale University.

56 Frobenius, *The Childhood of Man*, trans. by A.H. Keane (London: Seeley and Company, 1909), 85.

57 Frobenius, *The Childhood of Man*, 86.

58 Oswald Spengler, *The Decline of the West: Form and Actuality*, trans. Charles Francis Atkinson (New York: Alfred A. Knopf: 1927), 21.

59 T.S. Eliot, *The Waste Land: A Facsimile Transcript of the Original Drafts*, ed. Valerie Eliot (London: Faber & Faber, 1971), lines 321, 373, 143, 145.

60 Ezra Pound, Letter to Douglas Fox, 26 February 1934, YCAL MSS 43, Box 17, Folder 775, Beinecke Rare Book and Manuscript Library, Yale University.

61 Pound, Letter to Douglas Fox, 26 February 1934.

62 Ezra Pound, 'The Jefferson-Adams Correspondence', *The North American Review*, 244:2 (1937/1938), 314–324, (316).

63 See, for example, Hugh Kenner, *The Pound Era*, 465. Kenner attempts to use this passage to exonerate Pound from charges of anti-Semitism.

64 Ezra Pound, Letter to Langston Hughes, 18 June 1932, *The Selected Letters of Ezra Pound 1907–1941*, ed. D.D. Paige (New York: New Directions, 1971), 241.

65 Ezra Pound, 'Significato di Leo Frobenius' (1938), reprinted in *Il Luto di Gassire, Legenda Africana di Leo Frobenius, con due scritti di Ezra Pound* (Milan: Vanni Schweiller, 1976)., 9. Translation my own.

66 Pound, 'Significato di Leo Frobenius', 6–7.

67 Pound, 'Significato di Leo Frobenius', 8–9.

4   Definition and Debabelization
Utopian Language in the Work of Ezra Pound and C.K. Ogden

A Poetry of Definition

On Christmas Day 1934, Pound wrote to Hugo Fack enquiring as to what he knew about Basic English. Pound claimed that 'all propaganda wd/ gain by using Bas/ Eng/ as much as poss[ible]', by which he presumably meant to imply that the explanation of economic theories would achieve a wider audience if they used C.K. Ogden's newly developed international language. In the letter to Fack, Pound outlines what he already knew about Basic English, noting (erroneously) that it had a 'vocab/ of 800 words (proposed for world language), with supplementary vocabularies for special and technical subjects. Very important that the econ/ vocab/ should be decently articulated'.[1] On the same day, Pound wrote to Philip Mairet, the literary editor of *The New English Weekly*, explaining that he wanted to write an article on Ogden as a means of demonstrating that 'the ARTICULATION of terminology had been neglected since Economics began'.[2] Pound clearly saw Basic English as a potential means for unifying his linguistic and economic theories, much in the same way that his appropriations of China and Fascist Italy were able to unify his cultural and historical interests with his political and economic sensibilities.

Basic English was a radical attempt at reforming English into an international auxiliary language (IAL) for scientific and commercial communication. It was a response to various attempts in the late nineteenth and early twentieth centuries to develop a world language for commerce, communication, and the facilitation of world peace. Unlike previous IALs which were largely artificial, such as Esperanto, Ido, Novial, and Volapük, it was a reformed version of an existing language. Basic English began in earnest with C.K. Ogden's foundation of the Orthological Institute in 1927. The Institute's work was published in the journal *Psyche*, which became Ogden's chief medium for psychological and linguistic discussion. Signatories to Ogden's permanent petition for Basic English, placed at the end of each issue of *Psyche*, included John Dewey, A. Lloyd James (linguistic advisor to the B.B.C.), H.G. Wells, and George Bernard Shaw. By 1935, the Orthological Institute had representatives in thirty countries.[3] In many ways, however,

Ogden was the latest iteration in a long-standing approach to debates around the nature of language.

Basic English depended upon an intense simplification of English grammar and a stark reduction of the vocabulary. Ogden first reduced the vocabulary of English to 400 general nouns, or 'names', 100 adjectives, 100 verbs, prepositions, and articles, 200 'picturable' things (such as body parts); 850 words in total, not including the numerous variations on those words. Ogden also encouraged simpler syntactic structures, and radically reduced the verb stock to sixteen Basic 'operators' (come, get, give, go, keep, let, make, put, seem, take, be, do, have, say, see, send, may, and will). The basic premise of this reduction is that most complex verbs in English could by and large be replaced by one of these operators being combined with a preposition, a qualifier, or an adverb: thus 'reduce' becomes 'make smaller' and 'retrieve' becomes 'get back'. See, for example, Ogden's Basic English introduction to *Debabelization* (1931), a book which outlines the 'argument' for the language: 'Basic English is an attempt to give everyone a second, or international language, which will take as little of the learner's time as possible'.[4] To both native and non-native speakers, this reads as a simple sentence in standard English, if a little paired down.

The grammar of the language follows a simple, structural logic: Ogden's sample sentences for Basic English included phrases such as 'I will put the record on the machine now', which appear as a kind of staccato, austere version of standard English. This is, in effect, the point. The grammatical machinery of Basic English is driven by a radical attack on the notion of the verb. Indeed, Ogden was sceptical about the verb's basis in reality, arguing in 'Basic English and Grammatic Reform' (1936) that 'what is called a verb...is frequently the disguise in which a variety of more fundamental symbols have been unobtrusively pooling their referential resources'.[5] What Ogden proposes instead is a logic of 'directional thinking', as illustrated in the following sentence: 'the dog went *after* the rat *by* the drain *across* the street *over* the wall *with* the fly *through* the door *against* the rules *to* the meet'.[6] There is only one 'operator' (go, in its past form) in the entire sentence, and yet Ogden is able to register an entire process in clear Basic English. On the one hand, Basic English is a simplification of English, a translation of complexity into simplicity, and a process of simplified definition. On the other, it is a method of creating intelligible English out of what Ogden believed to be linguistic building blocks of both pragmatic and logical necessity; an illustration of Pound's dictum in the *Pisan Cantos* that what is imperative in 'discourse' is 'to get it across e poi basta' (LXXIX.506).

What linguistic affinities brought Ogden, a Cantabrigian who moved in social and philosophical circles anathema to Pound, into the view of the author of the polylingual *Cantos*? Pound seems to have had a threefold interest in Ogden: first, Ogden was a well-known figure widely connected in networks of mid-1930s thought across the Anglophone world and beyond. Second, Pound seems to have been attracted to the impulse to reform language; he was interested in the creative potential of Basic English. Third, Pound shared with Ogden a distrust of abstraction and generalisation. In this sense, Pound seems to have been attracted to the potential of Basic English as a means of communicating across disciplines. By virtue of its definitional simplicity, Basic English requires a contemplation of all that is necessary in a statement, and the logic of its language revolves around clarity. Given that Pound was concerned that economics and philosophy needed to have obscurity lifted, this was an attractive proposition. Above all, however, Basic English was a political and philosophical project, designed to facilitate pacifistic programmes and reform thought. The unification of a political programme with an aesthetic of linguistic clarity was clearly attractive to Pound.

In this chapter, I will explore the ways in which Pound's initial engagement with Ogden was based on a shared utopian vision: one in which linguistic and political principles coalesce. Within less than a year, this vision collapsed, and Pound's initial excitement with Ogden's project soon gave way to disappointment. Pound, however, took much from his brief encounter with Ogden, and it was a formative period in his thinking about both language and politics, and their relation to one another. Joshua Kotin has recently provided a brilliant account of Pound's utopianism in his *Utopias of One*. Where Kotin's account seeks to move beyond social critique and pessimistic notions of failure, my account here must, unfortunately, be grounded in both as these are the frames Pound himself sets up.[7] In order to make sense of Pound's utopian claims about language, I provide an outline of the idea of exact definitions, and then compare Pound's and Ogden's projects. This demonstrates that although his ideas were bound through idiosyncratic treatments and traditional images, Pound remained a thinker of his time, and if his premises led to extreme poetic and political conclusions, other thinkers dealing with similar premises thought otherwise.

Idols of the Marketplace

How did Pound come to see Ogden and Basic English as a crucial response to political and philosophical problems? The answer lies in Pound's understanding of the philosophical importance of definition. In the mid-1930s, Pound developed a thesis that would neatly unify his cultural, economic, historical, and philosophical concerns: to wit, in the Middle Ages, philosophy, which was generally the preserve of theologians, was largely conducted by precisely defining concepts and the words and phrases relating to them. With the advent of modern science in the Renaissance and the Enlightenment, where great advances were made with the aid of direct observation of the natural world, investigators of human knowledge neglected their previous tradition of careful enquiry based on definition. According to this theory, language in general decayed, with metaphysics, in particular, becoming increasingly abstract as a result of its abandonment of the mediaeval scholasticism which, in Pound's view, proceeded by careful and precise definition and was anchored in concrete particulars which existed in the world.

The collapse of scholastic methodology had, according to Pound's theory, dramatic effects: as Western society in general lost the imperative for clear definition, sophism reigned in philosophy, deceit became commonplace in economics, and the true basis of authority, 'right reason', became lost in abstraction and obscurantism. This had, for Pound, overt political and philosophical dimensions; the solution, therefore, would have to have a similarly wide reach. The seriousness with which Pound took this thesis is indicated in his introduction to *Make it New*, a 1933 collection of literary essays:

> As language becomes the most powerful instrument of perfidy, so language alone can riddle and cut through the meshes. Used to conceal meaning, used to blur meaning, to produce the complete and utter inferno of the past century...against which SOLELY a care for language, for accurate registration by language avails. And if men too long neglect it, their children will find themselves begging and their offspring betrayed.[8]

Thus, Pound's economic, literary, and political activities became inflected with this desire to discover and promote 'accurate registration by language'. He expounded, for example, on the importance of linguistic reform in a 1934 article for *G.K.'s Weekly*. Pound contended that 'Europe excited by the dawn of material science, drunk on Baconian greed for proof by experiment, jettisoned the care for *the word*' (emphasis in text).[9] What was needed was a method of 'registration' which would reconcile modern scientific materialism with long-standing traditions of European thought.

In the *ABC of Reading*, published the same year as his article for *G.K.'s Weekly*, Pound expanded upon his thesis by proposing not a return to the old scholastic method of definition but by developing a new, modern method, based on material science. The former, the scholastic method had not only decayed, Pound argues, but was flawed from the outset as it relied on a process of further abstracting a definition away from its meaning. Pound gives the example of a European man defining the word 'red': he suggests it is a colour, which he further defines as a vibration of light, which he then explains is a mode of energy, until he ends with a 'modality of being, or non-being' (*ABC/R*, 19). Pound contrasts this to the 'method of science', which is also the 'method of poetry', derived from Fenollosa's treatment of Chinese characters. According to

Pound/Fenollosa, when a Chinese man wishes to define red, he indicates it as the general quality shared by a number of particulars:

he puts (or his ancestor puts) together the abbreviated pictures of

ROSE	CHERRY
IRON RUST	FLAMINGO

That, you see, is very much the kind of thing a biologist does (in a very much more complicated way) when he gets together a few hundred or thousand slides, and picks out what is necessary for his general statement. Something that fits the case, that applies in all of the cases.

(*ABC/R*, 22)

This argument is the basis for Pound's 'ideogrammic method', a principle of literary practice revolving around the overlaying and juxtaposing of images in succession, allowing their discursive metanarrative to emerge through the reader's discernment of their similarities, rather than the images or references folding into an overriding, abstract theme.[10] In this example, though, the 'ideogrammic method' emerges as a principle of definition, and Pound's application of it in his poetic practice demonstrates that his primary linguistic concern is not, as for many of his contemporaries, the relationship between word and concept, or word and object, but rather the discursive connection between examples in an argument, or images in an ideogram, or poem.

There are numerous problems with Pound's contention here, not least that he and Fenollosa radically overstate the use of radicals in Chinese writing. In the *ABC of Reading*, Pound's outlining of a 'European' and 'Chinese' method of definition effectively corresponds to what are known in logical terms as intensional and extensional (or ostensive) definitions. An intensional definition proceeds by listing the set properties, qualities, and conditions that need to be fulfilled for a word to be used, such as defining 'red' as belonging to the category 'colour'. An extensional, or ostensive definition, by contrast, proceeds by demonstration, by listing examples in which a word is used. In his *Philosophical Investigations* (1953), Ludwig Wittgenstein famously points out the problem with ostensive definitions of the kind that Pound praises in the *ABC of Reading*. Imagine, for example, someone wished to explain the meaning of *two* by pointing at two nuts and exclaiming 'this is *two*'. It would not be clear to the observer, Wittgenstein claims, whether *two* referred to the number or to the foodstuff, and they would require further, intensional explanation. Wittenstein contends that this ostensive definition would only make sense if one had prior general knowledge of the word indicated and its usual connotations. Thus, the problem of defining words in terms of other abstractions returns.[11]

In many ways, Pound's and Wittgenstein's (and Ogden's) treatments of definition are modernist iterations of a long-standing philosophical concern. Although the conflation of symbols and referents had been formulated many times, at least as far back as the Presocratics, it is Francis Bacon's explication of this problem in *Novum Organum* (1620) that best captures the linguistic problem Pound identifies.[12] Bacon identifies the root of the problem in *idola fori*, or 'idols of the market place', so-called because such identifications between words and things are a by-product of the common, commercial use of language. He defines these as

> idols which have crept into the understanding through the alliances of words and names. For men believe that their reason governs words; but it is also true that words react on the understanding; and this it is that has rendered philosophy and the sciences sophistical and inactive. Now words, being commonly framed and applied according to the capacity of the vulgar, follow those lines of division which are most obvious to the vulgar understanding. And whenever an understanding of greater acuteness or a more diligent observation would alter those lines to suit the true divisions of nature, words stand in the way and resist the change. Whence it comes to pass that the high and formal discussions of learned men end oftentimes in disputes about words and names; with which (according to the use and wisdom of the mathematicians) it would be more prudent to begin, and so by means of definitions reduce them to order. Yet even definitions cannot cure this evil in dealing with natural and material things, since the definitions themselves consist of words, and those words beget others.[13]

Bacon argues that the only possible response to this is a reliance on concrete examples and individual instances, as we can therefore avoid the obfuscation of the material bases of thought and communication that results from a philosophical reliance on abstraction.

The market place is a fitting setting for Pound's treatment of this problem. If one part of Pound's concern with definition is language, the other is economics: these two areas of study meet numerous times in Pound's work, but nowhere more notably than in Canto XLV, the famous 'Usura Canto', written around 1935. This canto is a litany of usury's sins, listing the ways in which usury acts to inhere the relationship between humanity and natural process. It is also an exploration of two different kinds of definitional practice. On the one hand, we find Pound's preferred practice of extensive definition, the first of which outlines the usury's effects:

> with usura, sin against nature,
> is thy bread ever more of stale rags
> is thus bread dry as paper,
> with no mountain wheat, no strong flour

with usura the line grows thick
with usura is no clear demarcation
and no man can find site for his dwelling.

(XLV.229)

This is then followed by a more active account of Usura's working:

Usura is a murrain, usura
blunteth the needle in the maid's hand
and stoppeth the spinner's cunning.

(XLV.229)

In all of these processes, Usura is defined as the precise process of corruption, as the moment at which a practice or artisanal activity becomes
separated from its natural state and decays into pure artifice:

Usura rusteth the chisel
It rusteth the craft and the craftsman
It gnaweth the thread in the loom
None learneth to weave gold in her pattern;

(XLV.230)

The archaic language and evangelical tones of the text seek, by a process
of naming, to identify and thus exorcise the effects of usury. By defining
usury in terms of its concrete instances, Pound draws boundaries up
around the practice, preventing its spread (at least conceptually) through
delimiting acts. In the New Directions version of the text, however, this
is not where the poem ends. The final words of the canto are given over
to intensive definition, precisely of the kind from which Pound sought
to move away: 'N.B. Usury: A charge for the use of purchasing power,
levied without regard to production; often without regard to the possibilities of production' (XLV.231). Thus, Pound's 'Usura Canto', while
ostensibly about economics, is, implicitly at least, an exploration of the
possibilities of definition. The intensive, abstract, theoretical definition
which ends the canto should be juxtaposed to the extensive definitions
which seek to delimit the practice in poem; in the contrast between the
two methods, the one prosaic and the other poetic, we can see an illustration of Wittgenstein's observation that extensive definitions ultimately rely on prior knowledge of intensive ones. Nevertheless, Canto
XLV demonstrates the implications of extensive definition for Pound's
poetic practice.

In *Guide to Kulchur*, Pound claims that he was 'confronted with the
need of DEFINITION' (50) following his acquaintance with economics,
and provides another sketch of the supposed decay of philosophical procedure. Pound identifies the innovations of Gottfried Wilhelm Leibniz

as the last instance of the scholastic 'care for the word', and offers an account of the decline of language:

> Up till Leibniz you can find men who really struggle with thought. After Leibniz, the precedent kind of thought ceased to lead men. Before we had much material science, or during the two thousand years' lapse between the mislaying of what greek [*sic*] science there had been and the new science of Galileo and of the renaissance, the defining of terms, speculation, the measuring and testing of one thought on another and the attempt to lock thought in words HAD led men, it had even conduced to material science.
>
> (*GK*, 74)

According to Pound's brief sketch of philosophical history, without the material methods of scientific empiricism, mankind had only imagination and language (and the interrelation between the two) as methods of enquiry. As a result, language was a sharper tool for symbolisation, that is to say, one relied on it to a far greater extent for the dissemination of knowledge. The ways in which one put meanings together, or the ways in which one's words intended towards certain objects of meaning, were of more central value than the 'materialism' we have inherited from the Enlightenment. With the advent of empiricism and materialism, so this theory implies, a great extent of knowledge was lost; knowledge not only of language itself, but the knowledge which was embedded in language. Thus, in 'jettison[ing] care for *the word*', Western culture abandoned the theoretical basis of material science itself, driving a wedge between science and philosophy that allowed the latter to drift into abstraction, obscuring the natural basis of value.

Pound's castigation of Enlightenment philosophy and its aftermath by implication includes the work of his recent forebears and contemporaries. Pound, like Eliot, displayed little interest in German idealism, and, like Wyndham Lewis, displayed little but scorn for *fin de siècle* developments in British and American philosophy; he was, unlike T.E. Hulme (who had visited the university at Marburg and had engaged with work of Edmund Husserl), seemingly unaware at most of debates in phenomenology. In *Guide to Kulchur*, he disparages 'those courses in abstractions, philosophies and the verminous economics propagated 1901–1907' (312). And yet, for all of Pound's research in mediaeval and Renaissance metaphysics in attempting to find a solution for this linguistic decay, in the mid-1930s, he turned to a contemporary intimately entwined with the very milieu he repudiated.

The Development of Basic English

The political dimension of Ogden's thought was always at the forefront of Basic English. Orthology, or the study of the correct use of language, was the vehicle by which Ogden promoted his reformed and condensed version of English. The language was designed for two primary uses: as an introductory form of English for speakers of other languages, and as an international language in its own right. Alongside other attempts, such as Esperanto, Ido, and Otto Jespersen's short-lived Novial, Basic English belongs to a period of linguistic thought in which the development of an international language was a serious concern. All of the founders of international languages saw their projects in political terms. The founder of Volapük, the Catholic priest Johann Martin Schleyer, apparently conceived of a universal language through revelation, promoted it as a means of overcoming the difficulties in negotiating international postage systems, and expanded it to a pacifistic vision.[14] L.L. Zamenhof, founder of Esperanto, the most famous and successful IAL, developed his language in response to the various ethnic and nationalist conflicts that had engulfed his native Poland.[15] The renowned linguist, Otto Jespersen, founder of Novial, was keen to stress his credentials as a man of peace.[16] Basic English grew in the context of this political impulse.

As his biographer W. Terrence Gordon attests, Ogden is a notoriously difficult figure to define: 'when Ogden died in 1957, casual commentators and serious eulogists alike resorted to labels in describing him: polymath, monologist, intellectual entrepreneur'.[17] He had become famous for co-authoring *The Meaning of Meaning* (1923) with I.A. Richards in the early 1920s. *The Meaning of Meaning* is both a survey of linguistic thought and a sustained discussion of semantics, and its publication allowed Ogden to build upon what was his developing reputation at Cambridge as editor of *The Cambridge Magazine* and chair of the Heretics Society. These roles brought Ogden into close contact with the ideas of several figures in philosophy, literature, and economics, many of whom would come to be synonymous with the modernist period. The Heretics hosted discussions by T.E. Hulme, Bertrand Russell, Ludwig Wittgenstein, and Virginia Woolf.[18]

Although Ogden's early career is defined by *The Meaning of Meaning*, it was at Cambridge that he first conceived of the ideas that would occupy him for the rest of his life. First, he believed that all problems of understanding language could be understood as a lack of clarity with regard to symbolism; second, that the various peoples of the world were in conflict with one another as a result of linguistic differences (or, to give this thesis in its weaker form, that differences in language prevent the dialogue necessary to prevent war); third, that the solution to both of these problems was a new universal language with clear symbolism; and, fourth, given the predominance of English internationally, a reformed version of English is the best candidate to perform this role. In notes for a lecture that was to be given to the Heretics on Victoria Welby's significs in 1911, for example, Ogden claims:

Symbolic language would unite Sense and Meaning (with Significance always implied) and where possible must be always educational.

Differences in language make war possible. A new Universal Language would add one more?

[There are] 150,000,000 speakers of English. To cause the spread of English is to extinguish the possibility of war.

(47)[19]

Ogden's interests were as philosophical as they were political. On the one hand, this note speaks to a utopian vision of language that he would never fully abandon, maintaining his faith in Basic English's ability to bridge national differences; on the other, he is staunchly pragmatic, quantifying rather than qualifying the choice of English as the model. This would, of course, change as he developed his research in linguistics.

It is the generative logic of Basic English that is most relevant to our discussion. As James McElvenny has demonstrated, Basic English must be seen in the context of the conclusions about language reached in *The Meaning of Meaning*.[20] Ogden's and Richards's book is as much a survey as it is a sustained argument and reducing the text to a single theme is relatively difficult. In effect, the book is an investigation of the effects of the modern incarnation of *idola fori*, which the authors term 'word magic', or the ways in which people believe words to have power in and of themselves, that is, identifying words with the objects and ideas that they symbolise. Ogden and Richards propose two main solutions to the problem of 'word magic': first, a clear understanding of how symbolism works in language; second, a method of clearly defining symbols so as to eliminate misunderstanding. This enquiry produced what has come to be known in semantics as the 'semiotic triangle'.[21]

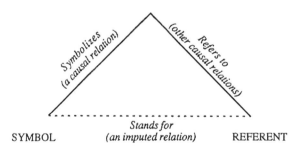

THOUGHT OR REFERENCE

*Symbolizes
(a causal relation)*   *Refers to (other causal relations)*

SYMBOL   *Stands for
(an imputed relation)*   REFERENT

Similar to Saussure, whose ideas Ogden and Richards nevertheless dismiss, the 'symbol' on the left side of the triangle has no natural connection with the 'referent', or object. Instead, a symbol only has a causal relation with a mental 'reference', and it is this mental reference which has a connection with referents. The 'word magic' that Ogden and Richards sought to clear away comes about when one believes there to be an actual connection between symbols and referents; their 'semiotic triangle' sought to disrupt this erroneous connection by placing 'thought or reference' at the centre of semantic understanding.

In many ways, *The Meaning of Meaning* provides less a general theory of semiotics than a specific theory of accurate description and definition. What regulate the use of symbols in a 'universe of discourse', Ogden and Richards propose, are six 'canons of symbolism'. These canons are a set of laws and definitions which are to be applied in any given sign situation, and are Ogden's and Richards's first attempt at achieving the 'debabelization' that prompted the former to develop Basic English. They are as follows:

1   'One symbol stands for one and only one referent' (88);
2   'Symbols which can be substituted one for another symbolise the same reference' (92);
3   'the referent of a contracted symbol is the referent of that symbol expanded' (that is, at different levels of interpretation) (93);
4   'A symbol refers to what it is actually used to refer to, not necessarily to what it ought in good usage, or is intended by an interpreter, or is intended by the user to refer to' (103);
5   'no complex symbol may contain constituent symbols which claim the same 'place' [in a universe of discourse]' (105);
6   'All possible referents together form an order, such that every referent has one place only in that order' (106).

The most radical implication of these 'canons of symbolism' is that they hold the referent to be the central feature: although this appears to be a theory of language, it is more specifically a theory of how to bypass symbols in order to reach the objects and ideas themselves. It is an implicit rejection of the centrality of language. While Ogden and Richards may seem to be outlining a systematic approach to language similar to Charles Sanders Peirce's semiosis or Saussure's semiotics, it is perhaps better to see their ideas in the context of the philosophical and social circles in which they moved. Like Russell and Wittgenstein, their approach to language was more rule-governed than it was semiotic, as epistemological as it was linguistic. In each sign situation, the so-called 'canons of symbolism' serve to counteract the effects of Bacon's *idola fori*.

Although Bacon is cited in *The Meaning of Meaning*, and features heavily in the work of the Orthological Institute, it was to Jeremy Bentham and his theory of fictions that Ogden turned to find a formulation of his views on 'word magic'. Bentham had argued that legal fictions were abstractions treated as if they were concrete entities, a contention that Ogden traces to the nature of verbs in 'Basic English and Grammatical Reform':

> verb forms such as *infect* or *cause* function grammatically like the true operators which Basic distinguishes from them. From such linguistic gadgets other, fictional, accessories such as the nouns *infection* and *causation*, which in turn mimic the behaviour of direct pointers like *chair* and *table*.[22]

And it is here that we can see Ogden's similarity to Pound's poetry of concrete instances. In his discussion of 'fictions' Ogden develops a philosophical approach to language which rejects metaphysical abstractions in the same way that Pound's poetry develops 'ideograms' out of particulars:

> So long as we are content to analyse our social and epistemological obsessions chiefly in terms of psychological fictions such as 'ideas', logical fictions such as 'propositions', legal fictions such as 'rights', physical fictions such as 'cause', biological fictions such as 'sex', saxophonic fictions such as 'swing', phonetic fictions such as 'rhythm', and pedagogic fictions such as 'correct English' – all of which may work well enough, at a purely descriptive level, when nothing is being reified or inferred – we shall continue to obscure the verbal background of our problems.[23]

Although Ogden admits that such fictions are 'inherent in the structure of all languages', he sees the task of philosophers, politicians, and writers (among others) as 'encourag[ing] all forms of awareness of both their uses and abuses, by the development of more adequate methods of interpretation'.[24] Basic English, then, although ostensibly a language of commerce was, in fact, a response to the linguistic problems exposed by twentieth-century philosophy. In *Basic English and Grammatical Reform* alone, Ogden cites Carnap, Frege, and Meinong, which suggests that his work cannot be divided into separate tasks: for Ogden, finding solutions to international intelligibility and to the logical problems raised by the logical positivists, among others, was one and the same task. Like Wittgenstein, whose *Tractatus* imagined a logically perfect language, Ogden attempted to discern the principles of an ideal language; unlike Wittgenstein, Ogden sought to do this in practical, pragmatic terms.

Ogden's method of definition in particular, and his theory of language as a whole, is underpinned by an understanding of reality which disavowed abstraction and generalisation. Ogden's language is constructed, as far as possible, out of concrete particulars. Pound was thus encountering the work of someone who had dedicated over a decade's thought to developing a method by which language could be reformed along strictly

nominalist lines: although Pound did not necessarily share the sheer aus-
terity of Ogden's approach, it certainly chimed with his desire for a reform of language which proceeded along the lines of material science.
Pound was not, however, the first prominent modernist writer to come
into contact with Ogden's work.

Basic English and Modernism

Ogden as modernist has attracted a greater deal of critical attention in
the last two decades, having been largely neglected in the latter half
of the twentieth century. Michael North compares Pound's 'aesthetic
campaign' for clarity and simplicity with Ogden's campaign for universal speech, relating both to Wittgenstein's project.[25] Damon Franke's
Modernist Heresies (2005) provides essential information on Ogden's
role in facilitating and taking part in a number of modernist debates on
language and literature, as well as within analytic philosophy. In her
Modernism and Magic (2013), Leigh Wilson outlines Ogden's struggles
with occult notions of language in his attempt to destroy 'word magic'.[26]
More recently, Megan Quigley's *Modernist Fiction and Vagueness*
(2015) contains extensive discussion of Ogden's place in relation to Joyce
and Wittgenstein. Quigley explores the ways in which modernist writing
is 'less defined by Eliotic structure and coherence than by its investigation of the borders of linguistic precision', and she allots Ogden a central
place in this discussion.[27]

As recent studies have sought to demonstrate, Ogden's position in
the first half of the twentieth century was more significant than scholars in the second half recognised. In philosophical circles, he was not
only well known for his role running the Heretics Society or for his co-
authoring *The Meaning of Meaning*, but also for his role in publishing
Ludwig Wittgenstein's *Tractatus-Logico-Philosophicus* in English.[28]
Richards's influence on both pre-war and post-war literary studies in
the Anglophone world is well known, but at the time Ogden was similarly involved in literary production. The Orthological Institute was
keen to promote the literary possibilities of Basic English. Literature
had played a prominent role in Ogden's career even before the founding of the Orthological Institute: Ogden's extensive list of contacts and
correspondents included T.S. Eliot and Wyndham Lewis. However, and
somewhat surprisingly, the most notable literary engagement of Ogden's
life was an author whose project could not, on the surface, have been
more different from his own: James Joyce.

In 1929, Joyce asked Ogden to write the introduction to *Tales Told
of Shem and Shaun*, a selection of extracts from his 'Work in Progress'. This was, perhaps, a surprising choice, but Richard Ellmann writes
that Joyce had hoped that Ogden would use his academic background
to focus on the linguistic and mathematical aspects of 'Work in Progress'. [29] This hope was in vain. Although Ogden neglected to discuss

mathematics, his introduction is a lively and engaging reading of Joyce's work in a linguistic context. Thereafter, Ogden helped Joyce record the *Anna Livia Plurabelle* section of what would become *Finnegans Wake* and wrote a translation in Basic English with his colleague Leonora Lockhart. Joyce similarly has a prominent place in the explanation of Basic English, with Ogden declaring in his introduction to *Basic English* that from the point of view 'of technology and of writers like James Joyce, the 500,000 words of the lexicologist are too few; from another, that of the occidentalizing oriental, the 10,000 words of the man in the street are too many'.[30]

As Damon Franke notes in his study of Ogden's contribution to modernism, Ogden's alliance with Joyce seems particularly strange due to the obvious differences in their projects. Franke characterises the apparent opposition of *Finnegans Wake* to Basic English, respectively: 'one is amalgamating, subversive, and liberating, the other isolating, directive, and colonizing'. Ogden, however, does not seem to have seen Joyce's project as compromising his work. Ogden, Franke explains, 'approached Joyce's work judiciously and saw the latter's linguistic experimentation as an illustrative contrast to his own language system. The feeling was mutual'.[31] Susan Shaw Sailer, in her seminal discussion of Joyce's and Ogden's literary collaboration, writes of a shared tendency towards universality, as embodied in the principles of the Enlightenment. According to Shaw Sailer, 'where Ogden conceived of Basic English as a potentially universal language, so Joyce meant *Finnegans Wake* to be a potentially universal work that is reflected in its structure, myth and language'.[32] Their collaboration was thus based on common ground and mutual interest and not simply linguistic curiosity. Ogden and his colleague Leonora Lockhart translated Joyce's *Anna Livia Plurabelle* in *Psyche* in May 1931, and it was republished in Eugene Jolas's *transition* the following year. Jean-Michel Rabate has neatly summarised this translation as 'Ogden want[ing] to prove that Joyce is indeed doing very complex things with simple means', a venture that similarly motivated Basic English.[33]

Ogden and Lockhart clearly chose Joyce's work for its renowned difficulty. They intended to demonstrate the flexibility of Basic English: if one could reproduce elements of *Finnegans Wake*, one could say anything in the language. Two short extracts from the text suffice to show the extent of their success. First, the original:

> The spot I'll seek if the hour you'll find. My chart shines high where the blue milk's upset. Forgivemequick, I'm going! Bubye! And you, pluck your watch, forgetmenot. Your evenlode. So save to jurna's end! My sights are swimming thicker on me by the shadows to this place. I sow home slowly now by own way, moyvalley way. Towy I too, rathmine.[34]

Not only the intense complexity of the language but also the density and specificity of the references make it difficult to read Joyce's text for those not immersed into the textual logic of *Finnegans Wake*, or who are at the very least unacquainted with large portions of the text. Ogden and Lockhart attempted to preserve the aural, lyrical qualities of the original while rendering its multiplicity of meanings in lucid Basic English:

> I'll give the place; let the hour be yours. My map is on high where the blue milk's moving. Quick, let me go. I'm going! So long! And you, take your watch, the memory flower. By night your guiding star. So safe to journey's end! What I see gets feebler among these shades. I'll go slowly now by my way, to Moyvalley. And so will I, to Rathmines.[35]

Although it is as faithful a translation as possible, and a remarkable achievement of Basic English use, Ogden's and Lockhart's version actually serves to expose the limits of their language. First, there is a question as to the extent to which a reader unfamiliar with the original would be able to follow the text. Second, although Ogden and Lockhart have successfully rendered the text in Basic English, they are the creators of the language and thus have a level of mastery (and flexibility) not accessible to language learners. In this sense, Basic English emerges as a simplification of a language already known, generated by a pre-existing mother tongue. As Pound would eventually discover himself, Ogden and his supporters had failed to translate the impressive detail of the language's regulatory logic into clear, useable instructions.

The Pound-Ogden Correspondence

The first letters represent Pound's genuine enthusiasm for the Basic English project. Most significantly, he was impressed enough with Ogden's work to offer to produce a Canto in Basic English in a letter of 28 January 1935 (*SL*, 265).[36] Regrettably, Pound did not follow up on this suggestion, and so it is difficult to gauge the extent to which this was a serious proposition. He also suggested that were Ogden to follow up his article and encourage a response from I.A. Richards, he would attempt to interest T.S. Eliot, as well as the American educationalist W. Wilbur Hatfield, editor of the influential *English Journal*. Pound offered to use his contacts in the Fascist government to encourage the implementation of Basic English as part of the educational curriculum in Italy. Presumably, this would have constituted the dissemination of Basic English and its theoretical implications to a wider academic audience in both Britain and the United States. Eliot's tripartite role as poet, critic, and publisher was to be complemented by Hatfield's position of influence in educational circles. Pound, somewhat erroneously, saw Basic English, and Ogden in particular, as a break from Anglophone literary and philosophical establishments:

> God knows the number of people who take any interest in thought (as distinct from the Christ/Dostoievsky/D.K. [*sic*] Lawrence SOUP) is small enough; so that the initial cube of the substance (however small) the interested shd/ be able to focus, communicate, and participate in the cognate amenities.[37]

Pound clearly dissociates the writers of the Orthological Institute from British and American academia, consistent targets of his criticism from the outset of his career. His aims were particularly grandiose at this point: on the one hand, it would represent a new departure in his thinking on language, and on the other, it would constitute a repositioning of Anglo-American philosophy.

Pound immediately followed up on his promise to contact Eliot, Hatfield, and members of the Italian government, even if Ogden does not appear to have explicitly encouraged this. He wrote to Hatfield first, on 21 January 1935, and Pound explained the ways in which he felt Ogden's project could benefit from his own personal expertise alongside Hatfield's influence.

> Heard from Ogden yesterday/ hoping I wd/ emit re Basic English. Seems likely the New English Weekly will let loose. At any rate the Basers follow up my lead.
>
> You [m]ight watch for results. AND: what about Eng/ Jrnl/ What about having the whole set of Basic books TREATED by someone (ONE, namely Ez P'O) who know something about lang-widg which [t]hese blokes do not.
>
> (as so far as I have gone, they ignore Fenollosa, Chinese, Levy=Bruhl [sic], Frobenius???/
> and the prof/ I am now reading uses 'literature' to mean PUNK literature, and has apparently never encountered any other.
>
> Also limited knowledge of specific languages shows through, and makes this their broth. They been readin hun profs/ and not people who knew enough about language to use it.[38]

Pound's insistence on specific languages as the focus of linguistic study clearly owes much to his philological background, as well as to his poetic practice. But this is tempered by his attack on 'hun profs', once again demonstrating his disdain for his contemporaries in philosophy. Hatfield, regrettably from Pound's perspective, felt that an article on Ogden in *The English Journal* would not generate enough interest and he was reluctant to engage with Ogden's work further.

The most significant of Pound's letters about Basic English was addressed to Galeazzo Ciano, who was Mussolini's son in law and the Minister for Propaganda in the Italian government. The letter reveals the political importance that Pound attached to Basic English. He made it clear in these letters that he saw the language as a starting point for non-native speakers of English as well as an important training ground for writers by virtue of its clarity and precision. He also outlined the benefits to Italy of adopting Basic English as a state-sponsored means of learning English, with Pound feeling that it would give the Italian government an advantage over rival nations:

> In the mean time I wish you could get the Capo del Governo ['Head of State'] to give ten minutes consideration to BASIC ENGLISH.
>
> This is a very serious proposition. Ogden has, by years of work, and very serious consideration of the MEANING of words, reduced the necessary English vocabulary to 850 words plus special vocabularies for specific sciences. It is not an 'artificial or freak language like Esperanto', but real English, and can be used [to] understand all discipline[s].
>
> It wont enable a man to appreciate psychological poetry, but can be used for all necessary TRANSMISSION; all commerce. The translation of the Duce's speech (made in English in 1931), into this BASIC, is given in 'Debabelization', and you can see that it retains ample force.
>
> The first European nation to use BASIC, as the basis of their teaching of English in schools, will get an immense advantage over all other[s].
>
> I shall be publishing an article on it in the New English Weekly, next month. (Considering it as a discipline for writers).
>
> You can SAY anything you like in it.
>
> I can have some books on it sent you. With the new Minister of Education. I take it a non-sentimental and practical idea is more likely to get into action, than it would under some aesthete or literary sentimentalist.[39]

The line 'can be used [to] understand all discipline[s]' is an altered version of the original 'can be used as literary discipline', which he crossed out. Nevertheless, he seems to have established three main aspects of his interest in Basic English: first, that it is a means of translation, in the sense that it translates complicated discourse into simple language as well as translating from foreign languages into English; second, that it can become a simple and useful language of commerce and trade; and third, that it is a useful foundation point for both native-speaking writers and foreign students beginning to learn English. Once again, however, Pound was frustrated in his efforts to elicit influential interest in Basic English, although he does claim to Ciano that he had been invited to Budapest to give a lecture on the language in the summer of 1935, an offer he appeared not to have taken up.[40]

Writing to Mairet in the week before his article was published, Pound restated his faith in Ogden's project: 'Og/ has at least heard of one or two foreign countries and of logical processes'. Pound also claimed that he could be a positive influence on Ogden with regard to literary and economic sources, writing that 'he don't [*sic*] happen to know any econ/ or literature/ and has had BAD economic company, from which I want to delouse him'.[41] It is possible that Pound is here referring to John Maynard Keynes and others centred around Cambridge during Ogden's time. The article itself, 'Debabelization and Ogden' appeared in *The New English Weekly* on 28 February 1935. Pound was less interested in the language as a whole and more interested in its literary and social implications. He outlines what he sees as the usefulness of Basic English:

I   As training and exercise, especially for excitable yeasty youngsters who want so eagerly to mean something that they can't take out time to think: What?

II As sieve. As a magnificent system for measuring extant works. As a jolly old means of weeding out bluffs, for weeding out fancy trimmings, and leaving Kipling and Hardy possibly somewhat improved. If a novelist can survive translation into basic, there is something solid under his language.

III [*sic*], this is our specific opportunity: the advantages of BASIC vocabulary limited to 850 words and their variants, plus the specific technical vocabulary for individual sciences, for the diffusion of ideas is, or should be, obvious to any man of intelligence.[42]

As a mode of scientific discourse, Basic English would be severely limited, but it is perhaps more useful as a means of explaining scientific discourse to non-scientists. Pound clearly had this point in mind when he insisted to Stanley Nott in May 1935 that 'readability in ECON. Comes from GOOD WRITING, it comes from ORTHOLOGY. (in my sense, as ameliorated from Ogden)'.[43] Basic English provides a foundational language into which technical terminology can be introduced as temporary affixes. The fundamental aspects of what any one discipline wishes to convey are contained within fifty or less technical terms supplementing an already fixed idiom.

Pound's choice of 'Debabelization and Ogden' as his title was particularly apt. Ogden's term simultaneously denotes a dismantling of the mythic and spiritual aspects of language while also seeking to redeem the chaos of international unintelligibility. According to Edward Sapir, the 'debabelizing' aspect of Basic English reflected the situation of modernity, as 'no national language really corresponds in spirit to the analytic and creative spirit of modern times'. Sapir was, however, sceptical as to the value of any one existing language. 'Perhaps the speakers of a national language are under profound illusions as to the logical character of the structure', he writes, in which case he believes that the speakers of said language 'confuse the comfort of habit with logical necessity'.[44] In *Debabelization*, a text heavily influenced by Sapir, Ogden explains why Basic English is superior to other IALs:

> it allows a maximum utilization of the economic tendencies of the present, and a minimum departure from the linguistic tendencies of the human race. It capitalizes the progress of five centuries, and it further develops the analytic tendency of the most adaptable language the world has yet seen.[45]

Ogden here falls for the fallacy against which Sapir warned: he attributes the ubiquity of English to intrinsic qualities of the language, rather than the political power of its speakers. While Ogden recognised that Basic English's success was dependent on the geopolitical situation of the time, he too readily ascribed that situation to the characteristics of the language. Pound agreed with Ogden's assumption on pragmatic grounds, writing that '[Basic's] immeasurable superiority to all languages invented ab initio is that it already has a full racy idiom, comprehensible to hundreds of millions of people'.[46]

Pound's correspondence with Ogden became increasingly fraught and strained with obvious frustration in the weeks following the publication of 'Debabelization and Ogden'. He had repeatedly suggested that Ogden, or one of his colleagues, should follow up the article with a response indicating its usefulness to the Orthological Institute, or disagreeing with its claims. In any case, Pound was keen that their future correspondence take place in the public space provided by *The New English Weekly* and not simply in private. He expressed his frustration to T.S. Eliot on 28 March 1935, writing 'what about Og/ why aint he bin in Crit/?? Too slow, and stuck and constipé, so can only do one little egg per annum'.[47] As Ogden was a prodigiously hard worker, it seems unlikely that laziness on his part was the reason that no follow-up article was provided. Alternatively, Pound speculated to Philip Mairet that Ogden may have distrusted the article for its appearance in *The New English Weekly*, which was the main British organ for Social Credit economic and political theories. According to Pound, Ogden was 'probably shy – thought he was *only* being wooed for Social Credit'.[48] As Social Credit was not mentioned in the correspondence, and Ogden always displayed an openness for engagement with disparate groups, this seems like Pound's attempt to avoid embarrassment.

Basic English and the Chinese Written Character

Interestingly, Pound seems to have been unconvinced by certain aspects of the language itself. He seems to have struggled with the verbal dimension of Basic English, finding it unclear. His main source for this was provided by Ogden's colleague, Leonara Lockhart. Her *Word Economy* (1931) constitutes not only a survey of the developing discipline of interlinguistics, but also a critical study of how linguistic theories affect Basic English. It is the most detailed outline of the linguistic situation to which the Orthological Institute responds. Its chief concern is the economy of language: the essential effects on the transmission and cultivation of meaning by the reduction of words. 'Economy', Lockhart suggests at the start of the text, 'is possible at three different levels: it may be achieved by the contraction of ideas, of vocabulary, or of words'.[49] *Word Economy* is, in fact, a more eloquent defence of the language than much of Ogden's own output, and Pound's disagreements with the text seem somewhat excessive. His main points of contention were with Lockhart's reliance on academics and scholars rather than writers and the lack of concrete examples of how Basic English functioned.

In his 'Debabelization and Ogden', Pound explicitly calls for the kind of economising suggested by Lockhart, and yet he was unimpressed with her work. He outlined his disagreements with Lockhart in an undated letter to Ogden. Pound began by criticising Lockhart's writing style and concluded with a strong disagreement with the verbal taxonomies of Basic English as a whole:

> I note a lack of articulation in Lockhart. Word Econ/ p. 24.
>
> Better GROUP those verbs acc/ their families
>
> come/go be/seem   do/make
>
> get/give,   take, have, keep, put, send
> let,
> say
> see
>
> question of parity between see/ hear/feel/smell not yet clear to me.[50]

Pound noticed that Ogden's project calls for a categorisation of its 'operators' along deeper philosophical lines. While Ogden was satisfied to extract these sixteen verbs on the grounds of frequency of use and necessity of purpose, Pound recognised that the *raison d'être* of the language depended on a stronger rationale than Lockhart and Ogden had provided. In *Word Economy*, Lockhart conceives of the operators as the culmination of a tendency in modern English to replace the majority of 'elaborate' verbs with a form combining simple operations (*put, take, go*) with spatial and directional adverbs or prepositions. As Lockhart suggests,

> This tendency has been used as the first principle of simplification in Basic English, an experiment which will be discussed at some length

in these pages because of the lesson in Applied Linguistics which it provides. In Basic English the verb system has been reduced to six-teen operators or verb –forms (*come, get, give, go, keep, let, make, put, seem, take, be, do, have, say, see, send*) and two auxiliaries (*may* and *will*). These operators, in combination with twenty-one prepositions or directives, act as substitutes for about 4,000 com-mon verbs. The reduction of auxiliaries is effected by means of vari-ous circumlocutions. Thus *ought* = 'it is right' *can* = 'be able', *must* = 'have to'.[51]

Lockhart is here, in fact, doing little more than summarising Ogden's explanations in *ABC of Basic English* and *The Basic Vocabulary* (1930), yet Pound found her articulation inadequate nonetheless. To an extent, Pound used Lockhart's work as a means of criticising Ogden's work by proxy. He suggested to Ogden that Lockhart was little more than a 'dil-igent pupil'. Ogden, dismissing Pound's criticisms of Lockhart, seems to have understood it this way.

At the same time as his engagement with the Orthologicial Institute, Pound was preparing Ernest Fenollosa's *The Chinese Written Character as a Medium for Poetry* for republication with the London-based pub-lisher Stanley Nott. With his potential collaboration with Ogden, Lock-hart, and others not proving as fruitful as he had hoped, he outlined to Nott his proposal for a 'post-Ogden' series of pamphlets to be named the *Ideogrammic Series* in a letter of May 1935.

This series is not run in opposition to C.K. Ogden. It is not a com-ment on his Psyche series, but it is definitely offered in CONTRAST. A number of the pamphlets are basic in a sense older than the spe-cial one associated with Ogden's simplified vocabulary. If the [in-tellectually] lively reader us[e] one set Ogden's tool as lever he may here find a useable fulcrum. The whole series is for[,] drives toward ORTHOLOGY.[52]

Despite his differences with Basic English, and his criticism of Lockhart, Pound seems to have still held hope in May 1935 that he and Ogden could work towards the same ends, if not collaborate directly. It is at this point, however, that the correspondence stopped.

Nevertheless, on the republication of *The Chinese Written Charac-ter* in 1936, Pound dedicated his short preface to a discussion of Basic English. This is a significant aspect of Pound's publication history that has been overlooked: although Ogden is a marginal figure in terms of Pound's engagement with him, that Pound would incorporate Basic En-glish into the republication of what is widely accepted to be one of the most important texts for Pound's understanding of language testifies to the significance that Ogden's thought held for him at this time. Before offering his own suggestions for improvement, Pound makes two criticisms of the language:

> My respect for Fenollosa's essay is very great; in reprinting it at this time, its bearing on Basic English is at least twofold:
>
> I   Many of the nouns in the Ogden list of 850 words could very well serve as verbs, thereby giving considerably greater force to that brief vocabulary.(
>
> II   Part of Ogden's simplification is more apparent than real, in so far as considerable idiomatic knowledge is required to grasp the shades of meaning inherent in its several simple verbs when used with adjunct prepositions.
>
> I also suggest that the limited gamut of actions included by Ogden in this essential vocabulary might be considered almost as declension of a yet briefer set of main root possibilities.[53]

The critique that Pound offers here is, in fact, more sophisticated than his praise of Ogden in his article for the *New English Weekly* and continues where he left off in the private correspondence. In the first remark, Pound seems not to have fully grasped that the 'limited vocabulary' of his verb stock was intentional, but it remains a valid observation. Although Lockhart and Ogden stressed that phrasal verbs such as 'put off' would replace 'elaborate' verbs such as 'delay' as part of a general tendency, they seem to have overstated the trajectory. Pound is prescient in stressing that Ogden's list of 'names' contains many words that we would today recognise as perfectly acceptable verbs. Pound recognised that the fundamental flaw with Basic English is that it is utterly reliant on standard English not only in terms of its word stock, but also in terms of its structures and idioms. A lot of what the Orthological Institute held to be self-evident about Basic English in fact turns out to be simply the result of the historical development of its mother language.

Reiterating his criticisms of Lockhart in the letter to Ogden a year earlier, Pound then turns his attention to the 'operators'. He clearly took issue with Ogden's failure to group verbs adequately.

> Seeing their sixteen verbal activities printed as follows, the reader may get my point:

be		do	let	make	
seem				say	
see					
get :	take :	have :	keep :	put :	send :	give
come					go

> To *seem* is the false case of *be*. It is the passive of the verb to *see*. To *do* is the more active mode of to *be*. To *let* is the permissive of *do*.

To *make* is the formative of *do*: it is a doing that leaves a concrete result. To *say* is a kind of making, leaving but a trace in the air.
Come and *go* are opposites of motion.
Get, take, are almost doublets: *have, keep,* also almost doublets.
To *take* is more active *getting*, to *keep* more retentive *having*.
And, to these, *put, send, give,* are relinquishings, standing in the possessive gamut, as *go* to *come*, in relative motion.
All this will seem very simple to anyone trained in ideogram. The running legs and the gripping hand of the Chinese pictures will give considerable vividness to the meanings and their relation.[54]

What is most interesting here is Pound's attempt to group these words conceptually. He understands them as related to one another not etymologically, but in terms of the relations between the ideas for which they stand. This implies that in Pound's view, the necessary reforms of language had to be accompanied by a fundamental ordering of human thought and activity. The relations between the verbs are categorised by conceptual links which precede them. It is regrettable that Ogden did not follow up this dialogue as Pound seems to have been agreeing with the model of language proposed in *The Meaning of Meaning* and relied upon in Basic English.

Ogden is also referred to in *New Directions in Prose and Poetry* (1936). This anthology was the first publication of the New Directions publishing company founded by James Laughlin, a Harvard graduate encouraged by Pound to become a publisher. Pound's Canto XLVI appeared alongside the work by Gertrude Stein, William Carlos Williams, Louis Zukofsky, Wallace Stevens, and numerous other writers of the period. It is a fine testament to the literary experiments of the 1930s and is dedicated to the founders of *transition*, the magazine responsible for the publication of much of Joyce's 'Work in Progress'. Although Pound was not responsible for assembling the anthology, one can easily discern his influence in Laughlin's introduction. In his preface, Laughlin refers to Ogden's and Richards's work:

> Language controls thought – as the Church Fathers knew when they insisted on continual care of terminology – as Ogden and Richards knew when they wrote 'The Meaning of Meaning' – and the fluidity and flexibility of thought depends upon the fluidity and flexibility of language.[55]

The phrase 'language controls thought' is perhaps a stronger statement of linguistic determinism than Pound would write, but the process of following the Church Fathers's 'continual care of terminology' with a reference to Ogden and Richards at the very least delimits a thought process remarkably similar to Pound's. Channelling Fenollosa, Laughlin admits that 'although it cannot turn English into an ideographic language where the material-metaphorical origin of every sign is *visible* in its structure, it can, by its limitation of the vocabulary and simplified syntax, shatter the old sound track to pieces' (emphasis in text).[56] Thus, to the writers in the *New Directions* Anthology, the significance of Basic English is similar to the significance of Joyce's 'Work in Progress' to Ogden; although they did not share every linguistic tenet, Ogden was a useful ally in disrupting a common enemy: the *babelization* of the world and the state of English.

As with Pound's use of his work in *The Chinese Written Character*, there is no evidence of Ogden responding to this endorsement of his work. For all his and Laughlin's interest, Pound's objection to Basic English would appear to be its limited creative potential. Writing in the preface to the *Chinese Written Character*, a book that takes poetry as its central concern, it is perhaps unsurprising that Pound's drive is to attempt to make Basic English more inherently creative. The word list and fixed grammatical structures of Basic English allow for the substitution of one word for another but the generative quality of the language, the ability of the speaker to create new imagery, for example, is limited. Pound offers Fenollosa's notion of the ideogram – the Chinese character which he believes to be stylised picture of natural images – as an equally orthological alternative. Pound's suggestion of Fenollosa, and Ogden's silence, constituted the end of any chance of collaboration; both men retreated into idiosyncrasy.

Orthology and the *Cantos*

With Ogden no longer responding to Pound's encouragement, he turned to his 'post-Ogden' orthology. Pound had attempted to gain a number of things from his engagement with Ogden's work: first, he had sought a kindred thinker who agreed that language could and should be rectified; second, he had hoped that Ogden would provide him with a list of British contemporaries who were broadly allied to Pound's way of thinking; third, Pound had wanted to expand the influence of his economic and linguistic thought; and, finally, Pound had seen Ogden's work as a potential point of synthesis for his political, economic, and cultural interests. In all of these senses, then, Pound's correspondence with Ogden was a relative failure. In 1936, Pound asked Herbert Read for a similar list of British writers and thinkers who would enrich Pound's knowledge and influence, and wrote, reflecting on the correspondence, that 'Ogden merely died'.[57] It would appear that it was Ogden's deeply held belief in orthology that affected Pound the most during their correspondence.

In 1935, following the publication of 'Debabelization and Ogden', Pound wrote two further articles for the *New English Weekly* entitled 'Towards Orthology' and 'Toward Orthology: Sargent Florence', appearing in the issues of 11 April and 20 June, respectively. In them, he outlined the necessity of clear and precise definition of terminology in order not to 'confuse perception of facts and relations'.[58] Between 1936 and 1938, the term appeared in the headlines of a number of his contributions to periodicals. The first was a short note in the 3 December 1936 edition of the *New English Weekly* reminding readers that 'as an intelligentsia [*sic*] we shall get *nowhere* until we start checking each other's actual terminology' – a statement with which Ogden would presumably have agreed.[59] Following these articles, Pound promoted his 'economic orthology' in the Italian press, writing 'Verso Un'economia Ortologica' and two further articles entitled 'L'economia Ortologica: Il Problema Centrale' and 'Economia Ortologica: Le Basi Etiche', both of which appear in the Italian economic magazine *Rassegna Monetaria* in the July and September 1937 editions, respectively. In these articles, Pound reiterates for an Italian readership many of the points regarding an accurate terminology made in the *New English Weekly*, calling for 'un nucleo coerente di tecnici pronti ad assumersi una responsabilità lessicografia' ['a nuclear core of technicians ready to assume lexicographic responsibility'].[60] Ogden's name does not appear in any of these articles, although he is undoubtedly the source of Pound's use of the term.

The nature of Pound's amelioration of Ogden's work is clearest in Canto LI, which concludes *The Fifth Decad of Cantos*. Although it is not immediately clear from a first reading, this canto is one of the most significant from a linguistic perspective. Pound wrote Canto LI between 1936 and 1937, at a point when his relationship with Ogden had already broken down, and the poem makes the fundamental differences between the two men's projects clear. If Pound had not produced the Basic English canto he suggested to Ogden, he appears to have at least used certain of the language's principles in this poem.

Canto LI opens with a loose translation of part of Guido Guinizelli's thirteenth-century poem *Al cor gentil rempaira sempre amore*, one of the most influential founding texts of the 'Dolce Stil Nuovo', and a significant combination of Neoplatonist philosophy and Troubadour love poetry. Guinizelli was one of the Dante's chief influences, and his treatment of love in *Al cor gentil rempaira sempre amore* points the way towards the latter's own treatment in *The Divine Comedy*. For Guinizelli, love is a unification of the earthly and the divine. The poem represents a series of analogies drawn between love and light. Since, according to the Neoplatonist tradition, both love and light were the creation of God, and their radiance is felt everywhere, they are evidence of divine intelligence manifested in earthly form. In other words, we can trace the light of the sun back to the first light, and the creator of the first light, God; we can trace our love for a person back to the first love and its creator.

Shines among the powers of heaven
   God the creator, more than Sun in our eye;
Each angel knows the Maker beyond its sphere,
   And turning its circle, obeys God's noble power.
And thus it follows at once:
   The blessed tasks of the Master transpire.
In the same way, in all truth, the beautiful lady
Should behave, for in her eyes reflects the desire
   Of a noble man
Who will turn his every thought to her command.

(V:41–50)[61]

In loving another human being, we not only enjoin ourselves to their fundamental essence, but also gain an insight into the 'primal love' of God. This is compared explicitly with the way in which we perceive light. As Neoplatonic philosophy conceives of a tripartite structure of the universe: the One, that is both omnipotent and nowhere, and the source of all creation; the *Nous*, or the realm of the intellect, which roughly corresponds with Plato's ideal forms; and finally, the realm of being, the limits of which are drawn by time and reality. The role of an individual is to connect one's intelligence with the *Nous* and thus with the primal creator, the One. Love and light are two such insights into this process.

Pound's rendering of this passage draws out the key aspects of the first two lines of the above stanza. He retains the word order from the Italian text and brings the movement down to earth with a humorous thud:

Shines
in the mind of heaven God
who made it
more than the sun
in our eye.
Fifth element; mud; said Napoleon

(LI.250)

The sun is here not as analogy, but as an essential link between different realms of existence (light travels from the world of being, through intellect, and on to the first moment of creation). As opposed to the delicate link between female beauty and divine inspiration that Guinizelli draws out in his poem, Pound brings the reader down to earth, stopping the passage of light with the opaque materiality of mud, presumably a dramatisation of the inhering effect that usury has on the divine light of 'right reason'.

The opening to Canto LI is a paired down rendering of a slightly longer extract among Pound's drafts for Canto XLVI in Yale's Beinecke Library. Pound's original rendering of this sequence can be reconstructed from a longer passage on single, loose page. It opens with a repetition of the Erigena quotation from Canto XXXVI, thus drawing on a wider array of Pound's Neoplatonist reading:

> Authority comes from right reason/
> Sapienza, amore, fede,
> but to prove fede by reason is treason,
> fede,
> that is tis but faith in logic; not faith
> in the Prime mover/
>   a barrier, based on assumption
> shines in the mind of heave[n], God who made it
> more than the sun in our eye.[62]

From a poetic perspective, it is clear why Pound abandoned such a formulaic explanation in favour of the more enigmatic lines which end the draft, but it is useful as an example of his thought processes and lends more clarity to the poem as a whole. *Fede*, or 'faith', cannot be proven by a process of reason, and to do so would be a betrayal of its very nature. What faith requires is belief in the vital universe. Pound's use of 'Prime mover' and 'God' should be taken as a reference to mediaeval thought as much as his to own belief system, and it is noticeable that he stops short of invoking revelation, but the implication is clear: 'right-reason' is intuitive and self-evident.

What follows in the poem is not, however, a continued descant on the theme of light as divine interpretation. This process is interrupted by the theme of usury, a dramatisation of Pound's theory that usury is best represented as an interruption of natural process. At first glance, this passage is a mere restatement of the main tenets of Canto XLV, but on closer reading, one can see that it bears the clear traces of Pound's reading in Basic English:

> With usury has no man a good house
> made of stone, no paradise on his church wall
> With usury the stone cutter is kept from his stone
> the weaver is kept from his loom by usura
> Wool does not come into market
> the peasant does not eat his own grain
> the girl's needle goes blunt in her hand
> The looms are hushed one after another
> ten thousand after ten thousand

(LI.250)

The reason for Pound's restatement of Canto XLV is unclear, but it may be that it gives structural unity to the whole sequence of *Cantos*, ending the section with a recontextualisation that mirrors the movement of

Pound's thought. Although a number of words would be disallowed according to Ogden's vocabulary list ('peasant', for example, would perhaps be rendered 'poor man' or 'farm worker'), and the passive 'is kept' contravenes the active principles of Basic English, the grammar of this passage initially works according to the rules of Ogden's operators. Pound changes 'a house of good stone' to 'a good house made of stone', which follows Ogden's dry, staid principles of description. Similarly, he changes 'Wool comes not to market' (XLV.229) to 'does not come to market', and 'usura/ blunteth the needle in the maid's hand' (XLV.229) to the 'the girl's needle goes blunt in her hand', a series of alterations in accordance with the way in which the operators 'come', and 'go' work in Basic English. It is clear, then, that Pound was writing with these principles in mind.

This passage is not an acceptance of Ogden's language, however. The first rupture in the Basic English rendering is the readmission of the Latin 'usura' in place of the initial 'usury', a usage which recalls the mediaeval origins of Pound's interest. The second more significant rejection of the Basic English grammar can be seen in the movement from the employment of operators to the return of the verb in the line 'the looms are hushed one after another'. Were Pound to remain in a Basic English idiom, he could have rendered the line 'the cloth machines go quiet one after one', but the sonic quality of 'hush', not to mention the kinetic force of the line, is possible only with the use of a verb. In the following line, Pound restores the power of verbs generally: usury supposedly 'destroys the craftsman', 'kills the child in the womb', 'breaks short the young man's courting', 'brings age into youth', and 'lies between the bride and bridegroom' (LI.250). As Pound always presents usury as a nefarious activity, as a poison in the act of coursing, the static presentation of Ogden's operators fails to suffice for his purposes.

Pound then continues the canto in the same vein as its predecessor, Canto XLV, listing a series of activities interrupted by the alleged falsity of usurious activity. He juxtaposes this to an account of fly-fishing, an activity which requires precise knowledge of natural cycles, reliant as it is on the time of year ('12th of March to 2nd of April', LI.251) and the time of day ('seven a.m. till eleven', LI.251). According to Pound, such natural precision is supposedly arrested by the unnatural process of usury.

The canto concludes with a series of references which together form a justification for the author's attempt to reform language. First, Pound outlines the ideal, honest action, 'that hath the light of the doer, as it were/a form cleaving to it'. Second, he quotes, presumably with approval, from Rudolf Hess's radio broadcast on 8 July 1934 that appeared to call for peace and collaboration between the races of Europe: 'Zwischen die Volkern erzielt wird/ a modus vivendi' ['between the peoples of Europe/A modus vivendi is achieved'].[63] If we read this passage in light of Pound's interest in the collaborative potential of an international language, it is reasonable to conclude that this is in part a utopian gesture. Such collaboration and international understanding is interrupted however, by usury's twin, the Dantescan figure of Geryon:

> circling in eddying air; in a hurry;
> the 12; close eyed in the oily wind
> these were the regents; and a sour song from the folds
> of his belly
> sang Geryone; I am help of the aged;
> I pay men to talk peace;
> Mistress of many tongues, merchant of chalcedony

(LI.251)

The passage is in part a summary of Cantos XI and XVII of Dante's *Inferno*. Although Geryon has its origins in Greek mythology, in *Inferno*, Dante conceives of it as a representative of fraud, symbolised by its various parts: it has a lion's paws, a dragon's wings, a scorpion's sting, but a human face. Dante and Virgil descend on Geryon's back down to the Circle of Fraud. In Pound's version, Geryon stands for the force which prevents youthful increase, which promotes war under the guise of peaceful talks, and which uses language to obscure clear meaning – all of which clearly relate to Pound's belief that capitalist arms dealers exploit and promote war for profit. David Moody has suggested that the phrase 'merchant of chalcedony' relates to Revelation 21:19, in which people sold off the foundation stones of the Temple of Jerusalem.[64] While this may certainly be the case, chalcedony was believed, from the Roman Empire to the Middle Ages, to confer the gift of invisibility upon those who carried the stone when it was formed into a heliotrope, a reading which aligns with the nefarious intrigue of which Pound accuses usurers.[65]

At the end of the Canto, Pound offers the ideogram of *Ching Ming* (正名) as the solution to the intricate corruption of Geryone and Usura. He translated *Ching Ming* in various ways, but it most often appears as 'right-naming' in his work, a phrase which recalls Ogden's 'Orthological' Institute. Canto LI stands as a microcosmic dramatisation of the effects of usury as well as a clear statement of what Pound felt to be the required response: call things by the right names. What this required was an effort of linguistic reform. Although Pound's correspondence with Ogden did not lead to the development of such a project as he had hoped, it clearly chimed with and sharpened his convictions. The placement of *Ching Ming* as a linguistic response to the sociopolitical effects (as Pound saw them) of usury is similarly a clear indication of Ogden's and Pound's shared conviction that their proposals for linguistic reform were inextricably bound up with the political milieu of the 1930s.

Pound's admiration for Confucianism and its influence on his *Cantos* is well known, but his use seems to be characteristically idiosyncratic. Feng Lan has argued that Pound's use of *Ching Ming* is peculiar, and largely takes it out of its original context. *Zheng Ming*, as Lan, in fact, transliterates it, originally appears to have referred to the rectification and fixity of certain feudal codes, such as those between rulers and subjects or fathers and sons. In other words, if the terminology of law is well defined, then the application and distribution of rules and law will be effective.[66] Pound's interpretation differs in that he uses the ideogram as a linguistic principle as well as a social doctrine. Lan explains that 'while Pound's revisionist version of *ming* reduces the feudalistic specificity historically deposited in the Confucian *ming*, it widens the scope of the term's application to ordinary instances of linguistic activity'.[67] In this sense, Pound is perhaps using *Ching Ming* as synecdoche, as a privileged example of his broader theories.

What remains to be determined, however, is whether or not Pound's interpretation of *Ching Ming* is the foundation of his linguistic principles or merely an extension of them. Hugh Kenner argues that 'the Ching Ming ideograph has levels of signification beginning with orthography and ending with the most intimate moral discriminations'.[68] It would appear to be the other way around: *Ching Ming* began as a principle of morality and was then applied as a principle of linguistics, notably by Pound himself. As a result, it may be seen that Pound came to the Confucian doctrine with a preconceived notion of orthography, allowing its original context to follow. This is the view taken by Peter Makin in his interpretation of 'right-naming' (as he translated the term).

> All Pound's discussion of right naming shows that he understood it to mean a stability in the relation between word and concept, to be achieved by explicit defining; and a conscious grasp, by anyone using words, of this relation. And this defining and this conscious grasp of defined and definable meanings concern individual words.
>
> It must be understood that the campaigns for *ch'ing ming* and for precise definition, as they operate together, are a campaign for definition, not only *by* words, but *of* words. That is a critical distinction.[69]

Makin believes that Pound's interest in this doctrine began in around 1935, the precise moment at which he is most fully engaged with Ogden's orthology.[70] Coupled, these two theories indicate that Makin is correct in his assertion that Pound is interested in definition 'not only *by* words, but *of* words'.

Indeed, if we trace Pound's understanding of *Ching Ming* throughout the subsequent division of his long poem, 'Cantos LII-LXXI', then Makin's assertion that Pound is seeking 'a stability in the relation between word and concept' generally holds. In the opening canto, LII, Pound offers a lyrical summation of the *Liji*, or *Book of Rites*, a collection of administrative and ceremonial rites, and a central text in the Confucian canon. Towards the end of the canto, he writes 'call things by the names. Good sovereign by distribution/ Evil king by his imposts' (LII.261), a line that, for all intents and purposes, suggests that there is a definite relation between things and the names designating them. Pound's is particularly praiseworthy in his treatment of Emperor Xuanye (1654–1722), known as 'Kang Hi' in the poem, on the grounds of his good governance, his interest in European science and philosophy, and, above all, his command that to his staff: 'qu'ils veillèrent à la pureté du langage/ et qu'on n'employât que des termes propres' ['that they care for the purity of the language/ and only use the correct terms']; in other words, 'CH'ing ming' (LX.334). Read in the light of structuralist and post-structuralist foci on the linguistic sign, it would appear clear that Pound is calling for a fixity of sign-object relations. However, if we read the injunction to care for the 'purity' of language in the light of Pound's concern with the regulation of language in terms of clear definition, that is, a process of careful explanation, and the use of commonly agreed terms, a slightly different picture emerges. It is not that an individual speaker (or indeed, writer or reader) needs to 'grasp' a pre-existing relation between word and concept, or word and object, but rather that a given speech community be clear in the ways in which this relation is to be understood at any one time. We can adjust Makin's assessment, then, into the following statement: Pound understood 'right naming' to be stability in the process by which one draws relations between words and concepts. This was Pound's foundation for the operation of good governance as it had appeared in history, the treatment of which in the *Cantos* is indicative of his 'post-Ogden' orthology.

Linguistic Utopias

On 24 September 1938, Ogden resumed their correspondence, writing to Pound challenging a remark in his *Guide to Kulchur* concerning Basic English. Pound had written of 'Ogden's scholars, often lucid in sentence, but feeble in concrete illustration. I mean they talk of language, of style, etc. and don't know it when encountered' (*GK*, 127–128). Ogden demanded that Pound explain himself. Pound's response was vicious, telling him 'you did not stand up to my remarks in Chinese Written character/ you did NOT mix and converse when I gave you the chance'. Ogden's response to this was that he had not seen any evidence that he should have replied and that Pound had not made this clear in his publications. In fact, Pound had explicitly stated this at the end of 'Debabelization and Ogden', as well as in their correspondence. Pound repeated the remark made three years earlier to Stanley Nott that Ogden was 'stuck', 'you had a good START with yr/ Basic propaganda/ and then you petrified', he wrote. [71] Ending thus in acrimony, the refusal of both men to cooperate on each other's terms put to rest any chance of collaboration.

Ogden does, however, appear in a 1939 article Pound submitted to *The Japan Times*. In the article, Pound outlines his belief that all inter-linguistic attempts at a universal language have failed, and proposes his own solution:

> I propose a tri-lingual system for world communications. None of the schemes for Esperanto or other universal language is at all satisfactory. Ogden's proposals for basic English could be developed. He has not the necessary tact or humanity to apply them. The greatest practical, that is possible, simplification would be a triple system: Ideogram, with the Japanese sound (syllabic) comment, Italian and English.[72]

Pound does not elaborate on how such a system would be developed or implemented, nor does he explain how Ogden's theories could be developed in line with this. The article is, in fact, rather introspective and refers primarily to an idea that Pound suggested to Erminio Turcotti, a professor of 'Eastern languages' at Milan. Turcotti had organised an Anglo-Italian symposium in 1938, the proceedings of which were published in *Fascist Europe – Europa Fascista* (1938), which included Pound's 'Ubicumque Lingua Romana' and a review of *Jefferson and/or Mussolini*. Pound had written to Turcotti in January 1938 outlining his belief in a tripartite structure for a new world language:

> I think for practical purposes. If you consider the combined populations of U.S.A. and Brit Empire you wd. do better to aim at a three language system.
> Chinese Ideogram, comprehensible to all China and Japan.
> Italian, gradually freed of a certain amount of academic red tape/
>
> and American, as middle ground.
> I mean that structurally Chinese ideogram is TOO FAR from the spirit of latin grammar to be translatable into Italian.
> whereas a literal American (English) version is comprehensible to several hundred million people.
> Who in turn who could quite easily learn Italian
> (a slightly OCCIDENTAL form of Italian...Occidental really brings in only Spaniard)
> an Italian with slightly freer grammar wd/ be as easy for Germans, Scandinavs and all speakers of English.[73]

Presumably, Pound advocated a less inflected form of Italian, reformed along the same lines that Ogden reformed English. As for 'Chinese Ideogram' being comprehensible to 'all China and Japan', Pound was probably aware that this is a gross and disingenuous oversimplification of a complicated issue. With his knowledge of language, and particularly of language history, Pound's statements in both the *Tokyo Times* article and the earlier letter to Turcotti seem curiously uninformed. However, when considered from a personal, pragmatic point of view, the logic behind Pound's suggestion becomes clearer: the three languages Pound proposes are the most common of his *Cantos*. Rather than prescribing a model of interlinguistic systems for the modern world, he, in fact, describes the interlinguistic system of his poetic attempt to render that world.

Pound's proposal for a trilingual interlinguistic system which would activate both his poetry and his politics comes up against a similar difficulty faced by most universal language planners: realpolitik. One major objection that can be raised to Jespersen's, Ogden's, and Zamenhof's estimations of language's prescribed role in world peace is that it claims to be a precondition for international harmony when it, in actual fact, presupposes it. Pound, Ogden, and the writers of the Orthological Institute were not alone in this conviction. John Chase's *The Tyranny of Words* (1938) is a curious account of the effect of semantics on human understanding. It is more a polemic essay than a scientific study, but it is remarkable for the author's genealogy of thought and arguments, both of which bear a striking resemblance to Pound's (even more so given Chase's leftist politics). The book's central thesis is that human society and its attendant conflicts (both physical and metaphysical) are the direct result of a lack of clarity in language; whether English, French, or Chinese, human speech is in urgent need of reform. Yet, Chase concedes, 'good language alone will not save mankind', but instead 'seeing the things behind the names will help us to understand the structure of the world we live in'. With the conviction of his utopian politics, Chase concludes that 'good language will help us to communicate with one another about the realities of our environment, where now we speak darkly, in alien tongues'.[74] From our perspective, the realities of the Spanish Civil War, in which a common tongue had done little to assuage rival groups, and the looming inevitability of Europe's second continental conflict in half a century both lend a shade of dramatic irony to the earnestness of Chase's endeavours.

One of the most interesting discussions of this problem was provided by the Swiss philologist Frederick Bodmer (1894–1960) in his *The Loom of Language* (1944), who assessed the various attempts at developing IALs over the first half of the twentieth century and proposes an ideal language drawn from all of them. Although he goes into great detail in explaining what the grammar and vocabulary of his ideal language would be like, he is at all points careful to note that an international language must proceed from, not precede, an international state. He writes that the 'creation of conditions for uniformity of educational practice by international agreement, as a prelude to universal bi-lingualism...is not a language problem. *It is a political problem*' (emphasis in text).[75] Such sentiment is unsurprising given that the book was written in the middle of the Second World War. Bodmer's ideal IAL awaits the existence of an international sovereign state with the means to regulate its use. In many ways, it would be the linguistic correlative to Bodmer's socialist politics, making use of central planning committees, methods of communication (such as radio and cinema), and regulating bodies (based on France's *Académie française*) in order to maintain and preserve the unity and purity of the language.[76] Bodmer's proposed reforms, which are based on an extensive analysis and a minimum of concrete suggestions, were made in anticipation of an imminent world socialist state.

The Loom of Language ends on a polemical note. Bodmer's politics, evident throughout, takes over the linguistic thrust of his argument and takes centre stage. While his argument is similar to Chase's in its ideology, it differs greatly in its notion of the extent of language's influence. He claims that even the possibilities opened to a world language by technological advances such as broadcasting, cinema, and air travel are limited by political situations:

> Of itself, no such change can bring the age-long calamity of war to an end; and it is a dangerous error to conceive that it can do so. We cannot hope to reach a remedy for the language obstacles to international co-operation on a democratic footing, while predatory finance capital, intrigues of armament manufacturers, and the vested interest of a rentier class in the misery of colonial peoples continue to stifle the impulse to a world-wide enterprise for the common wealth of mankind. No language reform can abolish war, while social agencies far more powerful than mere linguistic misunderstandings furnish fresh occasion for it. What intelligent language planning can do is forge a new instrument for human collaboration on a planetary scale, when social institutions propitious to international strife no longer thwart the constructive task of planning health, leisure, and plenty for all.[77]

We may see this as an eloquent outline of the weak form of the argument that linguistic reform can affect world politics. One objection may be that Bodmer's presupposition of a world socialist state for the success of his proposed linguistic reforms insulates the theoretical language from failure on its own terms: that is, he absolves himself from the responsibility of affecting his linguistic programme. The language would only emerge as a product of Utopia, rather than appearing as harbinger. Nevertheless, one can see in *The Loom of Language* the ways in which modernist speculations around the possibility of a world language were intertwined with the politics of the 1930s and 1940s.

With this in mind, we can return to Pound's use of Ogden. Where Bodmer advocates a weak form of the argument, Pound and Ogden seem to assign more power to language in itself, and thus outline a much stronger thesis. Where Bodmer argues that problems in language are reflective of political inequality and corruption, Pound and Ogden argue that problems of language are one of the root causes of the development of these issues. Pound approached Ogden with a view to achieving three principle aims: first, arresting the metaphysical 'decay' of the language that had resulted from the advent of positivist science and the supposed decline of verbal care; second, with a view to clarifying economics for the general population; and third, as a means of exposing and demystifying the elisions and obfuscations that allegedly served to cover up nefarious international capitalist activity. Canto LI dramatises Ogden's role in the development of his thought: it acted as a pivot from the nebulousness of Pound's Neoplatonist interests to the intersection of politics, economics, language, and writing in the figure of the *Ching Ming* ideogram. While Pound's brief interest in Ogden's work can seem to be a non-poetic excursion into half-forgotten twentieth-century linguistics, it, in fact, speaks to a central aspect of the thought underpinning the 1930s *Cantos*. Although Ogden was on the periphery of Pound's career, both men were drawn towards a similar gravitational centre: language as a political and philosophical tool, as the medium and mode of utopia.

In 'The Enemy is Ignorance' (written in 1944, published in English 1960), Pound recounts a visionary journey, undertaken in the midst of the calamitous war that would jeopardise both his poetic project and his personal freedom: 'On the 10th of September last, I walked down the Via Salaria and into the Republic of Utopia, a quiet country lying eighty years east of Fara Sabina'.[78] The date and the fictional (and impossible) location are significant. On 10 September 1943, Benito Mussolini and representatives of the German government were engaged in the formation of the Saló Republic, which would become, on 25 September, a remnant of the fascist state which had lasted twenty years. Fara Sabina lay near the southern border of the burgeoning republic. The setting of Pound's vision, then, is the prospective future of what was a precarious and largely undefined state. In the vision, he is struck by the 'cheerful disposition of the inhabitants' and enquires into the reason for their satisfaction, upon which he is told 'that it was due both to their laws and to the teaching they received from their earliest schooldays'. Pound's central question is thus: what is the basis of Utopian education? His answer: 'they maintain (and in this they are in agreement with Aristotle and other sages of East and West) that our knowledge of universals derives from our knowledge of particulars, and that thought hinges on the definition of words'.[79] This chapter has concerned latter.

The tone of Pound's article is admittedly comic, but it is derived from the linguistic principles which had, by 1944, become central to his conception of politics and philosophy. The notion that thought 'hinges' on the definition of words is a condensation of an argument he had sketched two years earlier in 'A Visiting Card'. Pound writes of how 'without the definition

of words knowledge cannot be transmitted from one man to another'.[80]
A definition, in other words, establishes and regulates the use of terms; it
is a clarification of language for the purpose of greater communal understanding, the laying down of a common code of discourse. He continues
to explain that 'one can base one's discourse on definitions, or on the recounting of historical events (the philosophical or the literary or historical
method, respectively)', even if, he admits, 'without a narrative prelude, no
one would have the patience to consider dry definitions'. Although Pound
is here referring to economic and philosophical writing, these assumptions
had long since served to lay the foundation of his poetic project.

Definition is a unification of linguistic and legal structures: it demonstrates that language is communally regulated. The definition of a word,
or law for that matter, serves as a drawing up of limits around a discussion. As the citizens of Utopia explain to Pound in his dream vision,
a society based on clear principles of definition is one that necessarily
avoids corruption in politics and obfuscation in philosophy:

> I was also informed that by learning how to define words these
> people have succeeded in defining their economic terms, with the
> result that various iniquities of the stock market and financial world
> have entirely disappeared from their country, for no one allows him-
> self to be fooled any longer.[81]

Definition serves two purposes, according to Pound. On the one hand,
it clarifies thought, establishing common limits around certain terms,
directing and regulating our use of language; on the other, definition
serves to diffuse built-up obscurity, ambiguities in thought, and slip-
pery corruption in legalese. In this, definition is both a creative basis for
thought, and a destructive weapon against economic, philosophical, and
political corruption.

Here Pound asks himself a very particular question, even if it is rendered in a satirical tone: what are the necessary conditions of an ideal
society? Pound's answer, a refinement of definition, thrusts him and his
work into a conversation with many of his contemporaries. The early
twentieth century was a time in which radical political and philosophical thought found profound expression and ready audience, and language was by no means exempt from utopian considerations. From L.L.
Zamenhof, the founder of Esperanto, to Ludwig Wittgenstein, first in his
Tractatus and then, more specifically, in *Philosophical Investigations*,
the question of what form the ideal language should take was central to
early twentieth-century thought.

What happened to the language of Utopia? By the end of the Second World War, both Pound's and Ogden's lifelong projects lay in jeop-
ardy. Although Pound's *Pisan Cantos* (1946) would eventually win the
Bollingen Prize, their author was imprisoned in St Elizabeth's Hospital

and was unable to receive the prize or much of his acclaim. The real model of Republic of Utopia into which he had imaginatively forayed in 1943 collapsed less than two years later. Ogden's Basic English seemed to have been faring better. It was even endorsed by Winston Churchill in a letter sent to Franklin Roosevelt on 20 April 1944. Churchill wrote of his 'conviction' that if the United States were to lend their support in promoting the language, 'Basic English will then prove to be a great boon to mankind in the future and a powerful support to the influence of the Anglo-Saxon peoples in world affairs'.[82] It is worth noting that Pound, who despised Roosevelt and Churchill, endorses exactly the same view in 'Debabelization and Ogden'.

Yet, the end of the war and the ascent of a new British government meant that the political support for which Ogden had always worked failed to materialise properly. Ogden's linguistic project remained in the formative, utopian stage, awaiting future delivery, a sad fate given that it was for a long time a serious proposition at least as prominent as Esperanto. It is clear from Pound's writing at this time that he similarly aligned the political and linguistic dimensions of his project with the establishment of a more harmonious world order: the terms on which this was to be done resulted in his name and poetry going down into infamy. As with so many Utopian ideas of the twentieth century, Pound's grand vision of political and linguistic reform came to be demonstrated ostensively by all too concrete particulars: namely 'the enormous tragedy of the dream in the peasant's bent shoulders' (LXXIV.445).

Notes

1 Ezra Pound, Letter to Hugo Fack, 25 December 1934, YCAL MSS 43, Box 16, Folder 701, Beinecke Rare Book and Manuscript Library, Yale University.
2 Ezra Pound, Letter to Philip Mairet, 25 December 1934, YCAL MSS 43, Box 32, Folder 1346, Beinecke Rare Book and Manuscript Library, Yale University.
3 W. Terrence Gordon, *C.K. Ogden: A Bio-Bibliographic Study* (London: The Scarecrow Press, 1990), 48.
4 Ogden, *Debabelization: With a Survey of Contemporary Opinion on the Problem of a Universal Language* (London: Kegan Paul, 1931), 1.
5 C.K. Ogden, 'Basic English and Grammatical Reform', in *C.K. Ogden and Linguistics*, Vol II (London: Routledge, 1994), 187–226 (194).
6 Ogden, 'Basic English and Grammatical Reform', 195.
7 Joshua Kotin, *Utopias of One* (Princeton: Princeton University Press, 2018), 2–3.
8 Ezra Pound, *Make it New* (New Haven: Yale University Press, 1933), 7.
9 Ezra Pound, 'Such Language', *G.K.'s Weekly*, XX (1935), 373.
10 For a detailed discussion of Pound's 'ideogrammic method', see Girolamo Mancuso's 'The Ideogrammic Method', in *The Cantos' in Ezra Pound's Cantos: A Casebook*, trans. Peter Makin (Oxford: Oxford University Press, 2006), 65–80.

11 Ludwig Wittgenstein, *Philosophical Investigations*, trans. G.E.M. Anscombe, M.S. Hacker, and Joachim Schulte (Chichester: Blackwell, 2009), 18.
12 It is worth noting the importance that Bacon seems to have held for both Pound and his wife, Dorothy. See Dorothy Pound's reference to *Novum Organum* in a letter dated 25 September 1945 in *Letters in Captivity* (New York: Oxford University Press, 1999), 91–93.
13 Francis Bacon, *The Works of Francis Bacon*, Volume 4, trans. Spedding, James, Ellis, Robert Leslie, Heath, Douglas Denon (London: Spottiswoode, 1858), 60–61.
14 See Roberto Garvia, *Esperanto and Its Rivals: The Struggle for an International Language* (Philadelphia: University of Pennsylvania Press, 2015), 21–22.
15 See Daniele Archibugi, 'The Language of Democracy: Vernacular or Esperanto? A Comparison between the Multiculturalist and Cosmopolitan Perspectives', *Political Studies*, 53 (2005), 537–555 (545).
16 See Otto Jespersen, *Selected Writings* (Abingdon: Routledge, 2010), 469.
17 Gordon, *C.K. Ogden: A Bio-bibliographic Study*, 4.
18 Damon Franke, *Modernist Heresies: British Literary History 1883–1924* (Columbus: Ohio State University Press, 2008), xiii–xiv.
19 C.K. Ogden, "The Progress of Significs", in *From Significs to Orthology*, Volume 1, ed. W. Terrence Gordon (London: Routledge/Thoemmes, 1994), 1–47.
20 James McElvenny, 'The Application of C.K. Ogden's Semiotics in Basic English', *Language Problems and Language Planning*, 39:2 (2015), 187–204 (191–192).
21 C.K. Ogden, and I.A. Richards, *The Meaning of Meaning: A Study of The Influence of Language upon Thought and of the Science of Symbolism* (London: Kegan Paul, Trench, Trubner and Co., Ltd., 1923), 14.
22 Ogden, 'Basic English and Grammatical Reform', 206.
23 Ogden, 'Basic English and Grammatical Reform', 210.
24 Ogden, 'Basic English and Grammatical Reform', 213.
25 Michael North, *Reading 1922: A Return to the Scene of the Modern* (Oxford: Oxford University Press, 2001), 60–61.
26 See especially Wilson's discussion of H. Blavatsky: Leigh Wilson, *Modernism and Magic: Experiments with Spiritualism, Theosophy and the Occult* (Edinburgh: Edinburgh University Press, 2013), 82–85.
27 Megan Quigley, *Modernist Fiction and Vagueness: Philosophy, Form and Language* (Cambridge: Cambridge University Press, 2015), 7.
28 Ogden has often been assumed to have been the translator himself, but it would appear that he was in fact a commissioning editor.
29 Richard Ellmann, *James Joyce* (Oxford: Oxford University Press, 1982), 614.
30 Ogden, *Basic English*, 11.
31 Damon Franke, *Modernist Heresies: British Literary History 1883–1924* (Columbus: Ohio State University Press, 2008), 202–203.
32 Shaw Sailor, 'Universalizing Languages: 'Finnegans Wake' meets Basic English', *James Joyce Quarterly* 36:4 (1999): 853–868 (853).
33 Jean-Michel Rabate, 'Joyce and Jolas: Late Modernism and Early Babelism', *Journal of Modern Literature*, 22:2 (1998–1999), 245–252 (251).
34 James Joyce, *Finnegans Wake*, 215.
35 Ogden and Lockhart, 'The Orthological Institute', *Psyche* 12:2 (October, 1931): 92–95 (95).
36 Although Pound did not produce a 'Basic Canto', I will demonstrate below that Canto LI incorporates many of Ogden's principles. I am deeply grateful, in this analysis, for remarks made to me by Daniel Katz and Kate McLoughlin.

37 Ezra Pound, Letter to C.K. Ogden, 21 January 1935, YCAL MSS 43, Box 38, Folder 1603, Beinecke Rare Book and Manuscript Library, Yale University.
38 Ezra Pound, Letter to Wilbur Hatfield, 21 January 1935, YCAL MSS 43, Box 15, Folder 688, Beinecke Rare Book and Manuscript Library, Yale University.
39 Ezra Pound, Letter to Galeazzo Ciano, 28 January 1935, YCAL MSS 43, Box 9, Folder 401, Beinecke Rare Book and Manuscript Library, Yale University.
40 Ezra Pound, Letter to Galeazzo Ciano, April 1935, YCAL MSS 43, Box 9, Folder 401, Beinecke Rare Book and Manuscript Library, Yale University. I have found no further evidence of Pound's claim, and he did not travel to give the lecture, but that is not to say that the invitation was not genuine.
41 Ezra Pound, Letter to Philip Mairet, 21 February 1935, YCAL MSS 43, Box 32, Folder 1347, Beinecke Rare Book and Manuscript Library, Yale University.
42 Ezra Pound, 'Debabelization and Ogden', 411. Ellipsis mine.
43 Ezra Pound, Letter to Stanley Nott, May 1935, *One Must Not Go Altogether with the Tide: The Letters of Ezra Pound and Stanley Nott*, ed. Miranda B. Hickman (Montreal: McGill-Queen's University Press, 2011), 164.
44 Edward Sapir, *Language: An Introduction to the Study of Speech* (New York: Harcourt, Brace & Company, 1921), 6.
45 C.K. Ogden, *Debabelization*, 28.
46 Ezra Pound, 'Debabelization and Ogden', *The New English Weekly*, 6:20 (1935), 410–411 (411).
47 Ezra Pound, Letter to T.S. Eliot, 28 March 1935, YCAL MSS 43, Box 15, Folder 664, Beinecke Rare Book and Manuscript Library, Yale University.
48 Ezra Pound, Letter to Philip Mairet, 7 March 1935, YCAL MSS 43, Box 32, Folder 1348, Beinecke Rare Book and Manuscript Library, Yale University.
49 L.W. Lockhart, *Word Economy: A Study in Applied Linguistics* (London: Kegan Paul, 1931), 10.
50 Ezra Pound, Letter to C.K. Ogden, 1935, YCAL MSS 43, Box 38, Folder 1604, Beinecke Rare Book and Manuscript Library, Yale University.
51 Lockhart, *Word Economy*, 24–25.
52 Ezra Pound, Letter to Stanley Nott, May 1935, *One Must Not Altogether Go With the Tide*, 114.
53 Ezra Pound, 'Foreword', in Ernest Fenollosa, *The Chinese Written Character as a Medium for Poetry: An Ars Poetica*, ed. Ezra Pound (London: Stanley Nott, 1936), 5.
54 Pound, 'Foreword', 6.
55 James Laughlin, 'Preface: New Directions', *New Directions in Prose and Poetry*, 1 (1936), vii–xii (ix).
56 Laughlin, 'Preface: New Directions', x.
57 Ezra Pound, Letter to Herbert Read, 3 May 1936, YCAL MSS 43, Box 44, Folder 1849, Beinecke Rare Book and Manuscript Library, Yale University.
58 Ezra Pound, 'Towards Orthology', *New English Weekly*, 6:26 (1935), 534.
59 Ezra Pound, 'Orthology', *New English Weekly*, 10:8 (1936), 159.
60 Ezra Pound, 'Verso Un'economia ortologica', *Rassegna Monetaria*, 34:5/6 (1937), 389–398 (398). Translation my own.
61 Guido Guinizelli, '*Al cor gentil rempaira Sempre Amore*', trans. Robert Edwards, in *Lyrics of the Middle Ages: An Anthology*, ed. J.J. Wilhelm (London: Routledge, 1990), 141–142 (142).
62 Ezra Pound, YCAL MS 43, Box 73, Folder 3303, Beinecke Rare Book and Manuscript Library, Yale University.
63 My own translation.

64 David Moody, *Ezra Pound: Poet*, Volume I (Oxford: Oxford University Press, 2007), 234.

65 Philip Ball, *Invisible: The Dangerous Allure of the Unseen* (Chicago: Chicago University Press, 2015), 24.

66 Feng Lan, *Ezra Pound and Confucianism: Remaking Humanism in the Face of Modernity* (London: University of Toronto, 2005), 46.

67 Lan, *Ezra Pound and Confucianism*, 51.

68 Hugh Kenner, *The Poetry of Ezra Pound* (Lincoln: University of Nebraska, 1985), 38.

69 Peter Makin, 'Ideogram, "Right Naming," and the Authoritarian Streak', in *Ezra Pound and China*, ed. Zhaoming Qian (Ann Arbor: University of Michigan Press, 2006), 120–142 (125).

70 Peter Makin, 'Ideogram, "Right Naming," and the Authoritarian Streak', 120.

71 Ezra Pound, Letter to C.K. Ogden, September 1938, YCAL MSS 43, Box 38, Folder 1604, Beinecke Rare Book and Manuscript Library, Yale University.

72 Ezra Pound, 'Tri-Lingual System Proposed for World Communication: Noted Scholar of Noh Suggests Bilingual or Trilingual Edition of Hundred Best Books on Japanese Literature', *Japan Times and Mail* (15th and 17th May 1939), 4, in 'C1510a', *Ezra Pound's Poetry and Prose Contributions to Periodicals*, ed. Lea Baechler, A. Walton Litz, and James Longenbach (London: Garland, 1991), VII: 450.

73 Ezra Pound, Letter to Erminio Turcotti, 9 January 1938, YCAL MSS 43, Box 53, Folder 2392, Beinecke Rare Book and Manuscript Library, Yale University.

74 Chase, *The Tyranny of Words* (New York: Harcourt and Brace, 1938), 361.

75 Bodmer, *The Loom of Language*, 481.

76 See Bodmer, *The Loom of Language*, 482–484.

77 Bodmer, *The Loom of Language*, 518.

78 Ezra Pound, 'The Enemy Is Ignorance', in *Impact: Essays on the Ignorance and Decline of American Civilization*, ed. Noel Stock, trans. John Drummond (Chicago: Henry Regnery Company, 1960), 98–117 (98).

79 Pound, 'The Enemy Is Ignorance', 98.

80 Ezra Pound, 'A Visiting Card', in *Impact: Essays on the Ignorance and Decline of American Civilization*, ed. Noel Stock, trans. John Drummond (Chicago: Henry Regnery Company, 1960), 44–74 (46).

81 Ezra Pound, 'The Enemy Is Ignorance', 99.

82 Winston Churchill, and Franklin D. Roosevelt, *Churchill and Roosevelt: The Complete Correspondence*, Volume 3, ed. Warren F. Kimball (Princeton: Princeton University Press, 1984), 105.

5 'In Nature Are Signatures'

The Problem of Universals in Modernist Poetry

The confidence of Pound's engagement with Ogden should lead us to conclude that in *Ching Ming*, in a method of 'precise definition', Pound had found the organising principle for his *Cantos*. Anti-metaphysical, founded upon sound linguistic and aesthetic practice, one would expect that Pound could invest his energies into the process of tying the loose ends of the *Cantos* together by virtue of this method. By the end of the 1930s, however, Pound can be seen to be developing a sense of unease with regard to the overarching themes of the *Cantos*. To give an overall structure to a poem, a precise definition must be in service of a clear vision or intention. His readings in anthropology and philosophy indicate a desire to articulate a universal, absolute framework upon which the various particulars of his poem can come to rest. As numerous readers have found, this was not forthcoming. Where I have outlined the progression of Pound's linguistic theories up until 1939, the outbreak of the Second World War and its aftermath mark a period of consolidation that would continue up until the end of Pound's career. It is also a period in which Pound attempted to synthesise his thought on language, politics, philosophy, and economics into a coherent vision of both literary aesthetics and paradisiacal harmony. The failure to achieve this is not, I argue, due to the obscurity of the language nor the difficulty of the method but a wavering in intention. It is a lack of coherence in philosophy and narrative structure (his eschewing of the latter being an intentional part of his method). This begs the question of how we reconcile the notion of a 'language of precision', a poetics of the *mot juste*, with the apparent obscurity of the *Cantos*. We cannot. What Pound developed was a linguistic conviction, a celebrated poetic methodology, but not a coherence of vision. Another reason may be that Pound simply ran out of time: as he wrote to Herbert Creekmore in February 1939, 'there is no *intentional* obscurity. There is condensation to maximum attainable. It is impossible to make the deep as quickly comprehensible as the shallow' (*SL*, 322–323). Precision must follow a vision.

Critical consensus tends to alight on the conclusion that there is not one single, overarching philosophical principle or theme to Pound's *Cantos*. Most critical discussions of Pound's work emphasise either the vast array of material and ideas which he tried to synthesise, or critics find a unity in the methodologies with which he sought this unity. The problems which Pound encountered in defining his philosophy can be seen in the numerous directions that scholarship can take in approaching the overarching dimensions of the *Cantos*. If we look to current approaches, three more recent studies of the centrality of certain philosophies to Pound's work demonstrate what appears, at first, an eclectic vortex: Feng Lan has written of the unification of the aesthetic, the ethical, and the philosophical in his *Ezra Pound and Confucianism* (2004), Peter Liebregts explores the Neoplatonic philosophy of light in Pound's work in his masterful *Ezra Pound and Neoplatonism* (2004), Mark Byron relates Pound's project to his reading of Scotus Eriugena and mediaeval philosophy more broadly in *Ezra Pound's Eriugena* (2014). In none of these excellent studies is a claim to totality made, but each one rather demonstrates one thread in the pattern of the poem.

While Pound has often been characterised as an ideological thinker with regard to both poetry and language, his career also indicates a strong tendency towards pragmatic decisions. To this end, Pound outlined the main principles of his aesthetic theory in a rough draft of a text entitled 'Pragmatic Aesthetics', which was written during the Second World War. Pound's identification with a pragmatic approach to poetic practice and artistic thought is certainly in keeping with the breadth of his interests and subject matter. As Stephen Sicari has pointed out, it is not only Pound's poetic form that is flexible and mutable, but also the central figures of his poem, with people and places occurring and recurring in different contexts with different meanings and in distinct forms. The loose metrical contract of the poem allows Pound to shift between poetry and prose, to negotiate between different languages, and to move from one particular to another. Marjorie Perloff, among others, has celebrated the variety of Pound's formal achievements and the mutability and plurality of the *Cantos'* content. Even then, Perloff notes the way in which Pound's poem increasingly tends towards a greater degree of separation between each particular as, according to her reading of the poem, his 'verbal composition was continuum rather than artefact. Increasingly as he wrote *The Cantos*, the question of genre was subordinated to the question of finding the appropriate phalanx of particulars'.[1] This was not, I argue below, for want of an attempt to find a universal theme to tie the particulars together, and it is clear that Pound's intention was not to delight in moving from particular to particular, but to build the poem up into an eventual generality. There has been a tendency in Poundian criticism to draw attention to Pound's theory of language in relation to the lack of a unified theme. It is my intention below to resist this argument by demonstrating that the perceived obscurity, disunity, and multivalence of the *Cantos* are not down to Pound's theory of language, but down to the lack of certainty in the theory of reality which it served.

Pound's theory of precise definition holds, I argue, regardless of Pound's position, but it cannot hold if he does not have clarity of vision to define. It is not my aim to tie Pound to any one particular doctrine, nor to offer a key to the *Cantos* as a whole, but rather to show that the strain between the obscurity of his later work and the precision of his understanding of language is not a conflict contained solely within the latter. I will do this by first addressing the question of Pound's theory of reality and relating it to modernism more broadly, before looking at the ways in which Pound's later thought emerges as a response to his correspondence with the philosopher George Santayana.

Was Pound a Nominalist?

One of the early interpretations of Pound's entire poetic project was provided by Harold H. Watts in 1952 under the title *Ezra Pound and the Cantos*, although many of the chapters had been published earlier. One chapter in particular was originally published under the title 'Philosopher at Bay' (1947) and Watts alleges that Pound's work revives the ancient 'problem of universals' and that the *Cantos'* argument is an outline of how philosophical nominalism offers a restorative problem for a world supposedly lost to usurious activity. Watts then proceeds to explore the ways in which Pound's work represents a revival of scholastic nominalism, a notion which he locates in the linguistic theories on which the *Cantos* seem to rely. According to Michael Coyle's and Roxana Preda's excellent history of the reception of Pound's work, the editors of *Cronos*, the journal in which it was published, sent a copy to Pound for comment. Pound, Coyle and Preda explain, 'managed little more than exasperated ejaculations ("nuts!") in the margin', and he left the article to Dorothy Pound, who wrote back to the editors of *Cronos*, dismissing the 'abstract discussion' as 'largely irrelevant'.[2] By considering Pound's work in the frame of the age-old debate of nominalism vs realism, Watts errs, Coyle, and Preda argue, in framing Pound's poetic activity in a way that 'establishes critical perspective at the cost of losing contact with Pound's actual texts'.[3] This is undoubtedly the case, as Watts's work is not supported by sufficient quotation from Pound's work, nor by engagement with his extensive critical writing.

Before we come to Watt's argument, it is important to have a clear understanding of the problem of universals, and the distinctions between nominalism and realism. Designating a starting point in philosophical discussion is always a dangerous task, and one must begin if not arbitrarily, then at a point of earliest known influence. In this sense, we may originate the question of the existence of universals in Socratic philosophy, although the formulation given in the works of Plato undoubtedly responds to debates which long pre-existed them. Plato's Socrates argues that all particular things in the intelligible world are images or copies of an ideal world of Forms, in which the original idea of any individual object exists.[4] In this sense, all trees are mere instances of an original, ideal Form of 'the tree'. The purpose of philosophy is to apprehend the true Forms of things, and all knowledge should be concerned with the truth of this metaphysical realm. Platonic realism, as this position is known, thus maintains that universals exist apart from and above particulars: should all trees on earth disappear, the original Form of 'the tree' would still exist. Particulars are thus mere instances of a fundamental universal. Aristotle, by contrast, maintains a more moderate form of this realist position. He agrees with Plato that universals exist, but he argues that the essence of an object is bound to its particular existence: take the quality of 'greenness', for example.[5] According to Plato, 'greenness' would be a property of an ideal form, and exists both through and beyond individual green things; for Aristotle, by contrast, 'greenness' is an existing universal, but it only exists so long as it is instantiated. Were there no longer to be anything green, then greenness would cease to exist. The Aristotelian position is one which agrees with Plato that universals exist, but ties it to the existence of particular instances. This position was further advanced by the Neoplatonic philosopher Porphyry, a student of Plotinus, whose *Isogoge* was a commentary and introduction to Aristotle's logical categories.[6] Boethius's Latin translation of *Isogoge* was the foundational textbook for much mediaeval thought on logic.

It is in the Middle Ages, however, that the problem of universals was elevated to a theological and philosophical dispute of the utmost significance. The mediaeval scholastic philosophers framed the problem of universals as the kernel of theological orthodoxies and critical philosophical debates, as well as the starting point of theories of language. If we conceive of a form of Aristotelian realism as the dominant position in Catholic theology at the time, then nominalism emerges in two senses: first, as a conceptual challenge to philosophical orthodoxy, and second, as an elevation of the role of language. Roscelin of Compiègne in the eleventh century is often seen as the founder of the nominalist position: although none of Roscelin's works remain extant, he was famous throughout the mediaeval scholastic world for advocating a doctrine which held that universals were mere words, that nothing except individual particulars exists, and that general qualities and ideas are linguistic abstractions. Peter Abelard, one of the first to outline a doctrine of this kind in print, argues in his *Logica Ingredientibus* that since Aristotle's position is that universals exist solely when they are instantiated by particulars, we must enquire as to how those universals exist: his conclusion is that they exist in the form of universal words and phrases, in our language.[7] And as our language refers, as Aristotle himself argues in *De Interpretatione*, not to things but to their mental representations, these universals exist solely in the mind and in language. This position was developed by William of Ockham in the fourteenth century into what has come to be known as a moderate form of nominalism, which Philotheus Boehner calls conceptualism. Like Abelard and Roscelin, Ockham maintains that only individual particulars exist in reality, but his thought departs slightly in maintaining that concepts, generalities, and essences do exist in the mind, and that it is this mental existence which is represented in language.[8]

Defences of the realist position were provided by Anselm of Canterbury, Thomas Aquinas, and Johannes Duns Scotus, among others. The latter is perhaps the most famous proponent of realism and is most known for his theorisation of two kinds of essences which subsist in particulars. Dun Scotus argues that any particular object or subject has two natures: first, a *quidditas*, or 'quiddity'. This is the object's 'whatness', that which makes it *what* it is: this is the essence which helps us define what kind of thing an object is: a particular tree is a tree by virtue of its *quidditas*. In addition to 'quiddity' an object has a second nature, its *haecceitas*, or 'haecceity'. This is the object's 'thisness', that which instantiates it as *this* particular object: it is by virtue of *haecceitas* that one tree is distinct from another. Haecceity and Quiddity are not in conflict with one another, they are not mutually opposed theories of an object, but rather the two poles according to which the nature of an object must be understood.[9]

It is important to remember that realism and nominalism are theories of reality, not theories of language: they belong to an epistemological tradition, first and foremost, and only secondarily to a linguistic one. Furthermore, it is important to understand the place of language in this debate: in both traditions of thought, language is composed of universals. As language revolves around communication within a speech community, the act of communication relies upon a replicable, universal understanding. If one takes a realist position, then all non-proper nouns refer to general universals which exist (whether in nature, or on a metaphysical plain); if one takes a nominalist position, denying the existence of those universals in nature, then one locates them solely within a process of abstraction taking place in language. Either way, language becomes a discourse of universals; the only debate is whether or not this universalising tendency has any bearing in nature.

Given Pound's lifelong concern for the relationship between language and phenomena, and his 'fear of abstractions', Watts's contention that Pound's work revives the problem of universals is not an interpretation which should be so readily dismissed, and his argument bears critical revision, particularly in the context of Pound's understanding of language. Watts's argument runs thus: Pound is a nominalist by virtue of his insistence on 'ideas in action', a phrase which Watts's argues means that should ideas be divorced from action they will cease to exist. Here Watts is slightly misled by his argument, as Pound's 'ideas in action' refers, primarily, to an ethical principle, rather than an epistemological one: an idea only has value, only passes the test of sincerity, if it can go into action. Of course, Watts is correct in that the implication of this principle may be epistemological if abstracted. A realist, according to Watts, would argue that ideas are superior to action and, as Pound always insists on the particular instance, on a poetics which seeks reality and experience, he 'contin[ues] the ancient nominalist-realist debate on the side of Abelard'.[10] Watts's interpretation of Pound's 'fear of abstractions', his promotion of the *mot juste*, and the insistence of the political value of *Ching Ming* lead to the conclusion that Pound 'is urging upon a distressed world the curative effects of holding to a nominalist attitude', which discredits 'the vapid idealism which usury permits to circulate'. By identifying usury with idealism and (scholastic) realism, Watts extends the argument of the *Cantos* to a philosophical realm while keeping its grounding in economic realities. Here Watts is on strong ground, in that Pound is often explicit about the problems of usury, namely that it is dislocated from reality and is based on the multiplication of abstract entities. It is here that Watts casts doubt on Pound's project, however, by questioning whether 'nature can be rearranged in the medium of language' in such a way which would adequately defend a modernist position.[11] Can language, in other words, escape the abstract and the universal? Certainly Watts believes that Pound's, at least, cannot, concluding that 'Pound's myth of language-as-it-ought-to-be coincides with the effects of language encountered in the actual poem'.[12] Watts concludes his reading of the *Cantos* by arguing that Pound still relies on abstractions, generalities, and an essentialist simplification of notions of good and evil, and that this comes through in his use of language in the poem; inevitably, despite Pound's efforts, the poem conforms to idealism about humanity, and forms a kind of 'simulated' realism.

Due to numerous flaws in Watts's work, not least its lack of citations and examples, it was not taken up as an example, but the conception of Pound as nominalist is one that has continued in literary criticism. A much firmer argument is provided by Marjorie Perloff. Perloff shares Watts's contention that Pound was a nominalist, but she differs in her assessment of his whole project. According to Perloff, Pound himself sought to advocate a Neoplatonic and Confucian ethical and philosophical doctrine, but his poetry is in fact sustained by nominalist poetics. She argues that 'what makes Pound a nominalist is his peculiar fixation on the uniqueness of a given word or object, its *haeccitas*. its *difference* from all other words or objects'.[13] Her primary example is the list of restaurants in Canto LXXIV: 'Sirdar, Bouiller and Les Lilas/ or Dieudonné London, or Voisin's' (LXXIV.453). In the midst of his internment, Pound remembers with affection the restaurants which he had frequented earlier in his career in Paris and London, naming them specifically. For Perloff, this is a sign of Pound's faith in particularity. Comparing Pound's writing across the breadth of his corpus to the work of Marcel Duchamp, Perloff makes a convincing case that the preponderance of proper names, real or fictional, across Pound's work demonstrates a conviction towards *haeccitas*, a grounding in 'thisness', in constructing a poetics out of concrete particulars alone. Using the example of the listing of restaurants in the *Pisan Cantos*, Perloff argues that 'the seeming excess of Poundian names...is thus offset by the recycling of a given unit in a context that changes its thrust in what is in fact a dense economy of meanings'. Furthermore, 'the acute awareness of difference is accompanied by the concomitant play of likeness – a linking of items that seem quite unrelated'.[14] Ultimately, Perloff concludes that Pound's focus on the natural object, on the nominalist particular, creates a situation in which the poem cannot cohere, but that this is where the value of the poetry lies, as this is reflective of the nature of reality.

Although Perloff's treatment of this question offers an excellent reading of the *haecceitas* of Pound's work, it, like Watts's, assumes that there is a strain between Pound's 'nominalism' and his grander intentions for the *Cantos*. In both cases, we are presented with a nominalism which fails, or which succeeds too well. In neither case is it questioned whether Pound is a nominalist. If we consider the list of restaurants, or the Poundian concept of the 'subject rhyme', however, we notice that it is not difference that structures Pound's work, but rather similarity – or, at the very least, the search after similarity. It is a similarity which is grounded not in abstraction, but in the delineation of particular people, objects, and events. Perloff is entirely correct to stress the importance of the 'thisness' of things for Pound's poetics – we need only think of Pound's celebration of 'primitive' language for its preponderance of specific details – but this preference for *haecceitas* is not necessarily a nominalist position. Particularity is the commonality between nominalism and realism: the debate does not revolve around the existence of particulars but of universals. Furthermore, haecceity and quiddity are both, in Scotist realism, essences of the particular; it is simply that *quidditas* is that which instantiates it as a kind, that which provides a link to its species. Indeed, haecceity was part of Duns Scotus's realist understanding of universals which William of Ockham repudiated.[15] Were we to accept, at least theoretically, the twin poles of haecceity and quiddity, then the question shifts from the former – which is determined solely by a separate existence in space and time – to the latter, to the essence of a thing's 'whatness'. Therein lies the question of the universal.

Regardless of the Pounds' dismissal of the question of universals, Watts and Perloff are indeed supported by numerous statements that Pound himself makes in both his poetry and his prose. Consider, for example, the following remark from *Guide to Kulchur* in which Pound seeks to provide a justification of certain philosophical principles of the ancient Stoic school of thought:

> They, the Stoics, did have some respect for terminology or 'representation' which gathered or seized the object with clarity.

WITH emphasis on the individual object 'reality existed only in the particular'. 'universals were to them subjective concepts formed by abstraction'.

(GK, 122–123)

It is difficult to read this any other way than evincing faith in an anti-realist position. It seems to fit perfectly with the semiotic aspects of Fenollosa and with Pound's aesthetics of the concrete and 'absolute' symbol, as well as his philosophical opposition to metaphysics. The position Pound ascribes to the Stoics is not necessarily nominalism as such, but rather conceptualism. As David Sedley has pointed out, the Stoical position looks forward to the British empiricists in conceiving of universals as mentally subsisting entities, themselves useful for understanding reality but not a part of reality itself.[16] Reading these lines through Pound, the implication is that the Stoical philosophy is dismissive of universals, though this is not quite the case.

The nominalist interpretation of Pound's work finds particular strength in the *Pisan Cantos*, where Pound's appropriation of the myth of Wanjina seems to imply an interpretation of *things* (emphasis in text) as being tied to discursive practice. The myth of 'Wanjina' was derived from an account of an Aboriginal rain god, 'Wondjina', narrated to him by some of Frobenius's students in 1939, following their exhibition to Australia the year before.[17] Pound relates the myth to Odysseus's answer given to Polyphemus who, having been blinded, demanded to know who had committed the act, as well as identifying the myth with 'Ouan Jin', seemingly a Chinese phrase of Pound's own invention.

'I am noman, my name is noman'
but Wanjina is, shall we say, Ouan Jin
or the man with an education
and whose mouth was removed by his father
> because he made too many *things*
whereby cluttered the bushman's baggage
vide the expedition of Frobenius' pupils about 1938
> to Auss'ralia
Ouan Jin spoke and thereby created the named
> thereby making clutter
the bane of men moving
and so his mouth was removed
as you will find it removed in his pictures
> in principio verbum
> paraclete or the verbum perfectum: sinceritas

(LXXIV.446–447)

The problem with interpreting this passage is that there are two potential moods at work in the poetry: the first is humorous. Pound provides a satirical account of his own condition. Caged at Pisa, awaiting extradition or execution on the grounds of treason committed while supporting the axis powers (and opposing the United States joining the allied effort), Pound seems to be using Wanjina as mythical martyr for freedom of speech. While this could be tacit evidence of a faith in the relationship between language and *things*, a more likely reading is that Pound uses *things* as a metaphor for 'truths'. Wanjina is punished for speaking realities, much as Pound believed himself to have been. Another reading, of course, implies that we should take the myth as a serious model for Pound's understanding of reality and language. If the 'named' is, in Pound's musical phrase, 'the bane of men moving', then it implies that a proliferation of language is antithetical to human activity. If we connect this to Pound's affinities with Ogden, a different interpretation of the passage emerges: Wanjina's father performs the role of the Poundian writer, cutting language down to what is necessary for the communication of idea, mood, or object. As Pound writes in a later Canto, 'to communicate and then stop, that is the/ law of discourse' (LXXX.514). Wanjina is thus contrasted to the 'paraclete', the light of the Neoplatonic tradition, and to the 'verbum perfectum' which is 'sincerity'. Sincerity was, for Pound, the true measure of an artist's work, but, once again, there is a problem of interpretation here. Is 'sincerity' in an art work its correspondence to reality or its coherence with regard to the artist's intention?

One answer to this question is provided in Canto LXXXII, where Pound reminisces over his old literary acquaintances. In a memorable passage comparing the influence of Ford Madox Ford to that of William Butler Yeats, Pound once again asserts his preference for a 'direct treatment of the thing', as opposed to linguistic sophistry:

> And for all that old Ford's conversation was better,
> consisting in *res* non *verba*,
>> despite William's anecdotes, in that Fordie
> never dented an idea for a phrase's sake
>
> (LXXXII.545)

Donald Davie problematises this passage by pointing out that for all of Pound's praise for Ford's sentiments, he does not follow them in vast amounts of his poetry. While Ford's language is praised for its grounding in *res* ('things') rather than *verba* (mere 'words'), Pound's poetry abounds in verbal proficiency which fails, often, to alight on the very things it praises. As Davie writes, 'Pound's transition seems to be from *verbum to verbum*...with no appeal over long stretches to the *res* supposedly under discussion'. 'Pound', he continues, 'moves often from signifier to signifier, leaving the signified to take care of itself'.[18] Davie's point is well made, but it suffers from the inevitable mixture of terminologies that Pound's text inadvertently encourages. *Res* and 'signifieds' are no more synonymous than are *verba* and 'signifiers' and Pound is, therefore, judged according to a semiotic structure he does not use. What Pound means by *res* here is that Ford Madox Ford's discursive practice revolved around concrete instances, rather than word play or abstract logic – that which results from *verba* alone.

Returning to the first of the *Pisan Cantos*, Canto LXXIV, we find the passage which begs the question of Pound's relation to the problem of universals most explicitly. Whether Pound held this to be central to his concern or not, it directly addresses the issue by summarising Aristotle's position:

> philosophy is not for young men
> their *Kathalou* can not be sufficiently derived from
>   their *hekasta*
> their generalities cannot be born from a sufficient phalanx
>   of particulars
>   (LXXIV.461)

Reading this passage alongside Pound's unfulfilled intention to provide philosophical coherence for his epic poem, we can see the anxieties in the lines. The notion that 'generalities' must be derived from 'a sufficient phalanx/ of particulars' is a key for reading the *Cantos*: out of the phalanx of particulars, we must build the general meaning. The *Cantos* do not proceed by a method of abstraction, but rather by a method of induction, such as that which Pound believed Fenollosa had discovered in the Chinese written character. The question this raises for the problem of universals is thus: are these generalities based in reality, or do they exist solely on the conceptual-linguistic plane? In order to answer this, we will have to turn to a modernist understanding of the problem of universals.

The Modernist Problem of Universals: The Concrete Universal

Jerome McGann argues that modernist writing is marked out by its nominalism. As he remarks with regard to the poetics of Gertrude Stein, 'in place of the substantiality of empirical phenomena, this writing poses the substantiality of language'. In terms which neatly summarise the ethos of an era he describes Stein's writing as 'neither structure nor system, equal to nothing but itself'. [19] McGann is supported in this interpretation of modernism by Robert Chodat in his enlightening account of nominalism in post-war philosophy and critical theory. Chodat builds on an understanding of modernism's 'nominalist disposition', citing the modernist critique of abstraction.[20] Pound's name is, unsurprisingly, associated with this disposition. While McGann and Chodat are undoubtedly correct in outlining the nominalist tendencies of certain modernist figures, and a general tendency in modernism towards the particular, there are grounds for exercising some caution in describing modernism as nominalistic as a whole. The grounds on which this claim is made is an interpretation of the Poundian 'fear of abstractions'. While Platonic realism naturally exposes itself to the 'abstract' label, it is harder to say this of moderate realism in the Aristotelian vein. There is a separation between an 'abstract' and a 'universal', and one way to think about this is in terms of what Hegel terms the 'concrete universal'. Hegel distinguishes between abstract and concrete universals in the following way: an 'abstract' universal is a property, such as redness, conceptually separated from a particular; a 'concrete' universal is an instantiation of a kind of being, such as a rose. It is universal by virtue of its being an instance of what it is: it is a *red* rose, a differentiated, instantiated type, and is therefore both individual and universal by virtue of the dynamic relationship of the two. As Robert Stern notes in his excellent account of the concrete universal, the abstract universal is opposed to the particular, whereas the concrete universal is not: it depends upon it.[21] Stern's argument is, in part, that the British Idealists adapted (and slightly deformed) this concept as an explanation for the foundational structure of reality. Interestingly, we find a reference to this concept in Pound's Canto VIII:

> And with him Gemisthus Plethon
> Talking of war about the temple at Delphos,
> And of POSEIDON, *concret Allgemeine*

> (VIII.31)

According to Carroll Terrell, Pound derived the line from Fritz Schultze's *Georgios Gemistos Plethon und seine reformatorischen Bestrebungen*, (1874), which argued that Plethon, a Neoplatonist philosopher, was within the realist tradition.[22] Compare this with Pound's approval of Thomas Aquinas's 'nomina sunt consequential rerum' or his definition of 'god' in *Pavannes & Divigations* as an 'eternal state of mind', and his claim that it is 'better to perceive a god by form, or by the sense of knowledge, and, after perceiving him thus, to consider his name or to "think what god it may be"'.[23] The 'concrete universal' is thus a state of mind taking form. This may not be an abstract realist position in the Platonic tradition, but it is equally not nominalist. In terms of modernist figures, Charlotte Baumann has recently argued that the Hegelian concept of the 'concrete universal' was of vital importance to Theodor Adorno.[24] Pound was thus not alone in finding this concept interesting.

In terms of Pound's acquaintances alone, one could look to Stephen Daedalus's treatment of Aquinas in Joyce's *Portrait of the Artist as a Young Man*. Stephen explains the notion of the 'esthetic image' and its relation to Aquinas's concepts of *integritas* and *claritas*, and this leads him to a discussion of *quidditas* which unifies the literary and the philosophical:

> I thought he might mean that *claritas* is the artistic discovery and representation of the divine purpose in anything or a force of generalisation which would make the esthetic image a universal one, make it outshine its proper conditions. But that is literary talk. I understand it so. When you have apprehended that basket as one thing and have then analysed it according to its form and apprehended it as a thing you make the only synthesis which is logically and esthetically permissible. You see that it is the thing that it is and no other thing. The radiance of which he speaks is the scholastic *quidditas*, the *whatness* of the thing.[25]

In the context of *quidditas* (and not *haecceitas*), 'the thing that it is' should be understood in terms of the 'kind of thing that it is', that is the apprehension of a basket as basket, an apprehension of the nature of the particular existing in space. When Joyce justified his always writing about Dublin to Arthur Power, a notion of the subsistence of *quidditas* similarly appears: 'because if I can get to the heart of Dublin I can get to the heart of all the cities of the world. In the particular is contained the universal'.[26] Part of Joyce's aesthetic, then, revolves around the revelation of universals in particulars, a notion which has more in common with a speculative kind of moderate realism than it does strict nominalism. Evan Cory Horowitz argues that Joyce's aesthetic in *Ulysses* revolves around a 'particular/universal *alchemy*' (emphasis in text), indicative of high modernism as a whole.[27] Where human language and human conceptual frameworks come in is in the drawing out of these universals: if universals do not exist solely in words, words are nevertheless necessary to circumscribe them, and to bind them to particulars in discourse.

Another modernist who sought to reveal the universal in the urban particular was William Carlos Williams, whose *Paterson* not only was influenced by the high modernist monoliths of *The Waste Land*, *Ulysses*, and the *Cantos*, but revolves around similar themes as well. Much like Joyce, Williams maintains that 'THE LOCAL IS THE ONLY UNIVERSAL: In proportion as a man has bestirred himself to his own locality he will perceive more and more of what is disclosed and find himself in a position to make the necessary translations'.[28] As verse experiment, *Paterson* is perhaps more radical than anything produced by Eliot or Pound by virtue of the concept of the work as a whole: in many ways, it is more akin to the metamorphic quality of *Finnegans Wake*. The poem revolves around four particular embodiments of the name 'Paterson': the city it-self (Paterson, New Jersey), the river after which the city is named, a per-sonification of the city in the form of a giant, and a man. Each particular blends into the name, instantiating it as what Williams calls 'facts'. It is in *Paterson* that Williams asserts that there should be 'no ideas but in things!', a phrase which could stand with Pound's 'make it new' as the conceptual slogan of the modernist manifesto. The philosophical aim of the poem is outlined in Williams's verse preface:

> To make a start,
> out of particulars
> and make them general, rolling
> up the sum, by defective means[29]

On the surface, this appears to be an outline of one of the two positions: either an Aristotelian approach which casts universals as real so long as they are instantiated, as an abstraction derived from the particular, or it can be seen as a nominalist 'making' of generalities by virtue of language. The linguistic element of the poem is consistently stressed by Williams. In the poem, however, language is conceived as an inadequate medium for the representation of events which 'forever surpass' the ca-pacity of linguistic systems which attempt to represent them. For the people of the poem (and the people of the actual city of Paterson; the people of modernity), the problem is that 'language/ is divorced from their minds' and it is for this reason that it 'fails them'.[30] In many ways, Williams attempts to compensate for language's failure to register events with more than a 'vague accuracy' by making this difficulty explicit. For Brian A. Bremen, this represents what he sees as Williams's attempt to negotiate his poem through the 'failure of language' as 'the frozen language of the prose history that the beauty of "things" will "forever surpass", the divorce of feeling from fact, and the silence caused by the failure of language, all combine here to thwart the attempt at commu-nion or cathexis'.[31] Williams's response is to formulate a language of violent breakage, associated most often with the power of the Paterson river which is always 'rolling in, top up/ under, thrust and recoil, [with] a great clatter'.[32] As Bremen explains, the explosive and destructive po-tential of the river – and by extension the natural world as a whole – is a necessary response to linguistic failure, as 'freeing the language, freeing the beauty – the poetry that lies hidden in the prose – always takes place through violence in Williams'.[33] In *Paterson*, the poet's struggle against language takes place within language itself, but this violence is always bound, conceptually at least, with regard to the physical. While a sur-face reading of Williams's dictum 'no ideas but in things' may seem to advocate a notion of 'no universals but in particulars', there is a further divorce between language and concepts that undermines this notion. What Williams's violent aesthetic tries to do is to force language and local world back together in order to disclose universal truths to man. It is only through locality, through an intense engagement with the objects of the world around him, that universals appear. This is, once again, a question of *quidditas*.

The revival of the problem of universals was not a curious quirk of literary modernism, however. In 1911, Bertrand Russell outlined his position on this age-old philosophical conflict in his 'On the Relations of Universals and Particulars'. Drawing on the work of Frege and Meinong before him, Russell's argument is a modern renewal of an old question. Russell grants, first, the existence of various particulars in space and time; second, he argues that universals also exist in space and time (a realist proposition in the Aristotelian vein) in the form of shared properties, such as colour, and relations, such as *to the right of*. What marks Russell's argument out is his solution to the problem of how to differentiate universals and particulars. If we grant that particulars, such as chairs, exist materially, and universals, such as *redness,* also exist materially, then how can we say that two red chairs differ from one another? They share both particularity and universal qualities. Russell's answer relies on the nature of the object's existence. The two red chairs occupy different positions in space and time: it is thus space and time that qualify their differences. The property *redness,* however, transcends space and time. The particular is that which is differentiated in space and time; the universal is that which is shared across it. To extend this discussion to language, the proposition 'is red' would denote a universal, where the nominal phrase 'the chair' would denote a particular, thus 'the chair is red' refers to an instantiation of a universal.[34]

Another figure who was concerned about the problem of universals, particularly in the face of what he saw as an increasing propensity towards nominalism, was the pragmatist philosopher Charles Sanders Peirce. Peirce held that nominalism was a threat to the advances of science as it undermined the grounds of scientific reason. As Paul Forster writes, 'Peirce's general complaint against nominalism is that it limits the scope and authority of reason and thereby yields far too much to scepticism in science, ethics and religion'.[35] Peirce associated nominalism with psychologism, phenomenalism, and materialism. Although Pound maintained sceptical approaches to a wide variety of philosophies, his concern for the authority of 'right reason' was one of the features that attracted him to the thought of Anselm and Scotus Eriugena. In *Guide to Kulchur,* Pound implies that it is precisely a lack of values that prevents him from accepting materialism (*GK,* 189). Yet it was not Peirce but another philosopher in the pragmatist tradition against whom Pound would come to measure his philosophical ideas: George Santayana. In the following, I will, first, outline Pound's engagement with Santayana, the reasons for their correspondence, and, then, demonstrate the ways in which Santayana remained a measuring stick for the *Cantos'* philosophical position. I will then tie this to Pound's theory of language.

Approaching Santayana

Pound first appears in Santayana's correspondence in a letter sent to his assistant Daniel Cory on Christmas Day, 1933, referring to lectures given by T.S. Eliot at Johns Hopkins University earlier in the year. The letter in many ways reveals Santayana's scepticism about modernist poetry in general, as well as his reservations about Eliot and Pound:

> What you say about Eliot's lectures is exactly what I felt. He wasn't inspired. He didn't make the subject personal enough. If he had explained why Ezra Pound is 'magnificent', and why he himself would prefer an illiterate public for his poetry, it might have been enlightening: and he would have had plenty of occasions to show how this newly discovered essence of living poetry, which had been running underground from Guido Cavalcanti to Ezra Pound was suppressed or possibly occasionally burst out unintentionally even in the interval. But Eliot is entangled in his own coils.[36]

The personal aversion to modernist poetry, or at least to the kind of aesthetic and historical arguments that modernist poets made, was the result not of Santayana wholly dismissing literary practice, but rather from his engagement with it. In a letter to Robert Shaw Barlow, on 3 November 1936, Santayana explained his regret over an uncomplimentary review of William Faulkner's *Sanctuary* and suggested that his aspersions would be more appropriately cast on 'someone like Ezra Pound'.[37] Prior to their first letters, then, Pound was not a figure whom Santayana held in great esteem, even if he did recognise the weight and gravity attached to his name.

Pound had first met Cory, and presumably sought to initiate contact with Santayana through him. Pound and Santayana seem to have held each other in high personal esteem. The cordiality of their personal relationship was established in Pound visiting Santayana unannounced in Rome in January 1939. Santayana's previously antithetical stance softened and he describes Pound in detail in his letters to Cory, although he makes it clear that they did not discuss philosophy:

> He is taller, younger, better-looking than I expected. Reminded me of several old friends (young, when I knew them) who were spasmodic rebels, but decent by tradition, emulators of Thoreau, full of scraps of culture but lost, lost, lost in the intellectual world. He talked rather little (my fault, and that of my deaf ear, that makes

me not like listening when I am not sure what has been said), and he made my breaks, such as he indulges in in print. Was he afraid of me? How odd! Such a dare-devil as he poses as! I had just been reading his article in the *Criterion*, so that I felt no chasm between us – 'us' being my sensation of myself and my idea of him.[38]

The letter is fascinating for its revelation of the breadth and longevity of Santayana's career, spanning from late nineteenth-century New England and the inheritors of the transcendentalists to the aftermath of war torn Europe in the 1950s, when Pound was working on *Rock Drill*. That Pound would remind Santayana of people once 'full of scraps of culture but lost, lost, lost in the intellectual world' is telling, and is consistent with his assessment of Pound's philosophy in correspondence. Pound's clearly deferential tone is itself remarkable during a period in which Pound's epistolary style becomes more and more fraught with authoritarian language.

Pound's interest in a correspondence with Santayana becomes clearer late in 1939. Santayana had written to Pound on 30 November from Venice, explaining that he was considering visiting him in Rapallo, and informing him that he had finished his 'opus maximum', *The Realm of Spirit*. Pound's reply was relatively self-effacing, jocular, and enthusiastic, clearly delighted at having been contacted by Santayana, and in it he reveals the reasons for his interest in the first place:

> You have obligingly finished the *opus* at the earliest date I cd. read it. I have also got to the end of a job or part of a job (money in history) and for personal ends have got to tackle philosophy or my 'paradise,' and do badly want to talk with some one who has thought a little about it. There is one bloke in England, whose name escapes me, who has dropped an intelligent aside in a small book on Manes. Otherwise you are the only perceivable victim.[39]

Pound's identification of 'paradise' with 'philosophy' is interesting, as it suggests that Pound conceives providing the *Cantos* with a unifying absolute; that the paradise of the poem will not be a narrative device but rather a totalising and unifying schema. Unlike his interest in Fenollosa, Lévy-Bruhl, Frobenius, and Ogden, Pound's background in a philological discipline was not enough for him to respond to the work and he clearly felt that he needed external guidance in the subject. In turning to Santayana, Pound does not rely on idiosyncrasy, but is rather seeking the sort of pedagogical guidance of the kind which he gave to Louis Zukofsky, Basil Bunting, and James Laughlin.

Pound sent Santayana copies of *The Chinese Written Character as a Medium for Poetry* and his translation of *Ta Hio, the Great Learning of Confucius*, which he had published in 1939. Santayana replied on 15

January 1939, explaining that he read both but had a number of reservations. Fenollosa, he wrote, gave him 'his first glimpse of what Chinese hieroglyphics are and how they are composed', although he wished that there had been 'more about them and less about romantic metaphysics'. He accepted Fenollosa's theory that the characters are stylised pictures of natural processes, although he also added that convention must play an important role in establishing exactly what form the images should take in order to be communicated to others. He admitted that he did not share Pound's faith in the fundamental vitality of the ideogram in relation to the importance of 'putting ideas into action' (*GK*, 188):

> If action is all...ideograms would be a most unfortunate medium of expression, since they are static. Spoken words would do better, and inflected and elaborately corresponding words, as in Latin, would do best of all. Substances and pictures are there but terminal points in a mesh of developing relations – just what romanticism loves.[40]

Pound was undeterred by Santayana's doubts, and responded at length. There are three particularly interesting remarks that Pound makes in his response of 16 January 1940. First, he explains what he perceives to be the development of the Chinese written character: 'one ideogrammic current is from picture often of process, then it is tied to, associated with one of a dozen meanings by convention'. Using terminology gleaned from his readings in Lévy-Bruhl and Frobenius, he suggests that it is part of a 'whole process of primitive association, but quite arbitrary, as: two men, city, night= theft'. These arbitrary, conventional elements that Pound reads into the Chinese character are an important moment in the development of his linguistic theory, as is his admission that it was 'not the picturesque element [he] was trying to emphasise so much as the pt. re. western man "defining" by receding'. He also states that he is 'not sure the lexicographers back [Fenollosa] up', the first admission of doubt in Fenollosa's project which I have been able to find. Whether Pound's faith in Fenollosa had not been as total as he implied in the first place, whether it had waned over the two decades since he published *The Chinese Written Character as a Medium for Poetry*, or whether his faith was shaken in the face of Santayana's doubts is unclear (*SL*, 430).

Pound asks Santayana whether he had indicated to him his 'letch toward *teXne*' which he claims to conceive as a 'kindred tendency'. Pound defines his interpretation of 'techne' as moving 'from the *thing* to the grouped things, thence to a more real knowledge'. It is significant that Pound indicates this interest in the Aristotelian notion of *techne* (or a practical, useful form of knowledge, such as the making of items, that Pound associates with art and creation) in a passage discussing language. Language was Pound's medium, and his aesthetic theory is undoubtedly based in his understanding of his art. Pound seems to have believed around this time that *techne* might provide the structural, philosophical unity for his project. Santayana does not appear to have commented on *techne* in detail, but his commitment to a pragmatic, language-in-use, approach which ties art to the materiality of existence at least means that Pound was correct in identifying an affinity.

There are reasons to believe that Pound's choice of Santayana as sounding board was not solely due to his humility and literary background. There are numerous philosophical affinities between the two which served to make Santayana more receptive of Pound's questions than others may have been and which make him a useful philosophical counterpart to Pound's work today. Pound's identification of a 'kindred tendency' was not misplaced, even if he failed to fully explain what that tendency was. Santayana's philosophy is multifaceted, complex, and, in many senses of the word, unsystematic. His philosophy is pragmatic in the sense that it accepts many of the arguments of idealist epistemologies while rejecting their value in practical life. There is a literariness to his style which proceeds as much by an investigation of the nature of poetic life as it does by an understanding of our perception and thought. Indeed, Santayana stresses the importance of the literary for the understanding of human existence in *Scepticism and Animal Faith* (1923) by stressing the ways in which literary discourse forms myths out of a 'natural setting':

> This natural setting restores literary psychology to its normal status: it is no longer a chimerical metaphysics, but an imaginative version, like a historical novel, of the animation that nature, in some particular regions, may actually have possessed. The fineness and complexity of mental discourse within us may well be greater than we can easily remember or describe; and there is a piety as well as ingenuity in rescuing some part of it from oblivion. But here, as elsewhere, myth is at work. We make a romance of our incoherence, and compose new unities in the effort to disentangle those we are accustomed to, and find their elements.[41]

Although his philosophy is built upon a materialism which rejects God as a metaphysical construct, Santayana insists upon the lasting value of spirituality and religiosity, both of which spring from the same myth-making tendencies (and necessities) as poetry. Broadly speaking, he was a materialist and a naturalist: his work is largely concerned with the philosophical implications of studying lived reality, and of seeing thought as an outgrowth of man's interaction with the physical, or, as he terms it, 'animal' world.[42] For Santayana, all human knowledge is grounded in the dynamic interaction between the human Psyche (which, in Santayana's terminology, refers to the complex of relations that make up our physical being) and the environment. Santayana's difference from phenomenology, which operates on similar terms and with which his work has much in common, lies in his scepticism towards the primacy of the structures of consciousness, which he sees as a secondary extension of the material world. His thought is sensory, in that it revolves around tactile interaction with the world and seeks to understand the nature of 'common sense', not as an idealisation of rationality but rather as the foundational similarity between humanity and the 'animal' world from which, Santayana argues, we always come and to which we always relate. It is from this starting point that his interest in human consciousness, language, and culture springs.

It is in Santayana's understanding of language and the arts of language, poetry, and prose, that we can see the greatest affinity with Pound, and it is here that we can begin to answer the question posed at the outset of this chapter. Santayana adopts a rational approach to language, distancing himself from treatments of language which either see it as a mythical medium or as the cornerstone philosophical systems revolving solely around the operations of linguistic logic. However, although Santayana clearly stresses the importance of maintaining a separation between language and the world ('the vocal and musical medium is, and must always remain, alien to the spatial'), he recognises that the unification between words' relations and objects' qualities that occurs in the use of language establishes 'a conflict which the whole history of language and thought has exemplified and which continues to this day'.[43] In terms of his definition of language, Santayana conceives of it in terms strikingly reminiscent of Pound's in 'I Gather the Limbs of Osiris' or in *How to Read*:

> Language is an artificial means of establishing unanimity and transferring thought from one mind to another. Every symbol or phrase, like every gesture, throws the observer into an attitude to which a certain idea corresponded in the speaker; to fall exactly into the speaker's attitude is to understand. Every impediment to contagion and imitation in expression is an impediment to comprehension.
>
> (41)

This understanding offers a way to conceive of language as wholly arbitrary and yet subject to the necessity of artistic control. Precisely because language is artificial, it must be controlled, and constantly measured against our encounters with reality, which it, in turn, mediates. In and of itself, language is simply a 'medium of intellectual exchange', that it 'like money' functions as a 'common denominator'. This means that language must develop a stable, regulatory system of value intrinsic to itself, as it must be stable in order to hold together the relations around it. A word, Santayana writes, 'by which a thing is represented in discourse, must be a part of that thing's contact with mankind'. In other words, language is the means by which humans structure the world and their relation to flux, and it is precisely because language qua language is theoretically divorced from the spatial, precisely because its sounds have only a conventional relationship to the objects it represents, that we can use it as a malleable medium to frame our relation to the world. 'Words', Santayana writes in a passage which nicely summarises his position, 'in their existence, are a material accompaniment of phenomena, at first an idle accompaniment, but one which happens to subserve easily a universal function' (327). Language is, then, an adhesive instrument, a medium which is used to bind thought and feeling, animal and world, and human to human; Santayana sees language in terms of a positive force, stressing its role in unifying ideas and action.

It is here that the analysis in the *Life of Reason* helps situate a response to the problem of universals. Santayana defines words as 'a material accompaniment of phenomena', a definition which captures the poetic immediacy he believes underlies language. As words are material substitutes which nevertheless operate according to their own system, 'they can be identified in turn with many particulars and yet remain throughout particular themselves' (328). From here, Santayana seems to move towards a nominalist position, noting that 'the psychology of nominalism is undoubtedly right where it insists that every image is a particular and every term, in its existential aspect, a *flatum vocis*' (328).[44] To translate this into Saussurian terminology, Santayana's suggestion is that nominalism, in recognising that signifiers stand in wholly arbitrary relations to their signifieds, arrives at a correct understanding of the relation between language and reality. This statement must be tempered, however, by Santayana's general treatment of language. He does not assign it the same foundational and constitutional role that nominalism does: on the contrary, Santayana sees language as secondary to the dynamic interaction between human and environment. Furthermore, he criticises nominalists for failing to recognise that 'images may have any degree of vagueness and generality when measured by a conceptual standard' (328), suggesting that the standard of measurement must remain grounded in external reality. While Santayana grants that nominalism provides a strong psychological account of language qua language, this is not to suggest that it provides an adequate account of its relationship to reality.

In fact, Santayana's naturalistic philosophy offers a way to accept the anti-metaphysical aspects of nominalism while undermining its assumptions about reality as a whole. According to Santayana, the philosophical tradition since Aristotle has relied on an assumption that we encounter objects as particulars and then abstract certain universal qualities from them. Colour, shape, line, and texture are all, according to this theory, abstractions derived from bounded, particular entities. Were they not abstracted from the concrete entity to which they belonged, these qualities could not exist in reality. This leads us to the supposition, common to moderate forms of both realism and nominalism, that only the particular exists in nature and the general exists solely in the mind. Santayana grants that this is correct in supposing the secondary nature of conception, but that it has misunderstood what it is that we encounter when we come up against objects in the world. He argues that so-called 'sense data' such as colour or line are not ideal abstractions derived from an object, but are, in fact, the real, physical properties that we experience; it is the object itself that is derived from this experienced data. To discover an object is rather to 'pack in the same part of space, and fuse in one complex body, primary data like coloured form and tangible surface', meaning that the sensible qualities of an object are not abstractions from it, but rather 'its original and component elements' (45). It is here that we can see the influence of pragmatism, as the object is conceived as a complex of real relations and the significance of said object is a composite of human relations and associations. As Santayana writes, 'the object is a concretion of my perceptions in space, so that the redness, hardness, sweetness, and roundness of the apple are all fused together in my practical regard and given one local habitation and one name' (46). The sensations, or perceptions of the qualities of objects, then recur, and each further encounter with them becomes a recurrence of a familial and general appearance. This generic encounter is the universal which Santayana claims was 'falsely supposed to be an abstraction from physical objects' (46).

We can see Santayana's affinities with Pound and many of the thinkers associated with him. In the first case, with Pound himself, Santayana derives his literary philosophy from conscious encounters with the world, from the dynamic interrelations and interactions between subjects and objects in the real world, and a preference for the particular over the general as a basis for discussion. Similarly, he shares with Pound an interest in the surface of material relations that constitute experience. Above all, both he and Pound see in a deeper understanding of poetry and the poetic use of language a restitutive project with which to dispel the fundamental assumptions of longstanding metaphysical traditions. In these matters, Santayana has numerous similarities to Fenollosa, in terms of his scepticism towards abstraction, his grounding in the interactions of the human and the environmental, and his philosophical treatment of poetic consciousness, even if he did not recognise these himself. We can draw a similarity to Frobenius on the basis of his understanding of language as incidental to a creative, primordial consciousness, though this would, of course, be very heavily tempered by Santayana's resistance to schematic treatments of human phenomena.

Santayana is useful for reading Pound (rather than vice versa) from a linguistic point of view. Santayana held deep reservations about Pound's philosophic and aesthetic theories, and in outlining those reservations he came across what would be a central problem for Pound's vision of 'paradise' in the later cantos: the establishment of general, universal values upon which Pound's particulars come to rest.

> When is a thing not static? When it jumps or it makes you jump? Evidently the latter, in the case of Chinese ideograms, you bring your thoughts.
>   And these jumps are to particulars, not regressive to general terms. Classifications are not poetry, I grant that, but I think that classifications may be important practically: e.g. poisons; how much? what number?
>   There is another kind of regression towards materials causes, genealogies. Pudding may not suggest pie, but plums, cook, fire. These are generalities that classify not data but conditions for producing the data.
>   When you ask for jumps to other particulars, you don't mean (I suppose) *any* other particulars. Although your tendency to jump is so irresistible that the bond between the particulars jumped to is not always apparent. It is a neutral grab-bag. A *latent* classification or a *latent* generic connection would seem to be required if utter miscellaneousness is to be avoided.[45]

Santayana was not able to read Chinese characters, and thus his interpretation of them is based on assumption (itself based upon a pre-existing aesthetic disposition), even more so than Pound. However, in responding to Pound's tentative attempts to outline a general philosophy, he raises concerns that are at the centre of the second half of Pound's epic. By 'jump', Santayana is referring to the practical effect of Pound's 'ideogrammic method' on the reader, whereby the actual connection between references is left unarticulated. In Santayana's case, as a first-time reader of the *Cantos*, he does not appear to have had the benefit of access to Pound's critical writing on 'luminous details' written over two decades earlier. The notion of a 'luminous detail' standing as a synecdoche of entire discourses, poetic dispositions, or even cultural events and epochs is useful in providing an exegetic methodology for critics and long-standing readers, but evidently Pound's method is not obvious to Santayana. Similarly, Pound explains in *ABC of Reading* that what he interprets as a Western tradition of 'definition by regression' is the precise opposite of the creative potential that he reads into the Chinese written character. For Pound, this 'regression' does not result in the analysis of the various components making up an object, as Santayana's example of the pudding does, but instead leads to further and further abstraction. His anecdote about Agassiz and the fish, also in *ABC of Reading*, suggests that such 'regressive' generalising results not in further understanding of an object, but in its loss of vitality. Yet, Santayana suggests, Pound's critical thinking has not led him to a general outlook which ties his poem together. As he writes, 'the bond between the particulars jumped to is not always apparent', and although this may be interpreted as a criticism of Pound's lack of clarity, Santayana's desire for Pound to outline a '*latent* genetic connection' would suggest that he believes there to be a lack of an underlying centrality or foundation to Pound's poetic vision. Santayana's assumption is, however, that Pound approached him in order to explain or clarify his vision, rather than to help him form it.

Santayana in Pound's Work

Pound's conversations with Santayana clearly left an impression on him, particularly Santayana's doubts as to his philosophy. This is shown by references to the philosopher in his poetry and prose. In Maria Luiza Ardizzone's remarkable collection of Pound's wartime Italian writing, *Machine Art* (1996), there is a short series of notes entitled 'Pragmatic Aesthetics of E.P.', in which Pound seeks to lay down the fundamentals of his aesthetic theories. As they are in note form, it is difficult to assess them in their totality, but what is interesting are his sources. These, he indicates in a note at the top of the first page, are 'writings by the poet, letters to G.S. [George Santayana], conversations with G.S.', though he makes no note of having used any of Santayana's work. Nevertheless, using the adjective 'pragmatic' is significant when considering Santayana's presence, and Pound delineates his use of the term:

> E.P. Pragmatic Aesthetics
>   which FUNCTIONS
>
> I To nurture the discrimination, the judgement, to predict the contemporary works that will outrun time, like race-horses.
> II And to stimulate the artists' production and improve the works to be done.[46]

The word 'functions' has two significant meanings in this context. Ardizzone believes that Pound implies that his aesthetics is functional, in that it is linked to the act of making, rather than a kind of abstract knowing. It is grounded in *techne*, in technical principles borne out in technical prowess. In a linguistic sense, Pound's aesthetics would thus be pragmatic in that he is interested in the conditions and contexts of language use, not simply its purely semantic value.

There is a second sense in which Pound may be using the word 'functions', which may relate to Santayana more specifically. Just as Pound ameliorated the word 'orthological' from Ogden and used it in the late 1930s in his series of essays 'l'economica ortologica' ['orthological economics'], he may be ameliorating the word 'pragmatic' from Santayana and using for his own ends. In this sense, Pound gains the kernel of a concept from his correspondence with Santayana, in lieu of the totalising philosophy that he had hoped to find. Towards the end of the notes, Pound outlines the compensation that literature can provide in the absence of a philosophical system: 'philosophy, philosophical expression [is] nothing but a vague fluid approximation; art achieves a MORE PRECISE manifestation'.[47] The problem with this note – and it is important to judge it as a note, rather than as a fully developed thought – is that it is not clear what it is that art precisely manifests. What is clear, however, is that the 'whatness', the quiddity, is what is missing, not the method of verbal manifestation.

It is my belief that although Santayana's philosophy does not play a major role in the *Cantos*, his dialogue with Pound was crucial in exposing and drawing out the tension between Pound's poetic method and his overall intention for his long poem. Indeed, Pound's anxiety to turn his 'disposition' into a philosophy provides the thrust of the final sections of the poem, *Section Rock-Drill de los Cantares*, *Thrones de los Cantares*, and *Drafts & Fragments*. It is difficult to argue that Pound's poem coheres as a whole. In these final sections, we see the poet wavering between gesturing towards completion, often predicated on Confucian articles of faith, and falling back into methodology. As the *Cantos* remain incomplete, criticism has tended to focus on Pound's methodology, looking particularly at the ways in which the language of the *Cantos* resists completion. This is the interpretation that Perloff, for example, values in her argument for Pound's nominalism. Watts makes a similar movement in his reading of Pound, arguing that it is as 'nominalist' that we must judge Pound, although his judgement then differs. Judging Pound as a nominalist is problematic as it is not clear he was one. Pound's argument, such as there is one in the *Cantos*, is one that tends in a realist direction. Nominalist readings of the poem put the unity of the poem down to a connection between language and reality which the thrust of the poem itself actually seems to resist. Completion and wholeness were intentions of the poem's author, however. It is clear from his discussions with Santayana that Pound sought after a philosophy which would tie the *Cantos* together, and, in the following, I will argue that the poem comes to rest on a realist disposition, that although Pound is keen to dispel the 'word magic' (to use Ogden's terminology) of abstraction, this is in the service of discovering the 'concrete universal' that will tie his poetry together.

Santayana's spectre haunts the last sections of the *Cantos*. He remained an important personage in Pound's understanding of philosophy, if not necessarily a philosophical model himself, and he appears in *The Pisan Cantos* as part of Pound's remembrance of his various correspondences and conversations. Santayana is established, for example,

as a touchstone of modern thought in Canto LXXIV, where Pound recounts an anecdote he told of Henry Adams:

> Said Mr Adams, of the education,
> > Teach? at Harvard?
> > Teach? It cannot be done.
> and this I had from the monument
>
> > > > > > > > > > (LXXIV.453)

Or in the following account of the man himself in Canto LXXXI:

> George Santayana arriving in the port of Boston
> and kept to the end of his life that faint *thethear*
> of the Spaniard
> > > as a grace quasi imperceptible
> as did Muss the *v* for *u* of Romagna
> and said grief was a full act
> > > > repeated for each new condoleress
> working up to a climax
>
> > > > > > > > > > (LXXXI.539)

That Pound chooses not to refer to aspects of Santayana's philosophy
would suggest that he failed to find any agreement strong enough to
form a coherent response to it, as the notation form of his 'Pragmatic
Aesthetics' demonstrates. Santayana, in turn, remembered Pound fondly
from a personal perspective and was pleased when Pound remembered
him after his internment in St Elizabeth's, as he informed Robert Lowell
in a long letter dated 29–30 December 1949.

> I have been reading Ezra Pound's 'Pisan Cantos' and have received a
> letter of his (which I didn't expect) with a Chinese character in the
> middle of the page, and below, in 'traditional' English the maxim:
> 'Respect the intelligence of a cherry that can make cherries.' I am
> touched by his remembering me, as I have not answered one or two
> earlier letters that were wholly unintelligible. But it is a pity that he
> prints so many mistakes in his foreign languages, even in the Greek
> alphabet. I thought some passages in these 'Cantos' very good; but
> why so much trash?[48]

Pound's line 'respect the intelligence of a cherry that can make cherries'
refers not to haecceity but to quiddity, to the essence of the thing: that
universal of which it is an instantiation. Pound's origin for this is the
Ta Hio of Confucius, though he later expanded it into a philosophical
principle unifying his support for a polytheistic understanding of the
universe, his *Ching Ming* convictions, and his interest in Neoplatonic

light philosophy. The following passage from Pound's Canto XCV is a summary of Pound's and Santayana's thoughts on this matter:

> 'O world!'
>   said Mr Beddoes.
> 'Something *there*.'
>   sd/ Santayana.
>
>   (XCV.666)

Noel Stock traces this quotation to Pound's overinterpretation of Santayana's polite responses to his philosophical speculations (such as 'respect the intelligence of the cherry stone').[49] While it is true that Pound tends to misinterpret polite remarks as endorsements of his own project (see his insistence on Mussolini as a reader of the *Cantos* in Canto XLI, p. 202), we should remember that these misinterpretations are valuable in that they reveal Pound's own position. This is shown by Pound's 'response' to this remark in the lines that follow:

> Responsus:
>   Not stasis/
>   at least not in our immediate vicinage
>
>   (XCV.666)

If Santayana's 'there' is used (by Pound at least) to refer to the natural world, and, in Pound's terms, it indicates respect for a kind of divine intelligence, then we may see this as evidence that the *Cantos* in their final stages grasp after universal understanding. The linguistic problem is how to bound this intractable universal through in language; a nominalist framework does not bring us nearer to finding a solution. This passage also reveals that Santayana remains the ideal counterpart to Pound's philosophical speculations, meaning that although theirs was not a philosophical meeting of minds as such, the philosopher remained the yardstick against which Pound measured his speculations. The issue here is that Pound's use of Santayana is not, as Stock believes, a strong affirmation, but rather that it is weak. Pound offers little more than a gesture in his quotation of Santayana and his reply is equally vague.

Responsus: Signatures in Nature

This notion of divine intelligence as underpinning the whole of the *Cantos* has led to Carroll Terrell's hypothesis that the *Cantos* are 'a great religious poem'.[50] The problem with this reading is not that it is inaccurate, but that it still does not give the poem enough structural unity. Terrell argues that, for Pound, the rites and practices of all religions are 'intracompatible', so long as they grounded in action in the world. What Terrell does not suggest, however, is what it is that makes religious rites intracompatible, and the reason for this is that Pound does not provide an answer. Given Pound's suspicion of philosophical systems, his poetry comes to rest on rite and practice, putting faith in praxis. But Pound's praxis, drawn as it is from a vast array of traditions, cannot affect the synthesis that the poetry requires: herein lies the strength of a nominalist interpretation of Pound's work. According to this, what binds the poem together is a theory of language grounded in a nominalist conception of reality, building a new kind of discursive praxis out of the particular, as this is an accurate reflection of reality. If Pound's *Cantos* do not cohere, it is because reality does not cohere.

It is here that I would like to suggest that a truly nominalist account of the *Cantos* falls down, however. Pound's faith in *Ching Ming*, his desire for 'precise definition', and his preference for '*res* non *verba*' would all suggest a grounding of linguistic practice in the natural, but as we have seen, they primarily concern the directionality of consciousness – they are rooted in states of mind. At crucial moments in the text, the moments where he comes closest to outlining his philosophical position, he seems to turn away from language and towards the natural world, locating the ultimate reality to which his poem intends outside of the text, and outside of the readers' interpretative strategies. In other words, at key moments in the poem, Pound appears to turn away from the discursive, ordering, and structuring patterns of language and evinces faith in the nature of reality. But once again, we must be careful not to reduce Pound's thought to our conception based on the structure of the sign. What Pound does in the *Cantos* is not to offer a linguistic map of reality, but rather uses a specific method of linguistic precision to try to affect our modes of perception and our states of consciousness. Pound's argument for language is not one that seeks to tie all language to the specific concrete particulars to which he refers, but rather one which seeks to bring about a paradigm shift where all language has a heightening of intentionality. The *Cantos* are not a plan for language, but a plan for the use of language.

Because Pound's project is not one which treats language qua language, but rather always language in a particular use or context, his ultimate appeals are outside of the linguistic system: to broader contexts and wider realities. Consider, for example, the following lines in which Pound seems to be advocating a strictly nominalist position:

> 'We have', said Mencius, 'but phenomena.'
> monumenta. In nature are signatures
> needing no verbal tradition,
> oak leaf never plain leaf. John Heydon.

> (LXXXVII.593)

Two lines later, we find another reference to Santayana: 'And old Jarge held there was a tradition,/ that was not mere epistemology'. If we are to assign Pound a role among the nominalists, then there appears to be a contradiction here. If there are only 'phenomena', then surely unity is provided solely by that verbal tradition Pound then immediately denies? And if this is not, as the reference to Santayana suggests, a question of epistemology, then where to locate this 'tradition'? Here Feng Lan's gloss of this passage is useful. Lan argues that Pound adapts James Legge's interpretation of Mencius's thought as positing a distinction between phenomena and noumena, adding to it the notion of 'signatures in nature'. As Lan writes: 'transcending the "verbal tradition" of human language, these signs in the text of nature designate the perfect design of a divine intelligence'.[51] John Heydon, to whom Pound refers in his initial 'Three Cantos', was a seventeenth-century mystic who, attempting to reconcile natural theology with the sciences, claimed to be able to read and interpret the 'signs' of nature. Heydon has, as Tomas Willard remarks, often confused Pound's interpreters, and it is not clear to what extent Pound took him seriously.[52] Nevertheless, even if he functions here solely as a mythic signifier, Lan's reading is supported: Heydon, at least, serves a gestural function. This divine intelligence at work in nature is beyond our 'verbal tradition'; indeed, it renders it superfluous in the face of the divine. On the surface, the line 'oak leaf never plain leaf' seems a nominalist gesture, much like the 'intelligence' in the cherry stone, but is this the case? Once again, we come to a distinction between a universal and an abstraction. A 'plain leaf' is an abstraction, but an oak leaf, like 'a' cherry stone, is concrete universal. While the name 'oak leaf' may have no bearing in nature, it reflects a categorical distinction that we discern in its difference from all other kinds of leaves. This difference, this particularity, is not made on the grounds of its haecceity, however, but on the grounds of its quiddity: its kind. What this line implies is that the universals of nature are grounded in divine intelligence, not abstract syllogism or logical formulae. They are, in other words, beyond 'mere epistemology'; they are grounded in the real.

That the thrust of Pound's philosophical speculations revolves around quiddity rather than haecceity is similarly shown in Canto XCIII, in which he meditates on the interrelation between love, divine light, and paradise. In a curious passage, however, he issues the following outburst against 'philologers' and 'biographers':

> And as for the trigger-happy mind
>> amid stars
>>> amid dangers; abysses
> going six ways a Sunday,
>>> how shall philologers?
> A butcher's block for biographers,
>>> quidity!
>>>> Have they heard of it?

(XCIII.651)

As readers of the *Cantos*, we may find Pound's criticism of those who go 'six ways a Sunday' somewhat ironic, and inevitably the present author may be in danger of following the same mistake, but it is important to grasp Pound's use of quiddity here. In Canto LXXXIX, we find a similar line: 'Quiditas, remarked Dante Alighieri' (620). This line is traditionally linked to Dante's *Paradiso XX* and *XXIV*, as the word appears in both.[53] The clearer definition of the phrase is given in *Paradiso XX* (lines 91–93): 'you do as one who learns the name of a thing, but cannot see its quiddity if another does not set it forth'.[54] This is an explicitly realist doctrine. Dante's separation between the thing known by name and the thing known by quiddity, by acquaintance through an act of faith, presupposes the possibility of acquaintance between things which transcends language. In this passage, we see Pound employing the phrase as a rebuke to philological readings which indulge in minutiae without getting to the point.

Pound's gesture towards quiddity raises serious questions about the success of his project. The movement towards *techne* as the basis for his philosophy could not be sustained: praxis is not a structural unity, and methodology, he clearly discovered, cannot perform the role of philosophy for long. According to Michael Kindellan, in a well-wrought phrase, the quiddity of the *Cantos* is 'the resistance to stable presentation', a notion which he demonstrates well in his account of the genesis of later *Cantos*.[55] This is not, however, the intended quiddity of the *Cantos*, nor is it the kind of quiddity which Pound has in mind. Indeed, the final sections of the *Cantos* display all too overtly a conflict between the power of *techne*, a root in practice, and the need for overarching structural unity. The following passage from Canto XCIX displays much of the intended 'essence' of the *Cantos*:

Han (IX, i. e. nine) believed in the peoples,
Different each, different customs
    but one root in the equities
One in acumen,
       with the sun (chih)
           under it all
     & faith with the word
Hills and streams colour the air,
    vigour, tranquillity, not one set of rules.

(XCIX.719)

Pound tries to unify three things in this passage: Confucian ethics, Neoplatonist light philosophy, and faith in the correct use of language. The line 'Hills and streams colour the air' is a powerful image of natural unity and the final line 'vigour, tranquillity, not one set of rules' is in keeping with Pound's praise for Confucian distinctions. The linguistic dimensions of such a vision, the 'faith with the word', are demonstrated a few pages later:

> This is not a work of fiction
>   nor yet of one man:
> The six kinds of action, filial, reciprocal,
> Sincerity from of old until now,
>   holding together
> Not shallow in verbal usage
>   nor in dissociations
>
>   (XCIX.728)

'The plan is in nature' (XCIX.719), Pound argues. It is incumbent upon a speech community to ensure that their conventions, their languages and laws, are rooted in natural processes, respecting natural differences, distinguishing between phenomena as nature does. It is not 'faith *in* the word' (my emphasis) but *with*, that is to say that one's faith must be watchful over the use of language to ensure it does not slip into abstraction and syllogism. This passage relies on a distinction between faith and language; faith can apprehend the true nature of things directly; language, which was for Pound, as we have seen, bound to thought, can only do so implicitly, and so it must be constrained.

Though Pound may begin with a position close to nominalism, particularly in his insistence on the centrality of *techne*, he moves increasingly towards a realist disposition as the *Cantos* stagger towards their end. In Canto CV, for example, we find a rather extraordinary reference to the ontological argument of Anselm of Canterbury. Anselm is given his exalted position in *Thrones* thanks to his conviction that faith and reason are not opposed, but his famous ontological argument seems to run against the current of Pound's insistence that man's thought be grounded in nature.

>   Anselm 'Monologion' scripsit, 1063
>   'non spatio, sed sapientia'
>   not in space but in knowing
>   non pares, not equal in dignity
>   rerum naturas
>
>   (CV.766–767)

The first reference, 'non spatio, sed sapientia' could refer to the following from the second chapter of the *Monologion*, in which Anselm, having defined greatness as that which is 'great through itself', clarifies his point: 'I do not mean great in terms of size, like some sort of body; but something which, the greater it is, the better or more valuable it is, like wisdom'.[56] Pound's poetic translation ('not in space, but in knowing') is, naturally, livelier and reveals a subtlety to his use of the concept. If we locate the greatness of divine force in 'knowing' rather than in 'space', must we not accept a realist argument at least on some level? Pound's translation shifts the concept from the static abstract 'wisdom' and locates it in the dynamic activity of 'knowing'. The second reference most likely refers to the following passage of the *Monologion*, which solidifies the ontological argument:

> Furthermore, if one considers the natures of things, one cannot help realizing that they are not all of equal value, but differ by degrees. For the nature of a horse is better than that of a tree, and that of a human more excellent than that of a horse, and to doubt it is simply not human. It is undeniable that some natures can be better than others. None the less reason argues that there is some nature that so overtops the others that it is inferior to none.[57]

This nature is, of course, God the Father. The model Anselm provides for Pound is one in which one may reason towards divine knowledge. As he does with Eriugena, Pound includes Anselm as a defender of reason against blind faith, and what Anselm does here is root Pound's speculations in a rationalist tradition.

What *Thrones* ends up affirming, then, is 'Anselm, Erigena,/ the fight thru Herbert and Rémusat' rather than, as Watts suggests in his account of Pound's 'nominalism', Roscelin and Abelard.[58] There is a tension in *Thrones* between Pound's desire to present justice ideogrammically, offering instances, anecdotes, fragments of that 'spezzato' paradise he glimpsed in the Pisan sun, and his need to find a philosophical tradition to structure the poem. The wavering between these two desires results in certain passages (such as the above quoted) seeming to be neither ideogram nor argument, caught halfway between. In the final completed Canto, Canto CXVI, we find this wavering extended into a poetic soliloquy, in which Pound retrospectively seeks 'to affirm the gold thread in the pattern' (CXVI.817):

> to 'see again'
> the verb is 'see,' not 'walk on'
> i.e. it coheres all right
> > even if my notes do not cohere
>
> > > (CXVI.816–817)

According to Michael Alexander, these lines affirm paradise by linking to the concluding lines of Dante's *Paradiso*.[59] This reading is rejected by Jean-Michel Rabaté who argues that such an interpretation leaves open too many 'indeterminacies', and as a structural ending it would be out of keeping with Pound's otherwise 'spezzato', fragmented Paradise

(LXXIV.458). Rabaté is surely correct when he argues that the problem in this passage is the word 'it', which could refer to any number of things, from the poem to language to reality. What Pound means by 'it' here may offer a key to the *Cantos* totality, but it is not forthcoming. This is, ironically, an imprecision of language, but it would be remiss to put all of the blame on Pound's linguistics. 'You can be wholly precise in representing a vagueness', Pound wrote in 'The Serious Artist', and so we cannot rule out that the 'it' to which he refers was even to himself too vague to submit to definition. Rabaté concludes that 'even if "it" speaks, "I" cannot utter it; its coherence is outside, in the realm of the Other, forsaken, foreclosed'.[60] That is to say, the *Cantos* conclude with a radical separation between language and the world, a foreclosure which we cannot know. How else to explain the following lines among Pound's final published notes?

> Do not move
> 　　　Let the wind speak
> 　　　　　that is paradise
>
> (Notes for CXVII et seq.822)

The paradise of which Pound conceives cannot be bound through in language, the best we can do is to gesture towards a divine presence outside of our linguistic system. It is difficult to read this as much other than a disappointment in light of the grand linguistic ambitions with which Pound set out, and it is more difficult still to deny Watts's thesis that Pound's project fails on its own terms. So is Pound's response to Santayana, 'not stasis', not something of a poetic disappointment? Does the poem not end, abruptly, after all that effort in silent attention to the wind? Pound's radical poetics were put into motion in service of a linguistic conviction, a belief in the restorative effects of precise language and precise definition, and yet we end up with silence. As readers we are left at the end of the poem at something of an impasse of language. Describing Pound as a nominalist seems to offer some conceptual unity to the *Cantos*, as we can argue that the proliferation of particulars cannot build up into a generality as this is a reflection of reality. This may be the case for us, depending on how we conceive reality, but such a reading denies the search after unity which characterises the final sequences, and obscures the understanding of reality to which Pound himself seems to have subscribed.

There is, however, a way out of this impasse between language and the world. What if there is no conflict of language in the *Cantos*? Pound's poetics of definition and his insistence on clarity and sincerity are entirely consistent across the long poem. In these final stages, it is not crisis of confidence in language as such nor even in his use of language that results in the despondent tone of the poem. Rather it is derived from what Santayana noticed, and what Pound attempted to rectify: the poem lacks structural and conceptual cohesion. Santayana was troubled by the particulars of the ideogrammic method, confused by the generalities it built up, but Pound's ideogrammic method is not, in and of itself, obscure. The problem is not with the method – this, for example, 'coheres all right' – the problem is with ultimate referent. Individual *Cantos* are contained, meaningful units, and across the poem there is enough dialogue between the sections to maintain insightful interpretations not only for the poem but for human society. There is, also, enough of Pound's fascist sentiment to be submitted to investigation; and we can easily link this politics of order with a control of language and a control of reason. But the truth remains that Pound was, at the end of the poem, still attempting 'to affirm the gold thread in the pattern' (CXVI.817) – a task which has been taken up by his readers.

As Pound's readers, particularly in academia, we are well acquainted with two statements that Wittgenstein makes in his *Tractatus*: first, '*the limits of my language* mean the limits of my world', and second, 'what we cannot speak about we must pass over in silence'.[61] Many of us accept a doctrine of this kind, and so we are left with a choice between hewing close to language and the known – the world of discourse, the world of signs – or a kind of blind faith in the unspeakable – the world of referents. Reading Pound carefully, however, we can see that the *Cantos* serve to take the two statements apart, offering us an alternative. In the final lines of the *Cantos*, Pound adopts a position which allows us to accept the latter, that 'what we cannot speak about we must pass over in silence' while rejecting the former, by insisting that, in letting the wind speak, we can direct our minds beyond linguistic limits. This is not a nominalist position. It is one that subjects language to faith, that grounds language in transcendent realities, and that asserts the poetic in the face of the purely logical. Pound's understanding of language may not give the *Cantos* unity, as Santayana noticed, but it does assert their contribution to twentieth-century letters.

Notes

1 Marjorie Perloff, *The Dance of the Intellect: Studies in the Poetry of the Pound Tradition* (Cambridge: Cambridge University Press, 1985), 78.

2 Michael Coyle, and Roxana Preda, *Ezra Pound and the Career of Modern Criticism: Professional Attention* (Rochester, NY: Camden House, 2018), 53.

3 Coyle and Preda, *Ezra Pound and the Career of Modern Criticism*, 53.

4 See Plato's famous 'allegory of the cave' (*Republic*, 514a–520a) in, for example, Plato, *The Republic*, trans. Robin Waterfield (Oxford: Oxford University Press, 1993), 240–247.

5 Theodore Scaltsas, *Substances and Universals in Aristotle's Metaphysics* (London: Cornell University Press, 1994), 28.
6 Peter Liebregts's outstanding *Ezra Pound and Neoplatonism* (Madison, NJ: Fairleigh Dickinson University Press, 2004) is the authoritative account of Pound's engagement with, and use of this tradition.
7 John Marenbon, *The Philosophy of Peter Abelard* (Cambridge: Cambridge University Press, 1994), 113.
8 Philoteus Boehner, 'The Realistic Conceptualism of William Ockham', *Traditio*, 4 (1946), 307–335.
9 John Duns Scotus, 'Six Questions on Individuation from His *Ordinatio* II. d. 3, part 1, qq 1–6' in *Five Texts on the Mediaeval Problem of Universals: Porphyry, Boethius, Abelard, Duns Scotus, Ockham*, trans. Paul Vincent Spade (Cambridge: Hackett, 1994), 57–113 (110–112).
10 Harold H. Watts, *Ezra Pound and the Cantos* (London: Routledge, 1951), 99. The text was not actually published until 1952 owing to undisclosed publication delays.
11 Watts, *Ezra Pound and the Cantos*, 117.
12 Watts, *Ezra Pound and the Cantos*, 119.
13 Marjorie Perloff, *Differentials: Poetry, Poetics, Pedagogy* (Tuscaloosa: University of Alabama Press, 2004), 44.
14 Perloff, *Differentials*, 59.
15 Paul Vincent Spade, 'Ockham's Nominalist Metaphysics: Some Main Themes' in *The Cambridge Companion to Ockham*, ed. Paul Vincent Spade (Cambridge: Cambridge University Press, 1999), 100–117 (111–112).
16 David Sedley, 'The Stoic Theory of Universals', *The Southern Journal of Philosophy*, XXIII (1985), 87–92 (88).
17 Jean-Michel Rabaté, *Language, Sexuality and Ideology in Ezra Pound's Cantos* (Basingstoke: Macmillan, 1986), 148.
18 Donald Davie, '*Res* and *Verba* in *Rock Drill* and After', in *Ezra Pound's Cantos: A Casebook*, ed. Peter Makin (Oxford: Oxford University Press, 2006), 205–220 (206).
19 See McGann's enlightening discussion of Gertrude Stein's 'non-referential language' in *Stanzas in Meditation* (1933) in *Black Riders*, 21–23.
20 Robert Chodat, *The Matter of High Words: Naturalism, Normativity, and the Postwar Sage* (Oxford: Oxford University Press, 2017), 3. For an excellent account of nominalism's post-war afterlife, see Chodat's Introduction.
21 Robert Stern, 'Hegel, British Idealism, and the Curious Case of the Concrete Universal', *Journal for the History of Philosophy*, 15:1 (2007), 115–153 (129–130).
22 Carroll Terrell, *A Companion to the Cantos of Ezra Pound*, Volume II (Berkeley: University of California Press, 1980), 40.
23 Pound, *Gaudier-Brzeska*, 84; Pound, *Pavannes & Divigations*, 23, 24.
24 See Charlotte Baumann, 'Adorno, Hegel, and the Concrete Universal', *Philosophy and Social Criticism*, 37:1 (2011), 73–94.
25 James Joyce, *The Portrait of the Artist as a Young Man* (London: Penguin, 2000), 230–231.
26 Arhur Power, quoted in Richard Ellmann, *Joyce*, 505.
27 Evan Cory Horowitz, 'Ulysses: Mired in the Universal', *Modernism/Modernity*, 13:1 (2006), 869–887 (870).
28 William Carlos *Selected Essays* (New York: Random House, 1953), 28.
29 William Carlos Williams, *Paterson* (London: Penguin, 1983), 3.
30 Williams, *Paterson*, 12–13.
31 Brian A. Bremen, *William Carlos Williams and the Diagnostics of Culture* (Oxford: Oxford University Press, 1993), 34.

32 Williams, *Paterson*, 5.
33 Bremen, *William Carlos Williams and the Diagnostics of Culture*, 36.
34 Bertrand Russell, *The Problems of Philosophy* (Oxford: Oxford University Press, 1998), 53–55.
35 Paul Forster, *Peirce and the Threat of Nominalism* (Cambridge: Cambridge University Press, 2011), 7.
36 George Santayana, *Letters of George Santayana*, Book 5, 1933–1936, ed. William Holzberger (Cambridge, MA: MIT Press, 2003), 71.
37 George Santayana, *Letters of George Santayana*, Book 5, 401.
38 Santayana, Letters, Volume 5, Book 6, 195.
39 Ezra Pound, Letter to George Santayana, 8 December 1939, YCAL MSS 43, Box 102, Folder 202, Beinecke Rare Book and Manuscript Library, Yale University.
40 Santayana, Letters, Volume 5, Book 6, 316–317.
41 George Santayana, *Scepticism and Animal Faith: Introduction to a System of Philosophy* (New York: Charles Scribner & Sons, 1923), 260–261.
42 Santayana is often described as a 'pragmatist', casting him in a role alongside John Dewey, William James, and Charles Sanders Pierce. The problem with this label is that it relies more on his disciplinary and institutional background in Harvard's Philosophy Department than it does on the nature of his thought. Such a label, though accurate in a disciplinary sense, obscures the independence of Santayana's work and thought.
43 George Santayana, *Life of Reason* (New York: Charles Scribner & Sons, 1953), 326. Subsequent textual references are to this abridged edition.
44 *Flatum vocis* – either 'vocal wind' or 'voice flatulence', depending on the spirit in which it is read – refers to a dismissive phrase used by St Anselm to summarise the position of Roscelin and the other nominalists: 'therefore those contemporary logicians (rather, the heretical logicians) who consider universal essences to be merely vocal emanations [*flatum vocis*], and who can understand colours only as material substances, and human wisdom only as the soul, should be altogether brushed aside from discussion of spiritual questions'. Anselm of Canterbury, 'On the Incarnation of the Word', in *The Major Works*, trans. Richard Regen (Oxford: Oxford University Press, 1998), 233–259 (237). We may assume that Santayana uses the term ironically.
45 George Santayana, Letter to Ezra Pound, 20 January 1940 in *The Letters of George Santayana*, Volume 6 1937–1940, ed. William G. Holzberger (Cambridge, MA: MIT Press, 2004), 318–319.
46 Ezra Pound, 'Pragmatic Aesthetics', *Machine Art*, 155–159 (156).
47 Pound, 'Pragmatic Aesthetics', 159.
48 Santayana, *The Letters of George Santayana, Book 8, 1948–1952*, ed. William G. Holzberger (Cambridge, MA: MIT Press, 2008), 222.
49 Noel Stock, *Poet in Exile: Ezra Pound* (Manchester: Manchester University Press, 1964), 251.
50 Terrell, *A Companion to the Cantos of Ezra Pound*, Volume II, xiii.
51 Feng Lan, *Ezra Pound and Confucianism: Remaking Humanism in the Face of Modernity* (London: University of Toronto, 2005), 74.
52 See Tomas Willard, 'John Heydon's Visions: "Pretty" or "Polluted"?', *Paideuma*, 16:1 (1987), 61–72.
53 Terrell, *A Companion to the Cantos of Ezra Pound*, 532; Stephen Sicari, *Pound's Epic Ambition*, 175.
54 Dante Alighieri, *The Divine Comedy, Volume 3: Paradiso*, ed. and trans. Robert M. Durling (Oxford: Oxford University Press, 2011), 404.

55 See Michael Kindellan, *The Late Cantos of Ezra Pound*, 235.

56 Anselm of Canterbury, 'Monologion', trans. Simon Harrison in *The Major Works*, ed. Brian Davies and G. R. Evans (Oxford and New York: Oxford University Press, 1998), 5–81 (13).

57 Anselm, 'Monologion', 14–15.

58 Abelard is, of course, approvingly mentioned in Canto LXXX (532) and in *Guide to Kulchur* (170) but solely in the context of his having fought for his academic position.

59 Michael Alexander, *The Poetic Achievement of Ezra Pound* (Berkeley: University of California Press, 1979), 195–196.

60 Rabaté, *Language, Sexuality, Ideology in Ezra Pound's Cantos*, 27.

61 Wittgenstein, *Tractatus Logico-Philosophicus*, 56, 74.

Afterword
Pound's Linguistic Legacy

I began this study by exploring the ways in which Pound's faith in the Flaubertian *mot juste* might offer a response to Hugo von Hofmannsthal's *Letter of Lord Chandos*. I wish to return to the problem that Hofmannsthal poses:

> And this for an odd and embarrassing reason which I must leave to the boundless superiority of your mind to place in the realm of physical and spiritual values spread out harmoniously before your unprejudiced eye: to wit, because the language in which I might be able not only to write but to think is neither Latin nor English, neither Italian nor Spanish but a language none of whose words is known to me, a language in which inanimate things speak to me and wherein I may one day have to justify myself before an unknown judge.[1]

In his problematisation of the relationship between language, states of mind, spiritual values, and the world around us, Hofmannsthal offers us a paradigm of language with which we are much more at ease than Pound's faith in a method of 'precise definition'. One reason for this is consistency. We are able to recognise in Hofmannsthal's lyrical prose a framework which, by not being able to speak the truth of reality, speaks to our understanding of language as unstable and indeterminate; in Pound's work, by contrast, we feel at all times a tension between a theory of language use and the results of the language on the page, or at least of our reading of them. In reading Hofmannsthal in 2019, one feels less distance than in reading Pound's writing on the same subject. The literary critic surely feels more professional comfortability in Chandos's admission of despair than in reading Pound's assertions of the 'MORE PRECISE manifestation' of his language. In this age of collapsed metanarratives, Pound's understanding of language feels further away from us than Hofmannsthal's.

It is difficult to see how Pound offers the same ways into thinking about language in light of the numerous advances of structuralist and post-structuralist thought as Hofmannsthal's *Letter of Lord Chandos* or the work of Stephane Mallarmé might. In the case of the latter, his work brings the following eloquent judgement of Frederic Jameson:

> It is by way of the very weaknesses of the verbal when evaluated against their sonorous competition in orchestration that the superiority of Poetry as such can be defended: even a poetry whose modernist possibilities are to be found in a gradual effacement of content as such, a reduction of language's well-known 'double-inscription' (dear to the linguists) to the play of the signifier alone. Yet language's natural lack turns out to be the deeper meaning of the poet's vocation [...][2]

One can, of course, make such judgements of Pound's work but this requires an act of critical separation between artist and artwork that would render such judgements too general, cutting them off from the particularities of the work itself. Jameson can ground his reading in Mallarmé, but Pound's understanding of language resists the idea of the 'play of the signifier alone', as his language is always intended towards something, always the language of a disposition, a mood, an emotion, an image, or a complex mixture thereof. His theory of language is at once too austere and too complex (this is less of a paradox than it is the result of a conceptual effort to force language to obey) to fit neatly into a critical paradigm.

What Pound's understanding of language requires, then, is a shift in our paradigm of modernist language. As critics, we tend to think of modernism as a period of literary history in which a sceptical attitude towards language became the norm, and while there is certainly much truth to the idea that this attitude was becoming widespread, Pound offers a way to see a modernist resistance to this interpretation. Depending on our critical stances, Pound's work may be used to demonstrate the slippage between signifiers and signifieds, but in order to demonstrate this we must wrestle with his lifelong aesthetic and critical effort to prevent exactly that slippage (and not on those terms). Pound's work offers a way to read Hofmannsthal and Mallarmé (and others) as diagnoses of a linguistic phenomenon which poetry attempted to find a way out of, rather than in to. In these final pages I wish to gesture towards other modernist and postmodernist figures whom we may situate within the paradigm of linguistic thought that Pound's work suggests.

The first is the American poet Laura (Riding) Jackson and her account of language in *Rational Meaning* (begun in the 1930s, but not published until 1997, six years after her death). *Rational Meaning*, a work Riding completed in collaboration with her husband, Schuyler B. Jackson, should stand with Ogden's and Richards's *The Meaning of Meaning* as a seminal text of modernist thinking about language but which has been, until recently, understudied. At around the same time that Pound approached Ogden with a view to forming a united front against 'word magic' and the 'idola fori' which (as they saw it) characterised modern thought, Riding similarly conceived of a crisis in the use of language. In words reminiscent of Hofmannsthal's (albeit more formulaically written), Riding recounts the problem she encountered:

> In the early 'thirties I began to feel a practiced sense of urgency about something that had long troubled me. This was, that the use of words was in a bad way. The factor of urgency in my feelings was a product of accumulating awareness of the direct cause of the general state of word-use: it became plainer and plainer to me that the use of words was in a bad way because the knowledge of words was in a bad way. I committed myself to trying to make a new opening into the area of word-knowledge – the knowledge, that is, of what words mean. There is no conception of word-knowledge as a unity of words-knowledges. The characteristic conception of word-knowledge is, what this or that word means; there is no conception of language-knowledge as knowledge of the meanings of the words of a language in their interrelation as such.[3]

Riding's radical focus on the power of words involves a relegation of language as system: 'know the words (know what they mean), and all the grammatical and syntactical processes will be found deducible from the knowledge'.[4] In her rationalist account of language, Riding defines words as 'language's apparatus of meaning'. In a Flaubertian movement, she begins from the starting point that there are no such things as synonyms, and claims her project's intention was 'to dissipate the fiction that there were such things as synonyms, that any word was "like" another in meaning'. Riding and Jackson proclaim faith in language as a rational means of communication, as an act of creative definition: 'we believe in the rationality of word-meaning, and have sought confirmation of the belief in the logical properties we take to inhere in language', they proclaim in their preface. This is based not in a mythical belief in 'word magic', but rather in a humanistic conviction that the problems of language are caused by our use of it and, thus, linguistic solutions must lie in the same repository of human behaviour. For Riding and Jackson, 'all that is capricious or indeterminate, rationally erratic, logically untenable, in verbal practice, and all theorizing based on it pertains to the abnormal in human linguistic sensibility and the anomalous in ideas of language'.[5] In the case of linguistic deterioration, the 'bad' use of language, Riding and Jackson place the blame squarely within the human use of language. They do not propose a rival theory of language qua language, but rather seek to offer pragmatic means of relating meaning and definition.

Riding began the project of 'word-definition' as an outgrowth of her poetic career. By the 1940s, however, she had turned away from practising poetry completely.[6] Jerome McGann nicely summarises the reason for her turning away: '(Riding) Jackson came to believe that poetry was merely the most seductive and deceptive of the betrayals of truth and language'.[7] McGann notes that this turning away from poetry was not a repudiation of her earlier work, but merely an admission that it was no longer the vehicle for her faith in the relationship between language and truth. McGann critiques Riding, comparing her understanding of language with the work of postmodern poets such as Ron Silliman and Lyn Heijinian, and other contemporary writers who 'think of their work in relation to (the philosophy of) language rather than (the philosophy of) imagination'. He concludes that 'the best writers of the past twenty years, therefore, have succeeded because they chose to enter the prison house of language'.[8] McGann's judgement is undoubtedly correct in its assessment of the most successful poets of the post-war era, but it does raise troubling questions for how we continue to read Riding (or, at least, her earlier work) and Pound. Must we dismiss accounts of language such as Riding's and Jackson's, Ogden's and Richards's, and Pound's as incidental to modernist poetics, even if these accounts of language inform those poetics? Are we, as readers and critics, also too trapped in the prison house of language to conceive a way out of it? Has the radical nominalism of the second half of the twentieth century subsumed entirely the various poetic projects of the first?

This is, as ever, a question of perspective and of intent. To what end do we read and write poetry? The answer can be provided by looking at the generation of poets who followed Pound and (Riding) Jackson. Although they would all come to distance themselves from Pound in some way, they all share convictions about poetic language that fit better with his ideogrammic method, and his language of 'precision' than they do with deconstruction. What they offer is, like Riding, a resistance in language to the prison house McGann so aptly describes. A good example is Charles Olson and his 'Projective Verse' (1950), in which the importance of individual vision and 'breath' are stressed over traditional metrics. Olson, like Pound, makes use of the notion of language in poetry as a transfer of energy. Although Olson's writing style differs significantly from Pound's, the latter's voice is clearly echoed in the claim that 'a poem is energy transferred from where the poet got it (he will have some several causations), by way of the poem itself to, all the way over to, the reader'.[9] Olson, in fact, credits Pound with the establishment of the syllable, rather than the metrical foot, as the main unit of poetic craft: 'Let's start from the smallest particle of all, the syllable', a unit chosen, he argues because, to begin with syllables is 'to step back here to this place of the elements and minims of language, is to engage speech where it is least careless'.[10] Olson comes to insist on the breath as the basis of all verse:

> Nature works from reverence, even in her destruction (species go down with a crash). But breath is man's special qualification as

animal. Sound is a dimension he has extended. Language is one of his proudest acts. And when a poet rests in there as they are in himself (in his physiology, if you like, but the life in him, for all that) then he, if he chooses to speak from these roots, works in that area where nature has given him size, projective size.[11]

Olson's use of 'breath' combines the unique voice of the poet with an act of primordial vitality, shared by all humans (in making clear that 'breath' is a human quality, it may be assumed that Olson does not use the term literally). 'Projective Verse' brings together poetic analysis, philosophical thought, and etymological speculation in a way that is strikingly reminiscent of Pound's critical writing, particularly 'I Gather the Limbs of Osiris' and *How to Read*. While Olson's style differs significantly, it can be seen as a continuation of the establishment of poetry and poetic voices as a commentary on the state of language more broadly and faith in the poet's ability to use and direct language.

Denise Levertov's 'Some Notes on Organic Form' is in many ways a continuation of Olson's theme, exploring the relationship between poetic form, content, and language itself. Levertov paraphrases Robert Duncan's claim that 'organic form' is simply 'the poetry of the linguistic impulse', a phrase combining unique poetic vision and the drive towards a concern with language. In this sense, organic form, much like Imagism, is a poetic movement that can be applied backwards across history as much as it is a manifesto for future practice. Levertov explains the 'linguistic impulse' in 'organic form':

> It seems to me that the absorption in language itself, the awareness of the world of multiple meaning revealed in sound, word, syntax, and the entering into this world in the poem, is as much an experience or constellation of perceptions as the instress of nonverbal sensuous and psychic events. What might make the poet of linguistic impetus appear to be on another tack entirely is that the demands of his realization may seem in opposition to truth as we think of it; that is, in terms of sensual logic. But the apparent distortion of experience in such a poem for the sake of verbal effects is actually a precise adherence to truth, since the experience itself was a verbal one.[12]

Levertov aligns the poetic impulses of the Black Mountain School as much with the innovations of Gerard Manley Hopkins (from whom Levertov borrows the term 'instress', or the process which holds a variety of complex perceptions and presentations together) as with Pound in this passage, but the general argument of the essay can be placed in the same ethos as Olson's and Pound's and Riding's critical work. Levertov argues that the 'apparent distortion of experience' in poems such as *The Cantos* or Olson's *Maximus Poems*, driven as they are by praxis and not by the conventions of discourse, may appear to run counter to logic, but they are, in fact, attempts to discern a more fundamental logic, one closer to the world as it is, and not as it has been made to appear. This is, she argues, the result of a close attention to language, and the veracity of each poet's vision of the world is not measurable by the conventions handed down to us by logic and rhetoric, but instead by a reader's immersion in that poetic world. Poetry for Levertov, as for Pound and Olson, reveals fundamental truths about the world and language unreachable in any other medium.

Robert Duncan, reflecting on the tradition handed down by modernist poetry in *The H.D. Book* (written 1960–1961), writes that 'the poetic urge, to make poetry out of a common language, is to make room for the existence of the poet, the artist of free speech'.[13] In other words, what Pound and others such as William Carlos Williams, H.D., and Gertrude Stein have most fully achieved is not only do poets remain, as Shelley once claimed, 'the unacknowledged legislators of the world', but they become its primary investigators and arbiters as well. The modern poet can draw on both shaman and anthropologist, ameliorating aspects of both in service of deeper, poetic truths.

By taking Pound's ideas seriously, by taking Riding's, Olson's, Levertov's, and Duncan's ideas seriously on their own terms, we may be able to close what can feel like a conceptual distance between ourselves and the figures we study. This does not mean agreeing with them, but it at least means trying to understand them and to speak of them in ways in which the authors themselves may have understood. Modernism is not a monolith, and there is no one 'modernist' approach to language, but there are numerous cross-currents and debates shared across the modernist era in anthropology, linguistics, literature, and philosophy. I do not claim to have outlined anything other than a foundation: there is much more to do with Pound and language, let alone with the other figures who share his convictions. None of the above is meant to stand as an endorsement of Pound's views of language, nor his views on anything else, but if we are to reckon with Pound's views on language, we must do so on his terms. They are terms that directly challenge many of our assumptions, and there is more reason to read him and his circle. This kind of post-Poundian poetics may not offer us the keys to escape the prison house of language, but we must reckon with the attempt. The linguistic faith that lies behind Pound's claim that 'you can be wholly precise in representing a vagueness' may not be a doctrine we accept, but it is one to which we must attend.

Notes

1 Hugo von Hofmannsthal, 'Letter of Lord Chandos' in *The Whole Difference: Selected Writings*, ed. J.D. McClatchy, trans. Tania Stern and James Stern (Princeton: Princeton University Press, 2008), 69–79 (79).
2 Frederic Jameson, *The Modernist Papers* (London: Verso, 2016), 321.

3 Laura (Riding) Jackson, and Schuyler B. Jackson, *Rational Meaning: A New Foundation for the Definition of Words and Supplementary Essays*, ed. William Harmon (Charlottesville: University of Virginia Press, 1997), 7.

4 Riding and Jackson, *Rational Meaning*, 13.

5 Riding and Jackson, *Rational Meaning*, 15, 20, 21.

6 For another excellent account of the 'end' of Riding's poetry to read alongside McGann's, see Tom Fisher, 'Reading Renunciation: Laura Riding's Modernism and the End of Poetry', *Journal of Modern Literature*, 33 (2010), 1–19.

7 Jerome J. McGann, 'Laura (Riding) Jackson and the Literal Truth', *Critical Inquiry*, 18:3 (1992), 454–473 (458).

8 McGann, 'Laura (Riding) Jackson and the Literal Truth', 473.

9 Charles Olson, 'Projective Verse', in *Collected Prose*, ed. Donald Allen and Benjamin Friedlander (London: University of California Press, 1997), 239–249 (240).

10 Olson, 'Projective Verse', 241.

11 Olson, 'Projective Verse', 247.

12 Denise Levertov, 'Some Notes Towards Organic Form' in *New and Selected Essays* (New York: New Directions, 1973), 67–73 (73).

13 Robert Duncan, *The H.D. Book* (London: University of California Press, 2011), 364.

Index

Note: Page numbers followed by "n" denote endnotes.

Printed in Great Britain
by Amazon

20593141R00136